The Experimental
Investigation of Meaning

The Experimental
Investigation of Meaning

A Review of the Literature

By **MARJORIE B. CREELMAN**, Ph.D.

Behavioral and Clinical Studies Center, Saint Elizabeths Hospital, Washington, D. C.

 SPRINGER Publishing Company, Inc. New York

Published January 1966
SPRINGER PUBLISHING COMPANY, INC.
200 Park Avenue South, New York, N.Y. 10003

Library of Congress Catalog Card Number: 65-26951

Printed in U.S.A.

To Doug

Preface

This is an account of what has been done in the experimental laboratory to try to discover what meaning is. It is primarily a critical review of the literature. Around the central problem of meaning, the book relates work from diverse fields of psychological concern, and emphasizes the issues common to the experimentalist and the practitioner in psychology. It maintains a scientific rather than a purely philosophical approach. The book does not offer any solution to the problem, but it does examine the limitations and possibilities that have been or could be applied to the problem. Not all work covered in this book has been directly concerned with meaning. Some of it has had other goals. The work has been included here because it seemed either to have interesting implications for the understanding of meaning, or to suggest methods that might be applied to the search for the meaning of meaning.

In the face of diversity of opinion about meaning, I have taken the position that the nature and functioning of meaning are unknown largely because the experimental strategies we have used have by and large been inadequate or inappropriate, and that it is important that we develop more adequate techniques and concepts. Perhaps my conviction that the domain of psychology includes the private as well as the public event is traceable to my Titchenerian-Watsonian-Freudian-Tolmanian background; however, it is a conviction that has been strengthened rather than weakened by subsequent exposure to Skinnerian principles and strategies, much as I admire the genius of the approach.

It is an equally strong conviction of mine that our failure to deal scientifically with the private event contributes to an unfortunate schism within the ranks of psychologists, between the "scientist" and the "practitioner." In many sciences, the close interaction between scientist and practitioner has been profitable to both. But such an interaction is impossible where the fruits of scientific effort are irrelevant to the requirements of practice and the fruits of practice are untestable hypotheses. In psychology accusations of triviality, irrelevancy and untestability are flung back and forth between the two sides. This constitutes not only a block to progress but also evidence of a misunderstanding by each side of the other —a misunderstanding of aims, goals, pressures, necessities, *and language*. Psychologists are great inventors of jargon which often renders one group deaf and mute to another. I have attempted, in this book, to keep the jargon at a minimum in the hope of enticing both sides to consider a problem that is of concern to both.

I came to my interest in meaning through many years of working with troubled, confused, or disorganized people, first in a research setting and then, much later, in psychotherapeutic settings with individuals and groups. In neither setting could the behavior of people be understood simply in terms of the "actual" events, either past or present, but only in terms of what those events *meant* to them. How does one make use of this simple observation?

The fact that people do not respond to an event but to its meaning has been recognized in certain psychological testing situations, but there is room for a more thorough understanding of its significance. Furthermore, this fact has immense significance in any psychological experiment that applies a stimulus or gives instruction (creates an event) to a subject and observes his responses.

Other questions of concern to all psychologists have to do with whether meaning is purely verbal, or whether it is nonverbal as well; whether it is purely conceptual, or whether other than conceptual processes are involved. Every therapist has encountered in his clients, if not within himself, certain kinds of behavioral or emotional responses that are essentially inextinguishable, even though more appropriate responses can be readily verbalized. Experimentalists have encountered similar problems when working with human subjects.

It seems to me, then, that the answers to such questions as what meaning is, how it is formed, how it functions, what effects it has on behavior, and how it can be altered or extinguished, are crucial not only to practitioners, (psychotherapists, educators, human engineers, and others) but also to the experimentalists.

Since meaning is a concept that is so complex, it is not hard to understand why the problem has been avoided or tackled piecemeal. I hope that there are some investigators daring enough to move with imagination from the beginnings here suggested.

The assembling of this material into a book was made possible by the support of my superior, Dr. Neil Waldrop, Director of the Behavioral Studies Research Branch of Saint Elizabeths Hospital,

Department of Health, Education, and Welfare. Although I am entirely responsible for the views here expressed, he is responsible for the fact that I was able to stay with the task to its completion. For this, and for his moral support and encouragement, I am grateful.

I also wish to express my appreciation to my voluntary assistants, Mr. Jonathan Steiner and Mr. Charles Jones, who spent many hours correcting and proofreading the manuscript. Most particularly, I thank my secretary, Mr. Anthony Marocco, whose pertinacity, accuracy and dependability made my task immeasurably easier. Without his patient, loyal, unswerving devotion to the task, it would never have been begun, much less finished.

MARJORIE B. CREELMAN

Washington, D. C.
December, 1965

Acknowledgements

Acknowledgement is gratefully made to E. F. Borgatta and William Lambert for permission to use material from their as yet unpublished book, *Handbook of Personality Theory and Research*. Permission to quote from previously published work is hereby gratefully acknowledged. My thanks are due the following:

McGraw-Hill Book Company for an excerpt by W. A. Bousfield from C. N. Cofer's *Verbal Learning and Verbal Behavior* (1961).

W. W. Norton & Company for an excerpt from J. B. Watson's *Behaviorism*. (Copyright 1924, 1925 by John B. Watson. Revised edition copyright 1930 and renewed 1957 by John B. Watson.)

Prentice-Hall, Inc., for an excerpt from C. W. Morris' *Signs, Language and Behavior* (1946).

John Wiley & Sons, Inc., for excerpts from F. H. Allport's *Theories of Perception and the Concept of Structure* (1955), and from H. Werner and B. Kaplan's *Symbol Formation* (1963).

The M.I.T. Press for excerpts from L. S. Vigotsky's *Thought and Language* (1962).

The University of Chicago Press for the use of material from A. Strauss' (Editor) *George Herbert Mead on Social Psychology*, Revised Edition, (1964).

The Academic Press, Inc., for excerpts from an article by D. A. Wicklund, D. S. Palermo, and J. J. Jenkins from the *Journal of Verbal Learning and Verbal Behavior* (1964); also from an article by G. R. Marshall and C. N. Cofer in the same journal a table entitled "Measures of Word Relatedness Based on Associative Norms" (1963).

Annual Reviews, Inc., for excerpts from D. E. Berlyne's chapter entitled "Emotional Aspects of Learning," in *Annual Review of Psychology* (1964).

The Journal Press for material from R. Chamblis' "Mead's Way out of the Basic Dilemma in Modern Existential Thought," from the *Journal of Social Psychology* (1963).

Southern Universities Press, publishers of *Psychological Reports,* for an excerpt from an article by C. D. Spielberger and L. D. De Nike entitled "Implicit Epistemological Bias and the Problem of Awareness in Verbal Conditioning: A Reply to Greenspoon" (1963).

The American Psychological Association for the use of material from *The American Psychologist* and *Psychological Review*.

Contents

PART THREE • DISCUSSION

PART
ONE
Background

General Orientation

If the translation out of common sense into science is to be made at all, psychology is the science in which the equivalent of meaning will be found [Titchener (1915) p. 118].

The search for the meaning of meaning has been pursued for hundreds of years by philosophers and theologians, but until recently only sporadic forays into this misty territory have been attempted by psychologists. It is understandable that this unmapped quagmire has been avoided, and that some hardy adventurers who set out to explore it bogged down. The difficulty of the problems can be appreciated by trying to talk about the meaning of meaning without using the word itself or one of its close synonyms. Yet, according to a standard word count,[1] the word "mean" is one of the commonest words in the language, and the concept is so taken for granted that we never wonder if we know what we mean when we say, "I mean." However, as Brodbeck (1963) pointed out, meaning is a term within science, and as such it must itself be given meaning. That this has not yet been accomplished is evident not only from the statements made by psychologists and philosophers, but also from the nature of the attempts to define the term in the psychologists' experimental laboratories and from the theoretical controversies which have arisen from those attempts.

Bertrand Russell pointed out (1940) that meaning has a hierarchy of meanings corresponding to the hierarchy of languages. It can refer to intention, or to relationships between words, objects, events. It may be denotative, or it may be defined in terms of the acts or incipient acts to which stimuli give rise. Later (1952) in his *Dictionary* he defined meaning solely in terms of conditioned responses, anticipating to some extent the position of some of the contemporary psychologists working with meaning in experiments in the area of verbal learning and verbal behavior. However, this

---

[1] Thorndike and Lorge (1959).

did not settle the matter, for as Chambliss wrote in 1963 (p. 217) the importance of a common point of view when engaging in a discussion of so vague a subject as meaning is evident. The term has such a variety of meanings that all too often a debate about meaning is only a babel of diverse tongues in which no meeting of minds is possible simply because those engaged in the debate are not talking about the same thing.

The purpose of this review is to indicate what has and has not been done within the purview of the experimental investigation of meaning. It was undertaken also in the hope of emphasizing the critical importance to psychology as a whole of a new awareness and understanding of the role of meaning in human development and behavior. Traditionally, psychology has concerned itself with attempts to describe systematically and finally to explain the content of experience, including such problems as sensation, perception, emotion, cognition. As the science of psychology began to develop out of philosophical speculation, its students became increasingly aware of the fact that their subject matter consisted of processes and dynamic systems rather than static structures or mechanisms. Its scope expanded to include the learning process or processes, personality development and organization. Increasingly the behavior of the individual became an important object of study, of interest in its own right as well as providing a basis for inferring underlying mental processes.

As behavior and its motives began to occupy the center of focus for psychology, problems of prediction became more cogent and pressing than the mere description or even explanation of behavior. Eventually questions regarding adjustment, mental health, and mental illness increasingly claimed psychologists' interest. As description became more dynamic, diagnosis became inextricably interwoven with questions regarding prevention, treatment and prognosis, and deviant behavior along with its determinants vied with mental process for the experimental and theoretical spotlight.

With these developments, the importance of prediction for a science of psychology was underscored, and a new issue emerged. This issue, the control of behavior, is central in the areas of training and education and of the development and growth of personality, as well as to the theory and scientific practice of psychotherapy and the evolution of psychotherapeutic methods.

Meaning, too, has been referred to in terms of content, structure, mechanism, and more lately, of process and system. The importance

of meaning in the areas of prediction and control is only just beginning to be recognized. It is our hope at least to indicate how the
problem of meaning is and has been involved in all these areas of
concern. One might go about realizing this hope in a variety of ways.
For a number of reasons—some practical and some related more
intimately to personal predilections, biases, capabilities and limitations—the approach adopted here is to survey the efforts to explore
in the experimental laboratory the psychological aspects of meaning, to review some of the attempts that have been made to identify,
define, and measure meaning as a psychological variable.

It is our intention to call attention to a wide range of experimental models, methods, and substantive issues, and to attempt to
relate them on the basis of their suggestiveness with respect to the
explication of meaning. Many authors will find themselves in odd
company. Some readers will find themselves wandering in strangely
populated pastures. The population was deliberately chosen from as
many different psychological worlds as possible because the meaning
of meaning is a universal problem with many aspects, and the ultimate solution probably can come only from a collision of different
conceptual worlds. If we can find a basic, common language in which
to communicate, the differing experiences of each may vastly enrich
the contributions of all. The "hardnosed" experimentalists have
something meaningful to say to the "softheaded" phenomenologists,
experientialists, and existentialists about meaning, and the soft-
heads can pose challenging problems for the experimentalists. The
former may need the latter to pull their eyes *off* the ground. The
latter may need the former to plant their feet *on* it. This is why it
seems timely to point out to the operationalists and phenomenologists, to the experimentalists and clinicians that they have problems in common, what some of these problems are, and how each
can help the others.

Scope and limitations

A relatively small amount of experimental effort has been expended
in a direct approach to the problem of meaning as such. Much
more work has been done in areas which are tangentially or im-
plicity concerned with meaning. The material presented here is
drawn from the already considerable and growing body of literature in both categories. Early experimental investigations of mean-

ing centered about the phenomenon called *semantic generalization,* or the transfer of a response from an object to its verbal designate, or from a word to its synonyms. Much of the current work which seems to have some bearing upon the understanding of meaning is directly descended from these early studies which were designed according to a classical conditioning model. It can also trace its lineage to classical associationism. But current experimentation in instrumental or operant conditioning with human subjects is being faced with problems which certainly involve meaning.

The literature which is in some way related to or descended from the early studies of semantic generalization or transfer, and of association, when it is considered along with the growing literature of verbal operant conditioning, forms such an extensive and complex collection that we have limited ourselves to those studies which fall roughly into these classifications. Thus experimental conditioning, association, and verbal learning studies, both American and Russian, are the focus of this endeavor to present the history, development, and current status of psychological experimental work which seems to this reviewer to cast the most light upon the nature of meaning, or to point up the deficiencies in our present understanding. The material which is covered has been selected from the vast array of possibilities because in the opinion of the writer it is intriguingly suggestive of possible directions which the search for the meaning of meaning might take. Others might have made other choices, omitting some of the material included, and including much that has been omitted. The writer is acutely aware that this overview is neither exhaustive nor conclusive, but if it arouses interest or provides an impetus to renewed efforts toward new definitions of the problem, our hope will have been realized.

Because of the breadth and complexity of the problem of meaning, many aspects will of necessity be neglected. Clinical researchers studying perceptual and conceptual problems, psycholinguists, information theorists, semanticists, philosophers and others may justifiably complain of being slighted. Linguistic definitions have been dealt with in a variety of ways by Carnap (1946, 1947), Whorf (1956), Chomsky (1957, 1959) and others. The relatively youthful discipline called *Psycholinguistics* has been recently surveyed by Osgood (1963). The philosophico-psychological aspects of meaning have been considered with profundity and from varying frames of reference by such authors as George Mead in 1934 and 1938,[2] C. S.

---

[2] See also Strauss (1964).

Peirce in 1940,[3] and C. W. Morris in 1946; by Ogden and Richards (1949), Suzanne Langer (1957, 1964), and May Brodbeck (1963).

Some philosophical approaches to meaning

It is not possible to enter into an extensive discussion of these philosophical approaches to meaning. However, it should be pointed out that some of these authors, especially Mead, Peirce, and Morris, were close to and influenced by the behaviorist movement in psychology and anticipated the experimentalists' application of behavioral concepts to the analysis and definition of meaning. Morris, for example, stated (1946, p. 19) that

> the term "meaning" . . . does not have the precision necessary for scientific analysis . . . "Meaning" signifies any and all phases of sign-process (the status of being a sign, the interpretant, the fact of denoting, the significatum), and frequently suggests mental and valuational processes as well.

Mead[4] held that meaning arises during cooperative group action, that internalized conversation (self-stimulation) frees man from the necessity of immediate and direct response to present stimulation by bringing past and future into the "act," and that there is interposed between stimulus and response a selection process in which the higher centers of the central nervous system are involved. He wrote[5]

> Much subtlety has been wasted on the problem of the meaning of meaning. It is not necessary, in attempting to solve this problem, to have recourse to psychical states, for the nature of meaning . . . is found to be implicit in the structure of the social act, implicit in the relations among its three basic individual components: namely, in the triadic relation of a gesture of one individual, a response to that gesture by a second individual, and completion of the social act initiated by the gesture.

Peirce's[6] view of meaning rests upon the supposition of a tendency for all things, including ideas and feelings, to acquire habits. The meaning of anything is the conception it conveys, and "conception

---

[3] See Buchler (1955).
[4] See Strauss (1964).
[5] In Strauss (1964) p. 169.
[6] See Buchler (1955).

lies exclusively in its conceivable bearing on the conduct of life."[7] The definition of meaning cannot be in terms of individual or private reactions, but in terms of that which is public, general, and communicable. Peirce, like Mead, thus insisted upon the social, or communicable, aspect of meaning, as well as upon the triadic nature of relationships involved in meaning.

It should be noted that both Mead's and Peirce's conceptions imply the notion of the instrumentality of the act, or behavior, in producing consequences which support the behavior. However, unlike the operant conditioners, they do not limit consequences to the external environment. A question of interest to the experimental psychologist is how the past and the future are brought into the act, for example, and how self-stimulation comes to replace external reinforcement. We shall see later how the work of some investigators, particularly the Russian experimenters, might be seen as providing a partial answer to such questions or at least as providing a methodological or theoretical base from which experimental investigators might move toward answers.

Morris' (1946) approach to meaning was behavioral, and owed a good deal to Mead, Peirce, Dewey, Tolman,[8] and Hull, among others—a debt which he freely acknowledged. He built upon Peirce's notion that in order to determine the meaning of a sign, we simply need to determine what habits it produces. He also found useful Peirce's version of semiotic[9] because it did not restrict signs to any particular medium or modality and thus could handle nonverbal as well as verbal signs (language).[10] Morris was also impressed by Mead's notion that the significant symbol allows man to become a self-conditioning being, and his theory incorporated and attempted to explain self-conditioning.

In summary, Morris (1946, p. 19) held that

since the factors operative in sign processes are all either stimulus-objects or organic dispositions or actual responses, the basic terms of semiotic are all formulable in terms appli-

---

[7] Peirce, in Buchler (1955) p. 252.

[8] Tolman (1926, 1932).

[9] A term, used by the Stoic philosophers and by John Locke as well as by Peirce, referring to the science of signs.

[10] It is tempting to consider how the Russian conceptions of first and second signaling systems (see below) might be applied to resolve Morris' particular and peculiar difficulties with mediational processes implicit in Mead's and Peirce's notion of triadic relationships, but such a discussion is beyond the scope of this treatment.

cable to behavior as it occurs in an environment. Semiotic thus becomes a part of the empirical science of behavior, and can utilize whatever principles and predictions the general theory of behavior has attained or can attain.

Furthermore,

until any particular theory of behavior explains in its own terms the phenomena of sign-behavior . . . it will be an inadequate instrument for dealing with the more complex and distinctive features of man and his culture [Morris (1946) p. 59].

General plan of presentation

The book is in three parts: the first dealing with background material; the second reviewing the contemporary experimental literature, American and Russian; and the third presenting a summary and discussion of contemporary theory.

Our first project is to orient the reader to the role of meaning in the various areas of psychological concern. Consequently, the first part is introductory in nature. Following the general orientation and plan of presentation of Chapter 1, Chapter 2 attempts to indicate the importance of an enhanced understanding of meaning to such widely diverse if intimately related topics as psychological process in general, the description, prediction, and control of behavior, the definition of stimulus and response; to such varied substantive issues as perception, emotion, learning, personality development, mental health and illness; to such practical problems as training, education and psychotherapy, all involving both internal and external control of behavior.

Since this review attempts to summarize some of the important studies from the Soviet Union, and to relate their hypotheses and findings to American experimental work, it is necessary for the reader to be familiar with such terms as "first and second signalling systems" and "orienting reflex," and with the nature of the concepts to which these terms refer. Definitions of these terms are presented in Chapter 2 in sufficient detail to indicate the relevance of Russian experimentation to the investigation of meaning.

Chapters 3 and 4 attempt to fill in the background against which contemporary experimental work should be viewed by summarizing early attempts to define meaning psychologically, first in cognitive, conceptual, or descriptive terms, then in experimental terms. Finally, both the early conditioning and association studies concerned with meaning are reviewed, and brief reference is made to some other experimental techniques for studying meaning.

There might be some reason to quarrel with the labels "early" and "contemporary." The division is somewhat arbitrary. With regard to conceptual definitions, a few recent statements are included in Chapter 3. There is not sufficient material on "contemporary" psychological definition to write a separate chapter without straying too far from the experimental base into the phenomenological realm. It is hoped that the reason for the division of the experimental material into "early" or "background" and "late" will be apparent. It does not imply that many of the issues and concerns of the "early" work are not still very much alive.

Part II is concerned with the contemporary experimental work which seems to the writer to be relevant to the psychological investigation of meaning, including conditioning studies, association, and learning experiments. It is obvious that definitions and methods of investigation tend to reflect the theoretical inheritance and postures of the investigators. Werner and Kaplan (1963) remind us that the "facts" obtained in experimental investigation are typically dependent upon the general approach followed and the particular method employed. "Men," says Guthrie (1959, p. 162), "help to make facts, and human purposes and motives enter into their selection and formulation."

Since a variety of theoretical biases and functional interests are represented among the psychologists who have grappled with the problem of meaning, it is not surprising that a number of different techniques for studying meaning have evolved. Classification is rarely a simple task, and here it is almost invidious because of the intrafamilial theoretical and methodological relationships involved, and because of the occasional combination of methods in a single experiment. However, the experimental work to be considered here falls roughly into the following categories, according to the principal method of investigation used: physiological methods, conditioning methods (other than physiological), learning methods, scaling methods, and association. Since much of the experimentation related to the problem of meaning has originated in Russian laboratories and is little known in the United States, an attempt has been made here throughout to cover insofar as possible the relevant Russian work and to relate it to American experimentation.

Chapter 5 reviews the relevant American conditioning studies, emphasizing those utilizing the classical conditioning model. The operant approaches to verbal conditioning are briefly considered.

Chapter 6 concerns itself with Russian experimental work in semantic and interoceptive conditioning. Chapter 7 returns to the United States for a review of American word association studies, semantic satiation, and work in verbal learning as it relates to the study of meaning. Within the latter area, the techniques of associative clustering and paired-associate learning are reviewed, insofar as these are used in ways that are related to meaning.

Part III attempts to indicate areas of theoretical controversy and to point the way toward future directions which might be taken in the further experimental pursuit of meaning. Chapter 8 discusses American theoretical issues, Chapter 9 takes a brief look at Russian hypotheses, and finally Chapter 10 attempts to assemble and relate the material here presented in terms of some of its implications for future research.

References

BRODBECK, M. Meaning and action. *Phil. Sci.,* 1963, *30(4),* 309–324.

BUCHLER, J. (Ed.). *Philosophical Writings of Peirce.* New York: Dover, 1955.

CARNAP, R. *Introduction to Semantics.* Cambridge, Mass.: Harvard Univer. Press, 1946.

——. *Meaning and Necessity.* Chicago: Univer. of Chicago Press, 1947.

CARROLL, J. B. (Ed.). *Selected Writings of Benjamin Lee Whorf.* New York: John Wiley & Sons, 1956.

CHAMBLISS, R. Mead's way out of the basic dilemma in modern existential thought. *J. soc. Psychol.,* 1963, *60(2),* 213-220.

CHOMSKY, N. *Syntactic Structures.* The Hague: Mouton & Co., 1957.

——. Review of *Verbal Behavior,* By SKINNER, B. F., *Language,* 1959, *35,* 26–58.

GUTHRIE, E. R. Association by contiguity.
In: KOCH, S. II. 1959.

KOCH, S. (Ed.). *Psychology: A Study of a Science.* II. General systematic formulations, learning, and special processes. New York: McGraw-Hill, 1959.

—— (Ed.). *Psychology: A Study of a Science.* VI. Investigations of man as socius: Their place in psychology and the social sciences. New York: McGraw-Hill, 1963.

LANGER, S. *Philosophy in a New Key*. Cambridge, Mass.: Harvard Univer. Press, 1957.

——. *Philosophical Sketches*. New York: Mentor Books, New Amer. Libr. of World Lit., 1964.

MEAD, G. H. *Mind, Self, and Society*. Chicago: Univer. of Chicago Press, 1934.

——. *The Philosophy of the Act*. Chicago: Univer. of Chicago Press, 1938.

——. *Social Psychology*.

In: STRAUSS, A. 1964.

MORRIS, C. W. *Signs, Language and Behavior*. New York: Prentice-Hall, 1946.

OGDEN, C. K., & RICHARDS, I. A. *The Meaning of Meaning*. London: Routledge & Kegan, Paul, Ltd., 1949.

OSGOOD, C. E. Psycholinguistics.

In: KOCH, S. VI. 1963.

PEIRCE, C. S. Philosophical writings.

In: BUCHLER, J. 1955.

RUSSELL, B. *An Inquiry into Meaning and Truth*. New York: Norton, 1940.

——. *Dictionary of Mind, Matter, and Morals*. New York: Philosophical Library, 1952.

STRAUSS, A. (Ed.). *George Herbert Mead on Social Psychology*. Chicago: Univer. of Chicago Press, 1964.

THORNDIKE, E. L., & LORGE, I. *The Teacher's Word Book of 30,000 Words*. New York: Teacher's College (Bureau of Publications), Columbia Univer., 1959.

TITCHENER, E. B. *A Beginner's Psychology*. New York: MacMillan, 1915.

TOLMAN, E. C. A behavioristic theory of ideas. *Psychol. Rev.,* 1926, *33,* 352–369.

——. *Purposive Behavior in Animals and Men*. New York: Century, 1932.

WERNER, H., & KAPLAN, B. *Symbol Formation*. New York: John Wiley & Sons, 1963.

WHORF, B. L. Language, thought and reality.

In: CARROLL, J. B. 1956.

The Importance of Meaning to Psychology

> *Meaning, a concept born under the malediction of introspectionists, bandied about by philosophers, overformalized by configurationists, disguised by behaviorists who could not afford to disown it, has long been a stepchild in psychology. Or perhaps it is like Cinderella, a ragged waif compelled by those who are ignorant of its identity to carry the burden of their theories without recognition until such time as it can be touched by an understanding that will reveal its true nature and illuminate the systems it has been compelled to serve* [Allport (1955) p. 575].

During the decade since Allport made this statement, Cinderella has emerged from the hearthside and gone to the ball. Yet even her most enamored swains have not succeeded in establishing the precise identity of the glamorous stranger. Scions of sociological, philosophical, anthropological, linguistic, and other families have pursued her, approaching her to varying extents. We must be content for the moment to ignore their competition, and concentrate on the disputes within our own family: psychology. The disputes concerned her identity and how to go about finding her, not the importance of doing so. Only one branch of the psychology family, strict stimulus-response (S-R) behaviorism, has denied the importance of the pursuit, and, as we shall see, even some members of this branch are presently being assailed by twinges of doubt over the denial.

Suzanne Langer (1964, p. 54) wrote:

> The concept of meaning, in all its varieties, is the dominant philosophical concept of our time. Sign, symbol, denotation, signification, communication—these notions are our stock in trade.

By "our" it is not likely that she was referring only to her fellow philosophers. These "notions" are also the stock in trade of psychology, whether they are regarded as terms to be operationally defined or as explanatory principles.

The problem of meaning is implicit in every area of concern to the psychologist studying or dealing with human behavior. Both meaning in general, and, more specifically, verbal or linguistic meaning, are phenomena which can no longer be ignored by either phenomenologist or behaviorist. Whether we are concerned with content, structure, or process; with description, explanation, prediction, control, or regulation; with partial or global functions; with clinical, social, or experimental problems—meaning is a variable to be reckoned with by psychologists concerned with human beings. Yet such a statement, which seems so obvious at one level, is quite meaningless at another, since the meaning of meaning, in general and as a psychological variable in particular, is so equivocal. The term may refer to anything from a simple act (the meaning of an object is the response it evokes) or a simple connection, to a "philosophy of life"—"anything from a stimulus-response relationship, to the wish behind a dream" (Langer, 1964, p. 55). Meaning can refer to designation, denotation, connotation, signification, causation, intention, purpose, interpretation, evaluation, emotion, action, or all of these. When the term is used, it is sometimes unclear in just which sense it *is* being used. Furthermore, these various meanings of meaning themselves need explication with respect to the psychological processes involved in them.

One group of psychologists focuses upon observable behavior (response) and the objective conditions which determine behavior (stimulus) as the legitimate subject matter of psychological concern. This research strategy is based upon the conviction that only those variables which can be directly observed, measured, and controlled can have experimental significance. The strategy has developed out of animal studies which present clear evidence that relationships between stimulus and response are lawful and predictable. It is obvious, then, that meaning in any sense is a concept which has no relevance within the model. Other groups acknowledge the simplicity, elegance, and parsimoniousness of this approach, but feel the necessity to include subjective determining conditions as significant variables. They complain that attempts to generalize from infrahuman to human behavior have met with less than complete success where more complex problems are involved, especially with respect to symbolic behavior. If one acknowledges the importance of the subjective as well as the objective determining conditions which define a psychological situation, then the connection between these conditions is relevant and important. Furthermore, if meaning lies in, or *is,* this connection (Pickford, 1950), then by understanding meaning it may be possible better to coordinate and verify the various aspects of psychological concern.

One such problem of concern to psychologists is perception. Allport (1955) in his exhaustive critique of psychological theories of perception complained that although nearly every theory of perception deals with the problem of meaning in some way, none inquires sufficiently into its nature. He insisted that meaning is not simply a verbal or linguistic problem. Perceptual significances antedate linguistic significances in individual development, as they must have done in phylogeny as well. "Young children learn the significances of what they see and hear about them long before they begin to learn the meaning of words" (Osgood, 1963, p. 285). Representational processes first become associated with nonlinguistic visual, auditory, tactile, proprioceptive, and other cues. Russian experiments have suggested that "other cues" might even include interoceptive stimuli. Thus meaning must be defined in terms which include processes other than, or in addition to, verbal processes.

Allport (1955) suggested further that meaning has a scope even wider than the perceived character of things, and enters into processes other than perception. He asserted (p. 534), for example, that personality itself

> . . . consists largely of the meanings that are characteristic of a particular individual. Aside from purely automatic habits and reflexes[1] there is scarcely any part of the whole field of behavior into which meaning does not enter.

Kelly's (1955) ideas about the importance of the way an individual construes his world have been developed into a theory of personality as well as a diagnostic and therapeutic method. His conviction that an individual will behave in a manner consistent with his own perceptions and ideas about the universe implies meaning as a central issue in both prediction and control of behavior, and echoes Asch's statement (1952, p. 646) that

> we act and choose on the basis of what we see, feel, and believe; meanings and values are part and parcel of our actions. When we are mistaken about things, we act in terms of our erroneous motives, not in terms of things as they are.

---

[1] As will be shown later, recent Russian experimentation suggests that some "purely automatic habits and reflexes" may have their genesis, development, and maintenance partly in meaning.

Or as Lawrence put it (1963, p. 189)

> ... behavior is determined by code items rather than directly by the events with which the items are associated; i.e., we react more to our symbolic representation of things than to the things *per se*.

Or we react to what things *mean* to us.

If solving the problem of meaning is important to the understanding of personality, then it is crucial to understanding personality disorders. In Binswanger's[2] view meaning is central to mental health and mental illness. Mental health is characterized by freedom and flexibility—the ability to shift meanings. Mental illness, on the other hand, is distinguished by impoverishment and shrinkage, through homogeneity of symbolic reference.[3] Erikson (1960) viewed neurotic disturbances as essentially originating in faulty qualities and quantities of internalized "yes" and "no" signals, or in other words, distortions of affirmative and negative meaning.

It is perhaps not surprising to find psychologists of a phenomenological bent emphasizing the importance of meaning. Behavioral and experimental psychologists on the whole have been content to ignore the issue, or nervously to explain it away in terms of some observable process, or more likely to deny that it has relevance to the understanding of behavior. However, quite recently even some of our tough-minded brothers have been forced to acknowledge the existence of the "ragged waif" without knowing its identity. One reason for this may be because a few intrepid operant experimenters have dared to move out of the rat's cage or the pigeon's box into the laboratory with human subjects.[4] Other influences probably can be found in the "mellowed maturity of older psychologists whose careers have spanned the ebb and flow of classical and neoclassical behavioristic theorizing and experimentation" (Koch, 1964). Guthrie (1959), for example, confessed that "It is not enough that (patterns of physical change) be available ... nor ... that the organism's attention orient sense organs to receive them; it is further necessary that they have meaning for the responding organism" (p. 165).

This underlines the dawning realization that an effective or functioning stimulus in an experimental situation may be something other than, or in addition to, that physical event defined by the

---

[2] See Needleman (1963).
[3] Rollo May in Needleman (1963).
[4] See, e.g., Weiner (1963, 1964).

experimenter as "the" stimulus. Prokasy and Hall (1963, p. 315) reminded us that

> . . . there is certainly no reason to assume. . . that the experimenter's delineation of a physical event and the subject's perception of it are isomorphic. What represents an important dimension of the physical event for the experimenter may not even exist as part of the effective stimulus for the subject. Similarly, the subject may perceive aspects of an experimental event which have been ignored by, or are unknown to, the experimenter.

Gibson (1960) and Clark and McFarland (1963) clearly summarized the disagreements and confusions surrounding the definition of stimulus, so crucial in the S-R approach whose basic assumption is that the stimulus is a known and controllable variable. Osgood (1963) agreed that the functional units of stimulus and response have never been adequately defined, even descriptively.[5]

This emphasizes a new area of importance which meaning has for psychology. If we cannot know what a stimulus or a response *is* without knowing what *meaning* either event has for the subject, meaning then becomes a crucial variable in any experiment, especially one using human subjects. It can no longer be dismissed as of no significance, or even as an assumed intervening variable the nature of which is of minor relevance to the obtained results. It must be understood in order to interpret results.

Meaning and language

Allport (1955) felt that the tendency to identify meaning with language has been the source of much confusion in the attempts to investigate meaning. In his opinion, we shall never understand either meaning or the linguistic process itself until we cease to restrict our study of meaning to the meaning of language signs, and come to understand the more basic processes. However, nearly all of the experimental work in the investigation of meaning has been formulated within some kind of verbal-behavior framework, the rationale being that we may solve the more inclusive problem through understanding meaning as expressed in verbal signs. Osgood (1963) himself having admitted the chronological primacy of meaning over language, contended that there is no special lan-

---

[5] See also Lawrence (1963).

guage *behavior*. "The phenomena of language are perfectly and completely coextensive with the phenomena of behavior in general, and an adequate theory of one is at once an adequate theory of the other" (p. 246). Brown (1958) made more modest claims, but pointed to the store of evidence, from psychological testing and other individual sources, that the single verbal response usually predicts a large number of other responses. However, it may be important to keep in mind Hunt's (1962) warning against confusing verbal responses with the symbolic processes underlying them. Laffal (1964) described the psychological study of language in terms of concern with how language works upon and for individual speakers (and listeners), the essence of which lies in problems of meaning.

Language has long been used as a tool in the study of human thought and behavior. It is more recently that language itself has been the object of psychological concern. Language was earlier viewed as the reflection of thought, and interest centered upon first the content, then the structure of thought. Currently language is seen as a variety of human behavior to be investigated as other kinds of behavior. The development of new techniques is making it feasible to study language or verbal behavior in ways that allow relatively free movement to those psychologists who prefer to remain external to the "black box," as well as to those who are concerned with what goes on within the cognitive and physiological structure of the organism. The growing realization of the importance and variety of functions served by language has attracted those more interested in the regulation, control, and shaping of behavior as well as those whose interest is primarily in the analysis or description of behavior. Woodworth and Schlosberg (1956) have conceded, for example, that even involuntary responses can be controlled indirectly by arousing symbolic processes that are associated with their stimuli. The experimental demonstration that one can link emotional responses to words through conditioning procedures, and of the techniques for doing so, could have immense consequences in increasing the reliability and effectiveness of psychotherapeutic methods, as well as in enhancing understanding of the development, functioning, and malfunctioning of emotion. Wortis (1962) considered the current interest in verbal behavior and the second signalling system to be an important bridge "connecting the physiological interests of the Soviet workers with the contemporary psychological and psychotherapeutic preoccupations of Western psychiatry"

(p. 21). One might add that the current interest in verbal behavior, and in meaning, could serve as an important bridge linking the concerns of two large segments of American psychology—experimental psychology and clinical psychology.

The signalling systems and the orienting reflex

References to the terms *first* and *second signalling systems* are becoming more and more frequent in American reports. It is essential, then, that the reader understand these and one other term, that is the "orienting reflex," all of which refer to central concepts in Russian theories of verbal behavior and are thus constantly used in the Soviet experimental literature. All three terms originated with Pavlov, but the systems to which they refer have been elaborated by many experimenters.

The term orienting reflex originally referred to the simple turning response observed in Pavlov's dogs when any new stimulus, either accidentally or intentionally introduced, occurred. The term is currently used to refer to the organism's innate response to *novel* stimuli. It is not a simple single reflex response, but one which is a configuration or complex patterning of physiological and behavioral reactions.

The three functional levels of the central nervous system distinguished by Russian experimentalists are 1) a system of unconditioned (innate) reflexes, including, but not necessarily exclusive to, the orienting reflex; 2) the first signalling system, a primary conditional reflex system formed from the individual's direct experience with objects and events; and 3) the second signalling system, a secondary conditional reflex system formed from the individual's indirect experience—i.e., his knowledge *about* subjects and events and their relationships.

While in animals the formation of new connections is superimposed upon unconditioned reflexes and the old conditioned reflexes closest to the unconditioned reflexes, in man the majority of new connections are acquired through the participation of a word or words as signal and reinforcement, and as the result of social interrelationships. These acquired connections may be of any degree of complexity and depth, from the simplest to the most complex, and the activity is carried out under conditions of ceaseless interaction between the first and second signalling systems, under the regulatory control (in the adult) of the latter. The orienting reflex plays a vital role in connection-forming activity, since it involves responses which bring into action both long-distance receptors and contact receptors; thus it first helps to make the acquaintance of the environment, and then leads to mastery and control.

It is this dynamic interplay between the first (sensory) and second (symbolic) signalling systems that distinguishes the mental activity of man from the higher nervous activity of infrahuman organisms (Boiko, 1961). Although the Russian experimenters do not in general speak of meaning, it might be not too broad an inferential leap to look for the meaning of meaning somewhere in this "dynamic interplay." Luria (1962) asserted that man's higher verbal functions represent complex reflex processes, social in origin, mediated in structure, with language as the principal instrument of mediation. As a basis for the second signalling system, language has one principal feature: the symbol, which replaces the object, but not the emotional situation. He does not tell us what replaces the emotional situation, but some of the Russian interoceptive-semantic experiments, which will be reviewed later, may suggest ways of answering this question along with clues as to the nature of meaning. Boiko (1961) cautioned us to remember that, according to Pavlov, the second signalling system is not restricted to speech (verbal activity), but constitutes a more general regulator of human behavior.

Meaning and the regulation of behavior

Recent American work in the operant conditioning of verbal behavior, as well as the Russian experimentation in the area of verbal regulation of behavior and of the semantic conditioning of interoceptive processes, is giving us a new appreciation of the role of meaning in the control of behavior, including control from *within* the organism. Doty (1960) stated that since input exists effectively only as a pattern of neural activity, it is obvious that an input or stimulus for a given behavior can be generated by activities entirely within the brain, without recourse to causes external to the organism.

Erikson (1960) pointed out the important implications of the regulatory function of speech in the development of conscience, which he defined as the

. . . internalization of "yes" and "no" and the capacity to develop an inner voice which gradually becomes silent and functions without the awareness that the voice once came from the outside. [See Luria (1960) p. 406].

Although Osgood (1956) did not refer to conscience, he spoke of *attitudes,* which he defined as persistent patterns of self-stimulation which give rise to and regulate both nonverbal and verbal behavior. Attitudes, then, could be regarded as organized and enduring systems of related *meanings,* since he defined meaning in terms of patterns of self-stimulation.

Against this background regarding behavioral regulation and self-regulation, an analogy drawn by Yakovlev (1962) between Pavlov's concept of the organism's response to three levels of stimuli, Jackson's neurological theory, and Freud's topology[6] draws together the framework of Russian theorizing and some Western psychiatric and psychological conceptualizations.

PAVLOV	JACKSON	FREUD
Stimuli levels	*Neurological levels*	*Strata*
Physical agents	Lower	Id
Sensory signals (1st signal system)	Middle	Ego
(Verbal) Symbols or signals (2nd signal system)	High	Superego

Fig. 1 Yakovlev's analogy [From Yakovlev (1962) p. 28].

Meaning and development

Luria (1960) demonstrated that although the self-regulatory function of speech is initially weak and plays no decisive role in organization, it later becomes a potent organizing factor. Verbal behavior, whether explicit or implicit, comes to mediate and regulate behavior as a child matures. This regulation replaces communication as the primary function of verbal behavior, and a social level of organizational behavior by way of speech is formed through behavioral experience (Simon, 1957).

[6] See also Magoun (1964) p. 9.

Luria's experimental work with children has shown, for example, that behavior conditioned without verbal associations is relatively unstable, depends upon constant reinforcement, and disintegrates at even a slight change in the method of presenting signals. In contrast, behavior conditioned by way of verbal associations is quickly acquired, stable, and widely generalized.

However, the regulatory influence of speech occurs only when speech is semantically meaningful. If, for example, a child subject is instructed by the experimenter to respond in a given way every time the stimulus is presented, and at the same time to say, "I see; I see," learning is slow and unstable; but if the child says "yes" with his response to the positive stimulus and "no" to the negative stimulus, he makes no errors from the beginning. Luria stated (1960, p. 391), that "Only differentially meaningful speech has an organizing effect." The semantic side of speech becomes effective somewhere around the age of four or five, at the same time at which speech is internalized and voluntary movements become more coordinated. Feebleminded individuals display the lower level of semantic organization (Bogachenko, 1961) as do people under intense excitement or emotion (Magoun, 1964). These experimental findings point to the importance of an understanding of meaning to developmental and educational psychology.

It is perhaps indicative of the relatively new emphasis on the psychological study of language and of the word—in both the Soviet Union and in the United States—that a work by Vigotsky which had been published in 1934 and then largely neglected in both countries, has so recently been translated and republished. Vigotsky (1962, p. 153) stated that

... thought and language, which reflect reality in a way different from that of perception, are the key to the nature of human consciousness. Words play a central part not only in the development of thought, but in the historical growth of consciousness as a whole.

Word meanings constitute the limits of verbal thought. He thus insisted that the proper approach to the relations between thought and speech (verbal behavior) is semantic analysis, and the study of the development, functioning, and structure of the meaning of words.

Since words are connected with both the external and internal stimuli coming to the cerebral hemispheres, signal and replace them, they are capable of evoking all the actions and reactions which the original stimuli produce. This complex semantic and generalizing significance of the word determines the force with which, as an actual conditioned stimulus, it affects the processes of man's higher nervous activity. As an articulate being, man produces words that can act as stimuli which differ qualitatively from other stimuli because they comprehend, generalize, and stand for a multitude of separate stimuli (Simon, 1957). The word signalizes the essential feature, the major meaning, of the object signified, irrespective of changes or fluctuations in the secondary features of the object. The essential feature, found in the concrete and single instance, remains unchangeable; it is common for objects of the same kind, and serves as a means of distinguishing these objects from other similar classes of objects (Liublinskaya, 1957). It is at this stage that the word has acquired the comprehensive character which distinguishes signals of the second system, different qualitatively and quantitatively from the signals of the first system.

Summary

This chapter has suggested some of the areas of psychological concern which might be illuminated by an understanding of meaning. These include such diverse problem areas as perception, personality and personality development, personality disorders, the definition of stimulus and response, the regulation of behavior. It seems to be important, therefore, that the meaning of meaning be investigated in such systematic and inclusive ways as to bring fresh insights to the endeavors of experimental, theoretical, and applied psychology.

Many more psychologists have pointed out the necessity for tackling the problem of meaning directly than have risked the difficulties and frustrations of doing so. The experimental literature specifically addressed to the investigation of meaning as a psychological variable is limited in quantity and scope. However, there is a great deal of work which has come from the laboratories of both the American experimental psychologists and the Russian physiological psychologists which has intriguing and suggestive implications with respect both to the possible nature, definition, and measurement of meaning, and to possible techniques for pursuing the problem further. For a variety of reasons, some theoretical and some pragmatic, most of this work has been limited to the investigation of verbal meaning, and has been conducted within the framework of linguistic studies of various kinds. Following a summary of the early attempts to define meaning, it is these studies which will be surveyed in this book.

References

ALLPORT, F. H. *Theories of Perception and the Concept of Structure.* New York: John Wiley & Sons, 1955.

ASCH, S. E. *Social Psychology.* New York: Prentice-Hall, 1952.

BOGACHENKO, L. S. Some characteristics of the formation of conditioned reactions to complex sensory and verbal stimuli in children at the end of the school days.
In: GARTSSHTEIN, N. G., & BOGACHENKO, L. S. 1961.

BOIKO, E. I. (Ed.). *Studies in Higher Neurodynamics as Related to Problems of Psychology.* Washington, D.C.: Office Tech. Serv., 1961.

BRAZIER, M. A. B. (Ed.). *The Central Nervous System and Behavior.* (Transactions of the third conference sponsored by the Josiah Macy, Jr., Foundation and the National Science Foundation). New York: Josiah Macy, Jr., Foundation, 1960.

BROWN, R. *Words and Things.* Glencoe, Ill.: The Free Press, 1958.

BROZEK, J. Recent developments in Soviet psychology.
In: FARNSWORTH, P. R. XV. 1964.

CLARK, R. K., & McFARLAND, R. L. Systems concept of stimulus. *Percept. mot. Skills,* 1963, *17(1),* 99-102.

DOTY, R. W. Quoted in SOKOLOV, E. N. 1960.

ERIKSON, E. H. Quoted in LURIA, A. R. 1960.

FARNSWORTH, P. R., et al (Eds.). *Annual Review of Psychology.* XV. Palo Alto, Calif.: Annual Reviews, Inc., 1964.

GIBSON, J. J. The concept of stimulus in psychology. *Amer. Psychologist,* 1960, *15,* 694-703.

GUTHRIE, E. R. Association by contiguity.
In: KOCH, S. II. 1959.

HUNT, E. B. *Concept Learning: An Information Processing Problem.* New York: John Wiley & Sons, 1962.

KELLY, G. A. *Psychology of Personal Constructs.* I & II. New York: W. W. Norton, 1955.

KOCH, S. (Ed.). *Psychology: A Study of a Science.* II. General systematic formulations, learning, and special processes. New York: McGraw-Hill, 1959.

—— (Ed.). *Psychology: A Study of a Science.* V. The process areas, the person, and some applied fields: Their place in psychology and in science. New York: McGraw-Hill, 1963.

—— (Ed.). *Psychology: A Study of a Science*. VI. Investigations of man as socius: Their place in psychology and the social sciences. New York: Mc-Graw-Hill, 1963.

——. Psychology and conceptions of knowledge.
In: WANN, T. W. 1964.

LAFFAL, J. Psycholinguistics and the psychology of language. *Amer. Psychologist,* 1964, *19(10)*, 813-815.

LANGER, S. *Philosophical Sketches.* New York: Mentor Books, New Amer. Libr. of World Lit., 1964.

LAWRENCE, D. H. The nature of a stimulus: Some relationships between learning and perception.
In: KOCH, S. V. 1963.

LIUBLINSKAYA, A. The development of children's speech and thought.
In: SIMON, B. 1957.

LURIA, A. R. Verbal regulation of behavior.
In: BRAZIER, M. A. B. 1960.

—— *Higher Cortical Functions in Man and Their Disturbances in the Presence of Local Brain Lesions.* Moscow: Moscow Univer., 1962.

MAGOUN, H. W. *The Waking Brain.* Springfield, Ill.: Charles C. Thomas, 1964.

NEEDLEMAN, J. (Ed.). *Being-in-the-World: Selected Papers of Ludwig Binswanger.* New York: Basic Books, 1963.

OSGOOD, C. E., Behavior theory and the social sciences. *Behav. Sci.,* 1956, *1*, 167-185.

——. Psycholinguistics.
In: KOCH, S. VI. 1963.

PICKFORD, R. W. Aspects of the psychology of meaning. *J. genet. Psychol.,* 1950, 77, 231-255.

PROKASY, W. F., & HALL, J. F. Primary stimulus generalization. *Psychol. Rev.,* 1963, *70*, 310-322.

SIMON, B. (Ed.). *Psychology in the Soviet Union.* Stanford: Stanford Univer. Press, 1957.

SOKOLOV, E. N. Neuronal models and the orienting reflex.
In: BRAZIER, M. A. B. 1960.

VIGOTSKY, L. S. *Thought and Language.* Cambridge, Mass.: M.I.T. Press, 1962.

WANN, T. W. (Ed.). *Behaviorism and Phenomenology.* Chicago: Univer. of Chicago Press, 1964.

WEINER, H. Laboratory studies of "non-adjustive" human operant behavior. *Tech. Rep.,* #15, *Behavioral Studies Branch,* St. Elizabeths Hospital, Washington, D.C., 1963.

——. Two case studies in the experimental analysis of "non-adjustive" human behavior. *Tech. Rep.,* #16, *Behavorial Studies Branch,* St. Elizabeths Hospital, Washington, D.C., 1964.

WOODWORTH, R. S., & SCHLOSBERG, H. *Experimental Psychology.* New York: Henry Holt, 1956.

WORTIS, J. (Ed.). *Recent Advances in Biological Psychiatry.* IV. New York: Plenum Press, 1962.

YAKOVLEV, P. I. The traditional and the new in Pavlov's theory of higher nervous activity.

In: WORTIS, J. IV. 1962.

Early Definitions of Meaning

> *Any definition of meaning should be regarded as no more than a working hypothesis. Its value will depend on how it works: On the help it can give in the description, interpretation and classification of semantic phenomena* [Ullmann (1962) p. 66].

Ullmann's statement could apply to either the conceptual or the operational approach to definition. Definitions, or hypotheses, can be heuristic on a conceptual or experimental level. The early definitions of meaning were conceptual rather than operational, and tended to focus upon the *content* of experience. They ranged from the notion of ideas and images to elaborations that added such concepts as context, relationship, purpose or direction, and reference points within the individual rather than the object. The twentieth century was well under way before anyone proposed that meaning might be thought of in terms of conceptual organization or process, rather than in the more static descriptive way. Even the somewhat more dynamic definitions involving relationships between and among parts and wholes were more structurally or descriptively slanted than process oriented. That the definition of meaning might encompass action or behavior was never suggested until behavioristic psychology threw out meaning because it had become unnecessary as an explanatory or even descriptive concept.

William James (1890) defined the dynamic meaning of words as the fringes of feelings of fitness to their contexts, and the static meaning of words as the sensory images awakened (in the case of concrete words) or the verbal associates (to abstract words). Echoes of the last part of the definition are to be found in the work of such contemporary investigators as Noble, Bousfield, and Deese, to name only a few. Titchener's (1909) more general definition of meaning referred to the mental context of images and other derivatives of sensation in which a given content appears in consciousness. The work of Russian investigators, concerned with semantic conditioning and with the transformations from the first to second signalling systems, arouses memory traces of this old conception, and anchors it to neurological and other physiological processes.

McDougall (1926) added a new dimension in that a connection to response is implied in his definition. He declared that meaning is richer than imagery in that it consists in the mass of experiences or knowledge of an idea or object which determines the particular mode of approach to the idea or object. Drever (1921) went farther and spoke of meaning as a *relation,* either of the situation to the self, or of the situation as a part of the whole, or as a part to other parts. In order for an object to have meaning, there must be a reference that is not in the object but in the individual. He insisted upon a distinction between primary and secondary meaning. Primary meaning, purely affective, is the feeling of relation between the object or situation and the impulse toward it (purpose, aim, or need). Secondary meaning, both affective and cognitive, is derived from primary meaning and arises through the future projection of present experience. This again is faintly reminiscent of the Russian concepts of first and second signalling systems, and of their derivation and interaction.

In 1924 Watson swept aside the traditional concepts inherited from British associationism and from Titchenerian introspectionism, and asserted that meaning is simply the reaction evoked by a stimulus. He asserted that meaning is nothing but what an individual does. If one experimentally determines all the organized responses to given stimuli, one exhausts meanings. In 1925 he wrote (pp. 200-201):

> If you are willing to agree that "meaning" is just a way of saying that out of all the ways the individual has of reacting to this object at any one time, he reacts in only one of these ways, then I find no quarrel with meaning. . . In other words, when we find the genesis of all forms of a person's behavior, know the varieties of his organization, can arrange or manipulate the various situations that will call out one or another form of his organization, then we no longer need such a term as meaning. Meaning is just one way of telling what the individual is doing. So the behaviorist can turn the tables upon his critics. They cannot give an explanation of meaning. He can, but he does not believe the word is needed or that it is useful except as a literary expression.

It is unnecessary here to elaborate upon the profound influence this bold stroke had upon subsequent psychology. However, not

all psychologists immediately abandoned the subjective or unobservable entirely. MacCurdy (1928) agreed that the study of meaning
is the study of associated reaction patterns, but added that meanings
may be expressed in behavior, in affect, or in the conscious knowledge of associated patterns. Of course, if one were to substitute for
the words "affect" and "conscious knowledge" such behavioral
terms as "neural or autonomic responses" and "verbal report,"
this definition would not be far from the concept of meaning implicit
in many contemporary behavioristic experiments.

Bartlett (1932) described meaning in terms of that which is
present when the significance of any part of an organized setting
goes beyond its descriptive character and leads on to some other
related part. To be understood, both organizations of motor responses or of psychological material *and* the relevant functioning of
action tendencies must be considered. This reference to "action
tendencies" foreshadows such contemporary concepts as mediators
which are implicit or partial responses (Osgood, Bousfield, and
others), abridged act-structures (Allport), and "dispositions"
(Brown).

Mead (1938) formulated what he called a philosophy of the act,
which some contemporary authors[1] regard as an adequate science
of meaning. In the simplest terms, the meaning of an object is the
response it evokes, which response may not be consciously made.
However, where a response to a stimulus is made unconsciously,
there is no awareness of meaning in the act, and there can be no
response to a significant symbol without consciousness. Thus Mead
regarded the response to a significant symbol as the conscious meaning of that symbol.

Stout (1938) equated meaning with the formation of cumula-
tive dispositions due to retentiveness involved in reproduction and
association. Meanwhile, Head (1926) was insisting on a notion
of retention which is not a purely mechanical accumulation of impressions, dispositions, or engrams, but rather a mode of adaptive
organization. To him, meaning resided in the vigilance of the nervous system and the schematic organization of the effects of past responses and experiences. Here was introduced an explicitly stated
process or functionally oriented approach which is reflected in contemporary speculation. But the definition of meaning itself is highly
reminiscent of the current Russian concept of the orienting reflex,
which is now thought to be more in the nature of a vigilance re-

---

[1]See, for example, Chambliss (1963).

sponse than investigatory, and which theoretically results from impulses caused by the difference between the neuronal model (neural "program") and the actual stimulus (Sokolov, 1960).

Many years later, Pickford (1950) defined meaning as a specialized abstraction which refers to and explains the synthesis of appropriate subjective or physiological processes (impulse, idea, feeling) and outside objects and conditions—a synthesis which makes response possible. This definition closely parallels the concepts which form the basis of much of the contemporary experimental work. Osgood's statements with respect to meaning (1952, 1956) expressed similar ideas in somewhat more operational terms. He preferred to regard meaning as a hypothetical construct, a mediator with both stimulus and response properties (1963).

Combining the internal-functional approach and the idea of action or behavior, F. H. Allport (1955) asserted that meaning must be some aggregate of relationships and happenings *within* the organism. He defined it as "an energically diminished and kinematically abridged behavioral act (act-structure)." Meanings originally come from actual contacts with and manipulation of the environment. In the ensuing modification of the act-structure, the event-cycle of the system concerned is abridged so that its operation is finally largely covert. His ideas about origins of meanings closely parallel the Russian concept of the development of the signalling systems, and his theory of closed but intercontacting cycles is reminiscent of Hebb's (1949) interacting "fringes of meaning."

Summary

Attempts at the psychological definition of meaning have ranged from the simple notion of its being the accumulated content of experience to the equally simple notion of its being the response to a given stimulus. In between have been attempts to introduce both structural and functional notions in terms of association, relationship, and the interaction of a variety of elements, along with yet other attempts to anchor the concept of meaning in neurological, physiological or psychological mechanisms. But the problem was far from solved, or even being adequately posed. By and large, definitions of meaning arose out of conceptual-theoretical soil, and failed to generate experimental hypotheses leading to experimental investigation. They were on the whole unfruitful within the deductive framework of experimental psychology, even though some of them could easily have been expressed in terms of experimental variables. Attempts at definition in other than experimental terms dwindled and all but disappeared from the literature.

It is interesting that a reawakened concern with meaning received its impetus primarily from an inductive frame of reference. It did not begin with attempts at definition, but rather with the necessity to explain a set of quite specific phenomena observed in the course of experimentation focused in other directions—phenomena which seemed to require explanatory concepts beyond those simple connections posited for animal behavior. One such phenomenon, observed in a series of conditioning experiments, which reawakened interest in the psychological investigation of meaning was the transfer or generalization of a response from one stimulus to another along a meaning dimension, a phenomenon which has been called semantic generalization.

References

ALLPORT, F. H. *Theories of Perception and the Concept of Structure.* New York: John Wiley & Sons, 1955.

BARTLETT, F. C. *Remembering.* Cambridge: Cambridge Univer. Press, 1932.

BRAZIER, M. A. B. (Ed.). *The Central Nervous System and Behavior.* (Transactions of the third conference sponsored by the Josiah Macy, Jr., Foundation and the National Science Foundation). New York: Josiah Macy, Jr., Foundation, 1960.

CHAMBLISS, R. Mead's way out of the basic dilemma in modern existential thought. *J. soc. Psychol.,* 1963, *60(2),* 213-220.

DREVER, J. *Instinct in Man.* Cambridge: Cambridge Univer. Press, 1921.

HEAD, H. *Aphasia and Kindred Disorders of Speech.* Cambridge: Cambridge Univer. Press, 1926.

HEBB, D. O. *The Organization of Behavior.* New York: John Wiley & Sons, 1949.

JAMES, W. *Principles of Psychology.* New York: Holt, Rinehart, & Winston, 1890.

KOCH, S. (Ed.). *Psychology: A Study of a Science.* VI. Investigations of man as socius: Their place in psychology and the social sciences. New York: McGraw-Hill, 1963.

MacCURDY, J. T. *Common Principles in Psychology and Physiology.* Cambridge: Cambridge Univer. Press, 1928.

McDOUGALL, W. *Outline of Abnormal Psychology.* Chicago: Charles Scribner's Sons, 1926.

MEAD, G. H. *The Philosophy of the Act.* Chicago: Univer. of Chicago Press, 1938.

OSGOOD, C. E. The nature and measurement of meaning. *Psychol. Bull.,* 1952, *49,* 197-237.

——. *Method and Theory in Experimental Psychology.* New York: Oxford, 1956.

——. Psycholinguistics.
In: KOCH, S. VI. 1963.

PICKFORD, R. W., Aspects of the psychology of meaning. *J. genet. Psychol.,* 1950, *77,* 231-255.

SOKOLOV, E. N. Neuronal models and the orienting reflex.
In: BRAZIER, M. A. B. 1960.

STOUT, G. F. *Manual of Psychology.* London: Univer. Tut. Press, 1938.

TITCHENER, E. B. *Lectures on the Experimental Psychology of the Thought Processes.* New York: Macmillan, 1909.

ULLMANN, S. *Semantics: An Introduction to the Science of Meaning.* New York: Barnes & Noble, 1962.

WATSON, J. B. *Psychology from the Standpoint of a Behaviorist.* Philadelphia: Lippincott, 1924.

——. *Behaviorism.* New York: Norton, 1925.

CHAPTER 4

Early Experimental Studies of Meaning

> *Generalization is a verbal act of thought and reflects reality
> in quite another way than sensation and perception reflect it.
> There is every reason to suppose that the qualitative distinc-
> tion between sensation and thought is the presence in the latter
> of a generalized reflection of reality, which is also the essence
> of word meaning; and consequently that meaning is an act of
> thought in the full sense of the term. But at the same time
> meaning is an inalienable part of a word as such, and thus it
> belongs in the realm of language as much as in the realm of
> thought. A word without meaning is an empty sound, no longer
> a part of human speech. Since word meaning is both thought
> and speech, we find in it the unit of verbal thought we are
> looking for* [Vigotsky (1962) p. 5].

> *In the beginning was the Word* (John I, 1).

Conditioning methods

Two kinds of uncertainty have surrounded the problem of meaning
throughout the history of psychological concern with it. First was
the question whether meaning belonged to the phenomenological or
to the behavioral realm, as mentioned in the preceding chapter. If
it belonged to the behavioral realm, a further question was whether
meaning should refer only to the verbal area, or to behavior in
general, or to both. Although many theorists insisted on the larger
and more generalized aspects of meaning, experimental work has
from the beginning been limited to the study of observable behavior,
and largely confined to verbal phenomena. It began with the observation of a phenomenon which was later called *semantic generalization*.

SEMANTIC GENERALIZATION

When a reaction conditioned to one stimulus transfers to another, the amount of transfer varying directly with the similarity between the two stimuli, the phenomenon is called stimulus generalization. Of this, semantic generalization is a special case in which the similarity lies in the *meaning* rather than in the objective physical characteristics of the eliciting stimuli. The term "semantic generalization" was used by Razran (1939a) to describe the work of some Russian experimenters wherein a response was conditioned to a word or a sentence and then was found to generalize to other words, irrespective of any *physical* similarity between the eliciting words.

The experiments that Razran (1939a) summarized had been conducted prior to 1930 in the laboratories of Krasmagorsky and Ivanov-Smolensky, and had already been reported in Russia by Swartz. Workers in these laboratories had noted that responses conditioned to a sensory stimulus (for example, a light or an object of some kind) transferred to the word standing for the sensory stimulus (e.g., the word "light" or the name of the object), or vice versa (i.e., from the word to the object). These experiments suggested that a response conditioned to an actual stimulus would generalize to other stimuli bearing a *meaning* similarity to the stimulus rather than a physical similarity. In other words, they constituted the soil from which the experimental analysis of semantic conditioning in the USSR subsequently grew.

THE SIGNALLING SYSTEMS

Although Russian experimentalists rarely use the word meaning except in a popularly accepted, undefined way, it seems reasonable to equate a psychological concept of meaning with their concept of conditioned connections formed, with the aid of the orienting response, through the interaction of the first and second signalling systems. In another sense, the first and second signalling systems themselves might be regarded as two levels of meaning. The first signalling system includes such phenomena as sensation and perception, and roughly corresponds to American conceptions of direct associative processes (meaningfulness). However, there is no strict correspondence here in terms of *stimulus,* since direct associations can be formed between two words as designates of concrete objective referents. The correspondence is perhaps greater in terms of the *process* involved (first-order conditioning, perhaps). The second signalling system embraces speech, ideas, thoughts, abstractions, generalization, and may be roughly comparable to areas listed in America under the rubric of concept formation (second-order conditioning). Words may belong to either the first or second signalling system, or more often to both simultaneously.

RUSSIAN CONDITIONING METHODS

In a review article summarizing the fields of research and methods utilized in his laboratories, Ivanov-Smolensky (1956b) conceived of the entire activity of the central nervous system as a response to the effects of the organism's external and internal environment, as connecting these effects with one another, and as consisting of unconditioned and conditioned connections. He defined unconditioned connections as permanent connections (reflexes) arising in phylogenesis, and conditioned connections as temporary connections acquired in ontogenesis. Conditioned connections include connections formed between any stimulus and voluntary movements, with the aid of verbal instructions or by means of speech reinforcement, and connections (associations) between words.

He distinguished two classes of conditioned responses: 1) conditioned-unconditioned responses [including all vegetative conditioned responses (CRs) and many involuntary somatic CRs]. These are conditioned connections differentiated, with respect to the *effectors* involved, by the fact that they reproduce and duplicate, with no essential changes, the unconditioned reflex which generated them; and 2) conditioned-conditioned responses (including all voluntary movement and acquired motor behavior). These are connections wherein the effectors do *not* duplicate the unconditioned response (UCR), regardless of whether the CR was formed with the aid of a UCR or of verbal instructions. With respect to the *receptors* concerned, both types of connections may be established by direct *or* by verbal stimuli and thus, they are not identical with the first and second signalling systems.

From this summary, it would seem that much if not all of the Russian experimental investigations of the orienting response, of semantic conditioning, and of other kinds of conditioned-unconditioned[1] and conditioned-conditioned[2] connections could be considered under the rubric of the experimental investigation of meaning.

---

[1] Corresponding to the American conception of "classical conditioning."

[2] The definition of this term suggests something resembling the American conception of instrumental or "operant" conditioning.

Objects of Russian research on the response side have included 1) vegetative conditioned responses, such as the salivary, pupillary, pilomotor, respiratory, and cardio-vascular responses; 2) involuntary (excitatory) conditioned responses, such as swallowing, sucking, defensive (electrocutaneous), protective (eyewinking) and knee jerk responses; and 3) voluntary (motor) conditioned responses. In addition, the vocal motor and speech-conditioned connections (verbal associations) have been studied. Methods have involved the use of food stimuli, stimulation of the orienting reflex, speech reinforcement of voluntary movements, kinesthetic reinforcement (passive movement combined with a signal), direct and successive imitation, stimulation of double-defensive responses, verbal tests, and a variety of combined methods.

SEMANTIC GENERALIZATION: EXPERIMENTAL

Early studies in what Razran has called "semantic generalization" were rather straightforward studies of, in Russian terms, the "dynamic transmission" from the first to the second signalling system. Korbatov (1956) later distinguished a "double character" of the generalization of conditioned responses: 1) generalization to similar stimuli (stimulus generalization) and 2) generalization to word-designates (signs) for the stimuli (semantic generalization). Dynamic transmission may be observed not only when there is a conditioned motor reaction, but also when the most varied vegetative conditioned responses are elaborated.

Thus, much of the early work dealt with generalization from object to designate, or simplest first signalling system transfer, or with simple transfer from first to second signalling system.

A few examples may give the flavor of early Russian work which proved to be so influential in both the East and the West, although in quite different directions. Kapustnik (1930) established conditioned salivary reactions to visual and auditory stimuli and found significant generalization to verbal signs for the original stimuli. Smolenskaya (1934) established a discriminative conditioned response to a pattern of colored lights. The substitution of color words for the visual stimuli yielded measurable amounts of generalization in about half the subjects. Kotliarevsky (1935) demonstrated generalization to the word "bell" in subjects in whom pulse retardation was conditioned to the sound of a bell.

Traugott (1934) established a positive conditioned response

to the sound of a bell, a negative conditioned response (conditioned inhibition) to a bell plus a blue light. Substitution of the words "blue-blue" for the light resulted in inhibition in 70% of the cases, whereas presentation of a red light resulted in inhibition in a significantly smaller percentage of cases. This suggests that the words "blue-blue" are more meaningfully similar to blue light than is actual light of another color. Furthermore, the inhibitory effects of the words "blue-blue" generalized more broadly to other previously conditioned reflexes than did the blue light as stimulus. Note that in this experiment, the exciting (positive) stimulus (the bell) is contained in the inhibitory (negative) stimulus pattern (bell plus light). Thus the bell alone "means" *respond,* whereas the same bell, qualified by the blue light, "means" *do not respond.* From the standpoint of the nature of meaning, this seems even more interesting than the generalization phenomenon, since the "meaning" of the stimulus seemed to be determined, after conditioning, by a word indicating the qualifying characteristic rather than by the actual physical stimulus.[3]

Combining conditioning and free association techniques, Traugott and Fadeyeva[4] (1934) first established a positive conditioned response to an auditory-visual pattern of bell-whistle-light, and conditioned inhibition to an auditory-kinesthetic pattern of whistle-touch. An element of the excitatory pattern is again contained in the inhibitory pattern, yet in a post-conditioning word-association test, the associations to words representing the conditioned excitors came more rapidly than to signs of the conditioned inhibitors. Furthermore, after extinction of the positive conditioned response, the associative reaction time lengthened, and the words given in association became genetically older in that they referred to pre-experimental events.[5] It would appear from this that the functioning of the excitatory and inhibitory processes themselves is facilitated through conditioning of a specific response to sensory stimuli, since there was transfer not only on the stimulus side (from the actual stimuli to their verbal designates) but also on the response side (from the CR to verbal associates of the verbal stimuli).

These studies and many similar ones focused on generalization on the stimulus side, on transmission of conditioning within the

---

[3] Further instances of the primacy of the second over the first signalling system will be discussed later.

[4] This name is rendered in some translations as Faddeeva.

[5] Other instances of such "chronogenetic disinhibition" will be discussed later.

first signalling system (from physical object or signal to its specific verbal designate), and in some cases on transfer from the first to the second signalling system. They used both voluntary motor and vegetative or involuntary responses, and conditioned inhibition as well as conditioned positive responses on the response side; but in general the experimental designs were relatively uncomplicated, and the interest was centered largely on observing the phenomenon of generalization.

In the United States, Razran (1935) reported an experiment in which he had used himself as the subject. When he measured the amounts of saliva secreted while he thought (pronounced sub-vocally) the word for "saliva" in several languages, he found that the degree of generalization appeared to vary as a function of his knowledge of, or the frequency of his use of, the different languages. Thus the more "meaningful" the word, it would seem, the more it was reflected in the reflex response. A few years later (Razran, 1939a) he reviewed the Russian experiments in what he termed "semantic generalization," and reported another experiment of his own in which subjects conditioned to secrete 249 mg. of saliva per minute to the words *style, urn, freeze,* and *surf,* transferred the response to *fashion, vase, chill,* and *wave,* but not to *stile, earn, frieze,* and *serf.* These studies illustrate a different order or level of semantic generalization than the earlier Russian work, for here we are confronted with something more complex than simple transfer from first to second signalling system, or transfer within the first signalling system (homonymic transfer). In these instances, the elaboration and generalization is within the second signalling system.

Meanwhile these same Russian experiments were beginning to influence the work of Luria—also in the USSR—who described his work in a significant report, coauthored with Vinogradova (Luria and Vinogradova, 1959). Previously, Luria (1929, 1930, 1932) had been following another, although related, line of investigation which had its roots in Jung's[6] word association studies. These earlier Luria studies, replicated in the United States by Huston, Shakow, and Erickson (1934), made use of extensions of and improvements in Jung's methods and called attention to generalization on the response as well as the stimulus side. A subject was trained to asso-ciate a motor response of his preferred hand (finger press) with every verbal response in a word association test. Pressure tracings

[6] See p. 47.

were taken simultaneously from the other, nonresponding hand which merely rested on a pressure-sensitive device. The test phase of the experiment revealed that any word response which the subject failed to make appeared in the voluntary movement of the reactive hand as a partial response. Furthermore, the pressure curve from the other, inactive hand tended to lose its smooth, regular character. Luria theorized that effective excitation not completely discharged in the verbal response resulted in persistence of movement in the preferred hand after the voluntary response. With large amounts of excitation, a further spread to other systems may occur, disturbing, for example, respiration and/or causing involuntary movement of the other hand (response generalization). These studies, along with much of the subsequent Russian experimental work in semantic conditioning, raise serious questions as to how adequately meaning can be understood in terms of simple, grossly observable responses, or even in terms of response or stimulus generalization unless the terms stimulus and response are themselves redefined and elaborated.

In the subsequent experimental series, derived from the work in semantic generalization, and unavailable in English until 1959 (Luria and Vinogradova, 1959), Luria found that a plethysmographically recorded vascular reaction, stabilized through conditioning to the Russian word for "cat," failed to generalize in normal children 11 and 12 years old, to words phonetically resembling the stimulus word. However, words relating meaningfully to "cat" gave responses directly varying in intensity with the closeness of the meaning relationship. Diven (1937) conducted a similar experiment with adult subjects. He presented a list in which the word "barn" was repeated randomly along with single presentations of words presumably related to "barn," and of neutral words. Presentations of the word "barn" were reinforced with shock, and were preceded by the word "red." Generalization of the galvanic skin response (GSR)[7] was observed to words in the rural category but not to neutral words.

During this time Razran (1938, 1939b) continued with and elaborated on his experiments in semantic generalization using the salivary reflex. He flashed words and short sentences on a screen while six adults were eating. The order of the projections was randomized, and the presentations were made at two-minute inter-

---

[7] GSR refers to a measure of changes in the resistance of the skin to the passage of a low-voltage electrical current.

vals. Generalization of the salivary response was greater to semantically similar words than to phonetically similar words (homophones). These results supported the findings of Traugott and others with respect to the dominance of semantic over physical similarity. However, in a series of reports on other experiments, Razran (1949a, b, c, d, e) showed among other things that conditioned single words lost some of their generalization strength when they were combined in sentences, and, in another study (Razran, 1940), that attitudes and values of the subjects had to be reckoned with as significant variables. For example, the subjects' opinions regarding the truth or falsity of the stimulus statement affected conditioning and also influenced the generalization value of the words. This suggests not only that meaning is undoubtedly a more complicated function than simple association, but also that we might do well to examine more critically some of our simple assumptions with regard to the definition of stimulus and response. For example, can we regard anything presented to a subject as a simple stimulus without regard to its context?

Riess (1940), using the same test words as Razran had used in his experiment, but using the GSR to a loud buzzer as a substitute for the salivary technique, confirmed the previous findings of greater generalization to synonyms than to homophones (semantic rather than physical similarity), but later found that in young children this tendency was reversed (Riess, 1946). These results, along with further developments from Luria and Sokolov's work with very small children and mental retardates, pointed the way toward studying genetic aspects of the semantic function, but little has been done along these lines in the United States. Wylie (1940) repeated the experiments of Razran and Riess, conditioning the GSR elicited by shock to certain words and testing generalization not only to synonyms and homophones of the words but also to words bearing no relationship to the stimulus words. She failed to replicate Razran's and Riess's results, but explained the failure in terms of the subjects' "set," which she considered as merely an artifact of her experimental setup. It is possible that the process which we call "set" could be an element of the complex meaning process.

Cofer and Foley (1942) published an article which was important not only because it reviewed the experimental literature in semantic generalization to date but also because it set the stage for the development of a new area of interest and investigation:

the area of verbal behavior and verbal learning. They classified previous studies under three major categories of research design: those studies in which

1) a conditioned response was established to a stimulus object, and a test made for generalization to its name;

2) a conditioned response was established to a word (sign) and a test made for generalization to its object; and

3) a conditioned response was established to a word (sign) and a test made for generalization to other semantically or phonetically related signs—or words.

In an experiment which they classified under their third category, Foley and Cofer (1943) required each of five groups of subjects to repeat one of four different lists of words, and then tested for generalization with a fifth list. The example below shows the kinds of words used to compose the repetition lists. These lists included homophones of the test word (like 1 and 2 below), synonyms of the test word (like 3 in the example), and derived synonyms (such as 4 in the example).

Test word	*Homophones*	*Synonym*	*Derived Synonym*
Sent	1) Cent, 2) Scent	3) Dispatched	4) Killed

Note that "killed" is a synonym of "dispatched" but bears no *direct* relationship to "sent." The selection of words was ingenious, and the results were positive for semantic generalization, but they have been criticized because of a "flaw" in design which failed to control for the possibility of the subjects' "catching on" to the homonymic relationship. As a matter of fact, most of the subjects reported awareness of the homonymic relationship, whereas few reported awareness of the relationship of synonymity. However, the synonym groups demonstrated significant generalization as well as the homonym groups. A sixth (control) group, having repeated a list of unrelated words, showed no generalization to the test list at all.

THE PROBLEM OF AWARENESS

This foreshadows a current controversy with some interesting implications for meaning that will be discussed in more detail later on. The controversy regards the importance of awareness or unawareness in interpreting results in both generalization experiments and verbal conditioning. Many American experimentalists would agree that the subject's awareness of reinforcement contingencies in operant conditioning or awareness of semantic connections in learning experiments vitiates the experimental results. Others argue that "awareness" is a variable to be studied rather than a reason for discarding data or disregarding results. This controversy has opened up the question of the role that verbal instructions and reports by subjects play in the experimental situation. The notion that instructions might be one element of a compound stimulus has for far too long been suppressed by American experimentalists[8] either by ignoring the problem, or by attempting to control instruction as a variable by "standardizing" the verbal instructions used. This is one area where American psychologists might look to Russian experimentation for new interpretations of an old problem. Ivanov-Smolensky (1956a, p. 389) asserted that speech activity is no more subjective and no less objective than all other activities of the human organism; and thus speech activity both on the stimulus side and on the response side, is studied like any other stimulus and response activity. Taken by itself this statement could have been made by Skinner (1957), but there are conceptual and methodological differences between the American behaviorist and the Russian approaches to the investigation of verbal behavior. Soviet experimenters often treat verbal instruction as reinforcement, and verbal report as a response variable which has important uses in studying the interaction between the first and second signalling systems, particularly in the form of distortions in the transactions from one to the other (distortions in meaning).

CLASSICAL CONDITIONING AND LEARNING MODELS

The earlier American studies reviewed by Cofer and Foley (1942) were modeled on the classical conditioning paradigm, an understandable consequence of the fact that their prototypes came out of Russia and an atmosphere dominated by Pavlov's work. The Foley and Cofer (1943) experiment clearly shows the evolution of the learning and transfer experimental model—more popular with American psychologists—from the strictly classical conditioning model of Russian research.

The relationship between the classical conditioning model and

---

[8] For notable exceptions to this generalization, see Edwards (1961), Gagné (1964), Wickens, Allen, and Hill (1963).

the learning and transfer model was foreshadowed as early as 1935 by Neil Miller in his doctoral dissertation. This work was summarized in a long footnote in the Cofer and Foley (1942) review article, although it is not generally noted in the semantic generalization literature. Miller (1935) established in his human subjects GSRs which differentiated between a specific number and a specific letter, and found differentiated generalization to other numbers and letters not experimentally subject to direct reinforcement. From this he concluded that previous associations influence generalization of subsequent conditioning, and that mediating responses (meaning) can thus play an important role in transfer. It is interesting to compare Miller's study to one by Volkova (1953), nearly twenty years later, in which she established an experimental "past history" which affected subsequent responses. She conditioned her subject to salivate to "ten," not to "eight," and gave him arithmetic problems with either "10" or "8" as the correct answer. There was positive differentiation even when the number "8" or "10" appeared in the problem itself [e.g., $88 - 78 = 10$ (salivate), or $10 - 2 = 8$ (no salivation)]. This is another experiment which emphasizes the troublesome question as to the nature of the stimulus in an experiment. A possible hypothesis might be that the *functional* stimulus is the meaning which a stimulus-event has for the subject, but this again would require the specification of what is meant by meaning.

DECLINE OF CLASSICAL SEMANTIC GENERALIZATION

A temporary halt to American experimentation based on the Russian-originated, classical-conditioning type of semantic generalization study seems to have been called by Keller (1943).[9] There was a marked dearth of published material in the area of conditioning studies of semantic generalization during the ten or fifteen years following her report. Until about 1957 the only studies really comparable to the early generalization work were some experiments by Razran, which have already been mentioned, and a study by Corn-Becker, Welch, and Fisichelli (1949). Razran considered some psychological factors in the generalization of salivary conditioning to verbal stimuli (1949a, b) and also developed a crude semantic gradient to traditional association categories (1949c, d). Corn-Becker, Welch, and Fisichelli (1949) presented a series of

---

[9] See below, p. 44–45.

words which were designates of the reinforcing stimuli used (e.g., "green," "music," "bell," etc.). The word presentations were reinforced by the presentation of the stimuli themselves (e.g., the word "green" was followed by a green light, "music" was followed by recorded music, "bell" was followed by the sound of a bell, etc.) and the GSR was recorded. Then when they introduced the words "electric shock" on the 8th, 12th, or 16th trial, 73% of their subjects gave a GSR to the words "electric shock" alone that was larger in amplitude or longer in duration than the GSR to any of the reinforced CSs. An unreinforced control group gave only 13% GSRs to "electric shock." This has some interesting parallels to some of the Russian work, but the authors were primarily interested in hypnotic phenomena, one reason why this study has never been referred to in the semantic generalization literature.

During this hiatus in such American experimentation, the Russian work continued unabated, but this work was largely unknown in the United States until the Luria and Vinogradova (1959) studies were published in English.

The seemingly influential Keller (1943) experiment, referred to above, was in actuality inconclusive rather than negative for semantic generalization, but *post hoc* judgments are easily made. She conditioned the GSR to a picture of a boy scout hat, then tested for generalization with a picture of a fireman's hat, the word "hat," and such control words as "duck" and "ball." Here there was more generalization to the picture of the fireman's hat than to the word "hat." She concluded that these results might be attributed to the physical similarity between the conditioned and test objects (stimuli), or that it might be a matter of conceptual identity (both head coverings) rather than physical identity. The physical similarity between a fireman's hat and a boy scout hat seems rather tenuous, although the fact that they were both pictures might constitute a physical similarity between stimuli. No control pictures were shown, only control words. This study again raises some interesting questions about the nature of the stimulus, and about the validity of the assumptions that are often made with respect to the designation of the stimulus in particular experiments. It also suggests a broader view of meaning than that implied by experiments built upon simple replacement of physical stimuli by their specific verbal designates, or upon generalization across simple associative bonds. Although generalization along a conceptual dimension had been suggested by the few experiments that had studied transfer within the second signalling system, this was the first time that the possibility was made explicit. The uncontrolled features of Keller's experiment, resulting in failure to support the predictions, could well have contributed to the investigation of meaning by enlarging the conception of the problem had some of the possible implications been pursued, but the immediate consequence seems to have been to interrupt the development of experimentation along these established lines.

Scaling methods

Meanwhile, other methods were being developed or adapted to the study of meaning. Bingham (1943) combined the use of a physiological measure (the GSR) and a scaling technique when he had 50 subjects rate each of 72 words in terms of their *M*eaningfulness, *S*ignificance, and *I*mportance; he then developed an MSI Index, and correlated this measure with the GSR of the subjects to each of the words. He found a high positive relationship between GSR and MSI index, suggesting the validity of the use of GSR as a possible measure of meaning.

THE SEMANTIC DIFFERENTIAL

Osgood (1956a and b) and Osgood and Suci (1952, 1955) developed the well-known scaling device, the Semantic Differential, whereby subjects allocated concepts which were represented by word stimuli, on a standard set of bipolar descriptive scales by means of a series of independent judgments (Osgood, Suci, and Tannenbaum, 1957). Osgood and his coworkers applied factor analytic techniques to their data and arrived at three independent dimensions which they believe can describe the connotative meaning of any concept. Thus the meaning of any word could be described by its location within the three-dimensional space defined by the three independent factors: evaluation, potency, and activity.

The Semantic Differential by many considered a crucial development in the field, possibly provides a precise method of measuring *changes* in meaning.[10] If it were possible to demonstrate experimentally that behavior tends to change in relationship to changes in the phenomenal world of individual meanings—and the Semantic

---

[10] See Rogers (1964) for a discussion of this point.

Differential may provide the tool to do this in at least a limited way—the consequences for education in general and psychotherapy in particular would be enormous, especially in regard to improved methods and reliability of evaluation procedures. In addition, the Semantic Differential gives us a map of the "semantic space" of a concept whose relationships (with regard to dimensions and change) to other concepts and to various kinds of observable behavior might be determined. Furthermore, this method, itself a device for *discovering* the meaning of words, can be used for *measuring* the amount of transfer or generalization in experiments utilizing conditioning, learning, or association methods, and thus its development gave new impetus to the study of meaning.

However, with respect to understanding meaning rather than measuring meaning defined in terms of the instrument itself, the problem is more complex. The development of the Semantic Differential, and its subsequent sometimes rather uncritical employment by others than its author (as if it were the final word with regard to the global definition of meaning), illustrates two rather characteristic tendencies in American experimentation. One is a tendency that borders upon solipsism, and more will be said about this later. The other tendency is to stay outside the "black box" with respect to stimuli and responses studied, leaving a wider area to inference, and thus, seemingly at least, ever complicating the mediation model necessary to fill the gap between stimulus and response. This is particularly so when it comes to experiments with human subjects and to attempts to investigate complicated processes which involve language or meaning.

For example, one wonders what lies between a subject's reading of a particular word (S) and his response (R) on the Semantic Differential (his placement of the particular word on a continuum from one extreme of a verbal bipolar scale to another). It is not hard to grant that a simple, direct associative process may be involved in putting the word "mother" next to the word "good" or "bad," but how about placing it somewhere between "wet" and "dry," or "black" and "white?" Osgood's mediation model is neat and parsimonious, but it tells us nothing about the nature of the postulated self-stimulation. The Semantic Differential seems to "work" in that it predicts group verbal responses, even across cultures, and consequently has many valuable applications. For example, when bilingual subjects take translation-equivalent forms of the Semantic Differential (Japanese-English, for example) at different times, analysis of the data reveals identical connotative factors as highly correlated as when they are obtained from Americans taking the test twice in the same language [Osgood in Cofer (1961)].

However, the range of applicability of the Semantic Differential as a measure of meaning has not been thoroughly explored. It would be interesting to know, for example, what relationship, if any, obtains between the predictable verbal behavior and other types of behavior across cultures, or even within a given culture. If the meaning of a stimulus is a more potent determinant of behavior than the physical nature of the stimulus (which seems to be the case), then an adequate measure of meaning should predict other than verbal behavior.

The work on the development of the Semantic Differential is thoroughly covered by Osgood and his coworkers (Osgood, Suci, and Tannenbaum, 1957) and need not be reviewed in detail here. The uses to which it has been put in studies of semantic generalization by other experimenters using conditioning, association, and learning methods will be reviewed in later sections.

Word association methods

Interest in word association as a method of studying a variety of psychological variables has a long, venerable, and essentially uninterrupted history, beginning in 1904 with Carl Jung's work which culminated in his *Studies in Word Association* (1918). Jung, searching for "complex indicators," presented words to normal and abnormal subjects who were instructed to respond with the first word that came to mind. Any unusual extension of reaction time or deviant word response was considered to be indicative of a "complex," defined as a constellation of ideas with associated affect.

Later innovations which were introduced into the "free" association experiment of Jung included the methods of delayed repetition of the word list and the GSR measurement of associated affect. In 1910 Kent and Rosanoff conducted a study in which they obtained responses to a hundred common English words from over a thousand subjects, and modifications of their counts of response frequency are still used as a normative base for contemporary studies of association. These innovations resulted in three main lines of interest, namely, 1) the utilization of complex-indicators as evidence of guilty knowledge (the lie detector), 2) the development of standardized tests based on the frequency of associative responses to certain words by normal and abnormal subjects, and 3) the study of meaning.

The study of meaning took two main paths: the one already described above (p. 38ff.) and explored by Luria and his co-workers in the USSR, emphasized physiological aspects. The other, followed by American associationists, focused on the verbal response itself.

MEANING AND MEANINGFULNESS

In 1925 Carr suggested a close relationship between association and meaning when he asserted that meaning, which is not an observable process or independent item of experience, has no existence apart from that which "means" and that which is "meant." From this time on, and continuing vigorously in contemporary experimentation, word- association techniques and norms have been used in a variety of ways to support the view that associative bonds alone can account for semantic generalization. Recognizing the limitations of this view as a psychological definition of meaning, however, associationists have substituted the term "meaningfulness" for "meaning," finally reducing even this term to the letter M or *m*.

MEANINGFULNESS OF NONSENSE SYLLABLES

Various investigators have attempted to define the association value, meaningfulness, or M, in numerical terms. Early attempts dealt only with the association value of nonsense syllables (M), and were precipitated not by interest in the problem of meaning itself, but by the need to control the effects of this variable in learning experiments.

Glaze (1928) and Witmer (1935) defined M as the percentage of *subjects* in a given sample who "had an association" to a given syllable. Hull (1933) defined M as the number of *associations*, out of 60 possible associations, for each syllable. Krueger (1934) also defined M in terms of the frequency of response to a syllable, but in another way. He assigned 100% associative value to syllables arousing the highest frequency of response. Then he calculated the M value of each syllable in terms of the ratio of the frequency of *its* associates to the actual frequency of the 100% value syllables.[11] Later, Mandler (1955) defined M as the mean number of associates given continuously for 30 seconds in response to a syllable. Noble, Stockwell, and Pryer (1957) used scale ratings of meaningfulness as an index.

THE MEASUREMENT OF MEANINGFULNESS

That the attempts to define meaning in operational terms had their beginnings in work with nonsense syllables probably had a profound effect on the development of meaning definition among the American learning theorists and associationists. Noble (1952) pushed the attempt to define meaningfulness beyond the purview of the nonsense syllable into a broader area, and in so doing contaminated the pure concern over meaning as a controllable variable in learning experiments with a new dimension: interest in meaning itself. From this point on, it is often difficult to assess from the experimental literature in this area whether the focus of interest is on the learning process and the extent to which this process may be influenced by meaning as one variable; or whether the focus is on meaning itself: how meaning is constituted, how it can be defined, measured, and controlled.

Noble defined meaningfulness of a word or a sign (m) as the average number of associations given to that word (or sign) in continuous free association during a period of one minute, arguing that the number of learned and generalized overt responses that a stimulus elicits must be proportional to the total number of individual connections.

He began with the proposition that the noun "meaning" refers linguistically to "a dyadic relationship between terms" which is "transitive, symmetrical, and reflexive," (Noble, 1963) and with the belief that a systematic approach to the quantification of meaningfulness should be based on this proposition. He pointed out that meaning is not a serial relation in spite of transitivity, and thus, like any relationship, is intrinsically nonmeasurable. Meaning refers to habit bonds, or connections, or relationships without consideration of their magnitudes, but meaningfulness (connotation) is simply the linguistic equivalent of association. A word or sign having many connotations is more meaningful than one having

---

[11] For a review of the early work in this area, see Underwood and Schulz (1960).

only a few; thus meaningfulness of a sign can be measured in terms of the number of associations which it elicits.

This conception has had a marked effect upon subsequent work in association, and indices of meaningfulness, associative strength, and the like have proliferated since Noble's proposition.[12] Conceptions of the mediating properties of associative meaning or meaningfulness issuing from these early studies, as well as the frequency norms developed from them, are currently used in studies which once again focus primarily upon the learning process rather than upon meaning itself, although there seems to be a continuing thread of acute awareness that the problem of the nature and importance of meaning is still far from solved. From the point of view of method, two major refinements, or rather combinations, of association and learning methods have taken over the center of the experimental stage: namely, the study of associative clustering in recall of learned material, and paired-associate learning, which combines conditioning concepts with association concepts in the study of verbal learning and verbal behavior.

Summary

The experimental study of meaning began with the investigation of a phenomenon, observed in studies of classical conditioning and reported in the Russian literature, called "semantic generalization." Early American experiments, like the Russian, used the classical conditioning paradigm and studied generalization from object to verbal designate. Gradual modifications were introduced into the experimental method so that a word came to replace the unconditioned stimulus, and the evolution from classical conditioning into a verbal learning paradigm was under way. Interest in semantic generalization flourished from about 1935 for some ten to fifteen years, and then waned. Meanwhile, word association techniques were beginning to be employed in the study of meaning, and the Semantic Differential was developed as a method for the measurement of meaning. The combination of associationistic and conditioning approaches, along with the use of the Semantic Differential as a measuring device, led to new methods of investigation.

In Russia, Luria and his coworkers combined word association techniques with classical conditioning to study developmental aspects

---

[12] See below, Chapter 7.

of the signalling systems and the operation of the orienting reflex, while in other laboratories elaborations of classical conditioning methods led to the more complex work in semantic conditioning which will be considered later.

The only new definition of meaning which came out of this early work was Osgood's definition of meaning as a hypothetical construct: a mediating response with both response and stimulus properties. What can be inferred from the conditioning and association work is a view of meaning as an associationistic or generalizing process.

References

BINGHAM, W. E., JR. A study of the relations which the galvanic skin response and sensory reference bear to judgments of the meaningfulness, significance, and importance of 72 words. *J. Psychol.,* 1943, *16,* 21–34.

CARR, H. A. *Psychology.* New York: Longmans, 1925.

COFER, C. N. (Ed.). *Verbal Learning and Verbal Behavior.* New York: McGraw-Hill, 1961.

——, & FOLEY, J. P. Mediated generalization and the interpretation of verbal behavior: I. Prologomena. *Psychol. Rev.,* 1942, *49,* 513–540.

——, & MUSGRAVE, B. S. (Eds.). *Verbal Behavior and Learning: Problems and Processes.* New York: McGraw-Hill, 1963.

CORN-BECKER, F., WELCH, L., & FISICHELLI, V. Conditioning factors underlying hypnosis. *J. abnorm. soc. Psychol.,* 1949, *44,* 212–222.

DIVEN, K. Certain determinants in the conditioning of anxiety reactions. *J. Psychol.,* 1937, *3,* 291–308.

EDWARDS, W. Costs and payoffs are instructions. *Psychol. Rev.,* 1961, *68(4),* 275–284.

FOLEY, J. P., JR., & COFER, C. N. Mediated generalization and the interpretation of verbal behavior: II. Experimental study of certain homophone and synonym gradients. *J. exp. Psychol.,* 1943, *32,* 168-175.

GAGNÉ, R. M. Verbal instructions as experimental variables in learning. Symposium: *Meaningful Verbal Learning.* Los Angeles: APA Convention 1964. *Ref.: Amer. Psychologist,* 1964, *19(7),* 469.

GLAZE, J. A. The association value of non-sense syllables. *J. genet. Psychol.,* 1928, *55,* 255–269.

HULL, C. L. The meaningfulness of 320 selected nonsense syllables. *Amer. J. Psychol.,* 1933, *45,* 730–734.

HUSTON, P. E., SHAKOW, D., & ERICKSON, M. H. A study of hypnotically induced complexes by means of the Luria technique. *J. genet. Psychol.,* 1934, *61,* 65–97.

IVANOV-SMOLENSKY, A. G. Paths and perspectives for the development of the physiology and pathophysiology of the higher nervous activity in children. a
In: IVANOV-SMOLENSKY, A. G., et al. II. 1956.
——. Developmental paths of experimental research into the work and interaction of the first and second signalling systems. b.
In: IVANOV-SMOLENSKY, A. G., et al. II. 1956.
——, et al. (Eds.). *Works of the Institute of Higher Nervous Activity: Pathophysiological Series.* II. Moscow: Academy of Sciences of the USSR, 1956.
JUNG, C. G. *Studies in Word Association.* London: William Heinemann, 1918.
KAPUSTNIK, O. P. The interrelationship between direct conditioned stimuli and their verbal symbols. (Trans. from Russian title.) *Psych. Abstr.,* 1930, *8,* 152.
KELLER, M. Mediated generalization: The generalization of a conditioned galvanic skin response established to a pictured object. *Amer. J. Psychol.,* 1943, *56,* 438–448.
KENT, G. H., & ROSANOFF, A. J. A study of association in insanity. *Amer. J. Insanity,* 1910, *67,* 37–96.
KORBATOV, B. M. Study of the dynamic transmission of a conditioned connection from one cortical signalling system into the other.
In: IVANOV-SMOLENSKY, A. G., et al. II. 1956.
KOTLIAREVSKY, L. I. Cardio-vascular conditioned reflexes to direct and to verbal stimuli. (Trans. from Russian title.) *Psychol. Abstr.,* 1935, *13,* 40–46.
KRUEGER, W. C. F. The relative difficulty of nonsense syllables. *J. exp. Psychol.,* 1934, *17,* 145–153.
LURIA, A. R. Die Methode der abbildenden Motorik bei Kommunikation der Systeme und ihre Anwendung auf die Affektpsychologie. *Psychol. Forsch.,* 1929, *12,* 127–179.
——. Die Methode der abbildenden Motorik in der Tatbestanddiagnostik. *Z. angew. Psychol.,* 1930, *35,* 139–183.
——. *The Nature of Human Conflicts.* New York: Liveright, 1932.
——, & VINOGRADOVA, O. S. An objective investigation of the dynamics of semantic systems. *Brit. J. gen. Psychol.,* 1959, *50,* 89-105.
MANDLER, G. Associative frequency and associative prepotency as measures of response to nonsense syllables. *Amer. J. Psychol.,* 1955, *68,* 662–665.
MILLER, N. E. The influence of past experience upon the transfer of subsequent training. Unpub. Ph.D. diss., Yale Univer., 1935.
NOBLE, C. E. An analysis of meaning. *Psychol. Rev.,* 1952. *59,* 421-430.
——. Meaningfulness and familiarity.
In: COFER, C. N., & MUSGRAVE, B. S. 1963.

——, STOCKWELL, F. E., & PRYER, N. W. Meaningfulness (m') and association value (a) in paired-associate syllable learning. *Psychol. Rep.,* 1957, *3,* 441-452.

OSGOOD, C. E. Behavior theory and the social sciences. *Behav. Sci.,* 1956a, *1,* 167–185.

——. *Method and Theory in Experimental Psychology.* New York: Oxford, 1956b.

——, & SUCI, G. A measure of relation determined by both mean difference and profile information. *Psychol. Bull.,* 1952, *49,* 251–262.

——, ——. Factor analysis of meaning. *J. exp. Psychol.,* 1955, *50,* 325–338.

——, ——, & TANNENBAUM, P. H. *The Measurement of Meaning.* Urbana, Ill.: Univer. Ill. Press, 1957.

RAZRAN, G. H. S. Salivating and thinking in different languages. *J. Psychol.,* 1935, *1,* 145–151.

——. Conditioning away social bias by the luncheon technique. *Psychol. Bull.,* 1938, *35,* 693.

——. A quantitative study of meaning by a conditioned salivary technique (semantic conditioning). *Science,* 1939a, *90,* 89–90.

——. Semantic, syntactic, and phonetographic generalization of verbal conditioning. *Psychol. Bull.,* 1939b, *36,* 578.

——. Conditioned response changes in rating and appraising sociopolitical slogans. *Psychol. Bull.,* 1940, *37,* 481.

——. Semantic and phonetographic generalizations of salivary conditioning to verbal stimuli. *J. exp. Psychol.,* 1949a, *39,* 642–652.

——. Attitudinal determinants of conditioning and of generalization of conditioning. *J. exp. Phychol.,* 1949b, *39,* 820–829.

——. Some psychological factors in the generalization of salivary conditioning to verbal stimuli. *Amer. J. Psychol.,* 1949c, *62,* 247–256.

——. Stimulus generalization of conditioned responses. *Psychol. Bull.,* 1949d, *46,* 337–365.

——. Sentential and propositional generalizations of salivary conditioning to verbal stimuli. *Science,* 1949e, *109,* 447–448.

——. The observable unconscious and the inferable conscious in current Soviet psychophysiology: Interoceptive conditioning, semantic conditioning, and the orienting reflex. *Psychol. Rev.,* 1961, *68,* 81–147.

RIESS, B. F. Semantic conditioning involving the GSR. *J. exp. Psychol.,* 1940, *26.* 238–240.

——. Genetic changes in semantic conditioning. *J. exp. Psychol.,* 1946, *36,* 143–152.

ROGERS, C. R. Toward a science of the person.
In: WANN, T. W. 1964.

SKINNER, B. F. *Verbal Behavior.* New York: Appleton-Century-Crofts, 1957.

SMOLENSKAYA, E. P. Verbal symbols of conditional and differentiated stimuli. (Trans. from Russ.). *Na Putyakh K Izuch. Rysshykh form Neirodin.* 1934, 304–315.

TRAUGOTT, N. N. The interrelation of immediate and symbolic projections in the process of the formation of conditioned inhibition. (Trans. from Russ.). *Psychol. Abstr.,* 1934, *9,* 1166.

———, & FADEYEVA, V. K. The effect of difficult extinction of food-procuring conditioned reflexes upon the general and speech behavior of children. (Trans. from Russ.). *Psychol Abstr.,* 1934, *9,* 1167.

UNDERWOOD, B. J., & SCHULZ, R. W. *Meaningfulness and Verbal Learning.* Philadelphia: J. B. Lippincott, 1960.

VIGOTSKY, L. S. *Thought and Language.* Cambridge, Mass.: M.I.T. Press, 1962.

VOLKOVA, V. D. On certain characteristics of the formation of conditioned reflexes to speech stimuli in children. *Fiziol. zh. SSSR,* 1953, *39,* 540–548. *From:* RAZRAN, G. H. S., 1961.

WANN, T. W. (Ed.). *Behaviorism and Phenomenology.* Chicago: Univer. of Chicago Press, 1964.

WICKENS, D. D., ALLEN, C. K., & HILL, F. A. Effect of instructions and UCS strength on extinction of the conditioned GSR. *J. exp. Psychol.,* 1963, *66(3),* 235–240.

WITMER, L. R. The association value of three place consonant syllables. *J. genet. Psychol.,* 1935, *47,* 337–360.

WYLIE, R. C. Generalization of semantic conditioning to the GSR. Unpub. M.A. thesis, Univer. Pittsburgh, 1940.

PART TWO
Contemporary Experimentation

Introduction

Contemporary developments in the search for meaning can be considered under the same methodological categories used in sketching in the background material. Some of the contemporary work in verbal learning is specifically concerned with meaning and meaningfulness as an intervening variable in learning experiments—as a mediator between stimulus and response, or in the facilitation of the learning process. This work stems methodologically from the old classical conditioning paradigm, and combines associative methods and/or utilizes associative norms with "conditioning" or learning methods. The focus of this work is the learning process—the concern with meaning itself being secondary. By and large, meaning as a mediating variable is assumed to be nothing but that which can be accounted for in terms of associative bonds between words. As we shall see later, there is a growing dissatisfaction with this assumption, and it seems likely that new attempts to discover the nature of meaning may develop out of the failure of the assumption to further the experimental investigation of the learning process.

Work in verbal association has continued, and further attempts to develop more sophisticated measures of meaningfulness have been and are being made. Beginning as an attempt to define meaningfulness, association indices have been developed and used in a variety of ways, primarily as a technique to study clustering in recall and to measure meaningfulness as a mediator in paired associate learning experiments.

How much such indices of word relatedness based on free or restricted associations to single words can contribute to the understanding of meaning remains to be seen. However, beginnings have been made toward a particular kind of measurement which, with further refinements and elaboration to take account of patterning and subtleties of relatedness among words and categories of words, may prove to be of value in the further definition of meaning. One thing which seems to have been achieved is the realization that meaning, or even meaningfulness, is not simple or unitary but rather highly complex, and that it will require more complex experimental techniques than we have yet devised to begin to unravel the problem.

Conditioning studies of meaning or semantic generalization in the old classical sense have all but disappeared from the American literature. Operant techniques are beginning to be applied in the area of verbal behavior, but the focus of concern at present is upon the control of behavior, not upon meaning. How relevant to the search for the psychological nature of meaning this development is remains to be seen. In Russia, however, experimental work using classical conditioning methods continues, and the relevance of this work for an understanding of meaning is more apparent.

Conditioning Methods, USA

A word is as real a conditioned stimulus for man as all the other stimuli in common with animals, but at the same time more all-inclusive than any other stimuli [Pavlov, quoted in Platonov (1959) p. 15].

Classical conditioning

In the United States, the term "semantic generalization"—although still used occasionally—refers mainly to early classical conditioning studies and appears in only a few contemporary studies closely following this model. The classical method seems to be less popular than the operant method in conditioning, and verbal learning paradigms are more popular than conditioning paradigms in the study of meaning. The terms "transfer" or "mediation" are used more frequently than "generalization" in verbal learning studies. Both these concepts emphasize simple association or associative chains, whereas the semantic generalization concept implies not only conditioned connections in the classical sense, but also the concept of stimulus generalization which has been attacked with some vigor by several American experimenters.[1]

In the revival of interest in the problem of meaning, two major types of conditioning studies were carried out. Some followed the old classical paradigm, conditioning a word by pairing it with an unconditioned stimulus (UCS), and measuring generalization of the conditioned response (CR). Others used a classical conditioning paradigm modified with respect to the unconditioned stimulus in that a word with some assumed or measured meaning was substituted for the UCS. This UCS was paired with another word or a nonsense syllable as conditioned stimulus (CS) during the training or "conditioning" trials, and generalization to related words, objects, or events was measured in test trials. Due to the develop-

[1] See Prokasy and Hall (1963) for a thorough discussion of the background and current status of the concept of stimulus generalization.

ment of the Semantic Differential and indices of association, the "meaning" of words could be predetermined and thus, it was thought, they could be regarded as adequate UCS. With this development, the distinction between the classical conditioning paradigm and the paired-associate learning paradigm became so tenuous as virtually to disappear. Indeed, the older type of conditioning study has been gradually displaced by the learning model in the United States.

CONDITIONING AND THE SEMANTIC DIFFERENTIAL

One example of this modified type of study emerged as a milestone, since it reawakened interest in the psychological investigation of meaning, and used a method which demonstrated the relationship between the old (classical conditioning) methods and the new (association and learning) methods of studying meaning. In addition, it made use of the Semantic Differential to determine the "meaning" of the UCS words. The authors of this study, Staats and Staats (1957), reasoned that if a nonsense syllable were presented and immediately followed by a meaningful word, it would be expected (if "meaning" is a response with mediating properties) that the meaning response elicited by the word would be conditioned to the nonsense syllable. In order to eliminate the possibility of explaining generalization or transfer by simple association, and in the face of the unlikelihood that conditioning would take place in a single presentation, the nonsense syllable was paired at each presentation with a word different from all other stimulus words, but having the same semantic differential meaning components. No synonyms were used, but instead words were taken from the Semantic Atlas,[2] whose meaning index (as determined by their position on the Semantic Differential Scale) was the same or similar. The nonsense syllables were presented visually, and the word aurally immediately after the visual presentation of the syllable. The subjects were instructed to pay attention to the syllables on the screen, but at the same time to listen to the spoken word and to pronounce it to themselves immediately after hearing it. Following the conditioning trials, the subjects were asked to rate the nonsense syllables on the Semantic Differential Scale. UCS words with evaluative components, with

---

[2] See Jenkins, Russell, and Suci (1957). The Semantic Atlas consists of words whose "meaning" indices as measured by the Semantic Differential have been determined by normative methods.

activity-passivity components, and with potency components were used, each meaning type with a different experimental group. Results showed generalization to the nonsense syllables from words representing all three meaning components.

In a study which is an extension of the Staats' experiment, Pollio (1963) used three nonsense syllables as the conditioned stimuli (CS), each set of three being paired with nine words as UCS. For one group of subjects, the nine words had high evaluative meaning; for a second group the words had low evaluative (negative) meaning; and for a third, the control group, the words were neutral. The words for all groups were chosen so as to control for intralist meaning similarity. The CS was displayed on a screen for five seconds, and after one additional second, the experimenter read the UCS word and the subject repeated it after him. This procedure was followed until each of the nine words had been paired with each of the three syllables. Following the conditioning or training period, the subjects were asked for their word associations to the CS syllables. A different group rated the obtained associates on the good-bad scale of the Semantic Differential. About 50% of the associates given were from the original list of UCS words, but new associates were also found to have Semantic Differential ratings congruent with the UCS ratings. Cohen (1964), however, in a replication of the Staats' study, found that when his subjects were classified as aware or unaware, there was no evidence of the conditioning of meaning without awareness. Hare (1964), using a similar method, also found transfer only in aware subjects who tended to rate the CS syllables in terms of their recalled relationships to the UCS words. He concluded that the subjects had regarded the experiment as a problem-solving task and therefore rated the syllables as they thought they were supposed to.

DiVesta and Stover (1962) went a step further. Using fifth-grade children as subjects, they demonstrated generalization of evaluative meaning over a three-step process: 1) nonsense syllables were conditioned by pairing them with words with evaluative meaning; 2) nonsense figures were paired with the nonsense syllables which had *acquired* meaning; 3) generalization was obtained to the figures.

In a further elaboration Staats and Staats (1958) conducted two experiments to test the hypothesis that attitude responses elicited by a word can be conditioned to a continuously presented, socially significant verbal stimulus. In one experiment, two national names

(Swedish and Dutch) were paired with words with positive and negative evaluative meaning, respectively; in the other study, familiar masculine names (Tom, Bill) were used. Evaluative meaning of the national and masculine names was then tested for on the Semantic Differential Scale, the results yielding evidence that the meaning responses were conditioned to the names without the subjects' awareness. De Montmollin and Le Ny (1962), using French subjects and the French language, later failed to replicate these results.

In an attempt to replicate an experiment of Volkova (1953), Acker and Edwards (1964) used a classical paradigm but they substituted a vasomotor response for Volkova's salivary response. The results for both experiments were positive for generalization. In both experiments a response was conditioned to the words "good" and "bad," the subject in Volkova's experiment being conditioned by food reinforcement to salivate to "good" and inhibit to "bad." Volkova tested for generalization to sentences whose "meanings" were "good" or "bad," according to an *a priori* judgment. Her subject subsequently produced the conditioned salivary response to such sentences as, "The children are playing well," and "The fisherman caught many fish," but did not respond to such sentences as, "The pupil was fresh to the teacher," "The pupil failed . . .," "Brother insults sister," and "The facists destroyed many cities."

Acker and Edwards used white noise to condition a vasomotor response in their subjects' index fingers to either the word "good" or "bad." As a test for generalization they used words which the subjects had previously rated on a good-bad bipolar scale (the Semantic Differential). They found that the evaluative meaning dimension predicted accurately the words to which transfer of vasoconstriction would or would not occur, and there was no difference in transfer between a group instructed to evaluate each word as presented and a group receiving no instruction.

One might conclude that through such discriminative conditioning to evaluative terms, it would be possible to measure directly not only the nature but perhaps also the intensity of evaluative meanings attached by a given subject to a wide variety of concepts. An interesting elaboration of the Acker and Edwards experiment might be to test out the correspondence between the other Semantic Differential factors and generalization of a physiological response to words rated on the scale for *those* factors. Such tests seem necessary to lend validity to the assumptions implied by the use of the Semantic Differential as a definitive measure of the meaning of a word or words in experiments which use "meaning" as a starting point to investigate other variables. Even more essential is to find out whether the correspondence between any of the Semantic Differential factors and physiological responses to words, if found, would hold up if more complex concepts were substituted for single words. An experiment reported by Tanaka (1964) seems to suggest that they do, even cross-culturally. However, criticisms such as those by Triandis (1964) regarding the susceptibility of the Semantic Differential to response sets, by Carroll (1959a and b) and Deese (1964) on the basis of the statistical assumptions involved in the derivation of the factors, and by Thompson (1962, 1963) and Mordkoff (1963) regarding assumptions of polarity, have not been adequately answered.

A most interesting experiment related to the question of whether or not the Semantic Differential can be regarded as a measure of meaning may well be reviewed here. Although it is not a conditioning experiment, its results raise some important questions regarding the interpretation of results from conditioning experiments that use the Semantic Differential to measure semantic generalization. Beier (1964) constructed three different "polar" scales comparable to the Semantic Differential scales—except that one consisted of near opposites, one of non-opposite emotional words, and one of randomly selected nouns. He had his subjects rate such concepts as son, daughter, father, etc., on these three scales, and found that the distance between such concepts as son-daughter, son-father stayed reliably alike without regard to the reference points against which the concepts were measured. From these results he concluded that a subject rates a given distance into a random scale as into a good-bad scale, and that it is not unlikely that the rater is concerned with placing distance between the rated concepts rather than with the meaning of the reference points. One wonders what kind of "meaning" dimensions a factor analysis of scales such as these would yield.

CONDITIONING AND ASSOCIATION

The modified conditioning paradigm of Staats and Staats has almost completely metamorphosed into the paired-associate learning paradigm which will be considered in a later section. A method, intermediate between true classical conditioning and the learning method, using both conditioning and paired associate learning, is illustrated by an experiment conducted by Phillips (1958). She paired Turkish words with various shades of grey and then, using a loud tone as UCS, conditioned the GSR to a particular word (CS). She found that the GSR generalized to other words related to the CS by the previous pairing of the words with greys. The magnitude of the generalization effect was an inverse function of the grey associated with the CS and the grey associated with the test word. That is, the less the distance between the two greys (or the greater the similarity in "meaning" of the greys), the greater the generalization.

Another type of study combining conditioning and association methods was one designed by Bousfield and Cowan (1963) to test Bousfield's (1961) partial-response-identities theory which holds that the immediate response to a word is its implicit emission,

> (which) interpretation makes possible the useful assumption that a word functions both as a response and as a stimulus. The representational response develops as a consequence of repeated constant stimulation, and it is typically a part of the total response [Bousfield and Cowan (1963) p. 52].

This notion may be extended to account for a verbal response to a nonverbal stimulus which elicits a nonverbal representational response plus one or more verbal responses (labels), such represensational processes representing an absent stimulus. This concept is basic to Bousfield's mediation model which we shall encounter later. Since he asserts that the concept of meaning is superfluous,[6] it would be inaccurate to label his theory of partial response identities a theory of meaning, but it refers to a model which corresponds to mediation models proposed by other authors as equivalents for the concept of "meaning" or "meaningfulness." Bousfield and Cowan made the assumption that, according to the requirements of classical conditioning of a motor response, the sequential occurrence of a nonverbal CS and a nonverbal UCS should also establish connections between the verbal associative responses elicited by the CS and the UCS, even when the subject only observed the CS-UCS connection.

The conditioning procedure involved an apparatus which dropped a ball (UCS) on the subject's hand unless the subject withdrew it in response to a light flash signal (CS). Thus a conditioned

---

[6] See p. 176.

avoidance response was established to a flash of light. The verbal associates to the CS were "light," "flash," and "blink," and to the UCS "drop," "ball," and "fall." Each of these words was embedded in a list of neutral words, and each was used as the stimulus in a forced-choice association test of forward and backward associations. Three groups of subjects were used: the first was conditioned to the avoidance response, the second observed the light flash followed by the ball's dropping in the apparatus, and the third (control) group never saw the apparatus, but was given the subsequent association task. For this test, each group was divided into two, half being tested for forward associations (e.g., light $\longrightarrow$ ball) and half for backward associations (e.g., ball $\longrightarrow$ light). The results demonstrated parallel associative connections between the family of verbal associates to the CS and the UCS as a result of both conditioning and observation; no difference was found between forward and backward associations. The authors interpreted these results as supporting the response-identities theory, in that—instead of an associative response—a labeling response was given which is representational in nature and produces feedback, thus providing a representational stimulus. However, to the extent that the experimenters' conclusions are based upon the finding of equality between forward and backward associations, their argument is weakened by the demonstration by Asch and Ebenholtz (1962) and Horowitz, Brown, and Weissbluth (1964) that verbal association is symmetrical if its units are equally available.

ABSTRACT CONDITIONING

A conditioning study by Waters and Kodman (1962) was based upon a notion of "abstract conditioning" and bears a closer resemblance to Russian work in semantic conditioning than to American studies in semantic generalization. "Abstract conditioning," a term proposed by Welch (1947), is defined as generalized conditioning resulting from "conditioning factors of past associations."[7] It is perhaps because the early work of Welch and others was done in an attempt to explain suggestibility during hypnosis that it is not referred to in the literature concerning semantic generalization, although it has interesting implications for the study of meaning.

Waters and Kodman's (1962) experiment used a method which was essentially a replication of the Corn-Becker, Welch, and Fisi-

---

[7] Corn-Becker, Welch, and Fisichelli (1949).

chelli (1949) experiment discussed above. Using suggestible and nonsuggestible groups, they conditioned subjects by pairing projected verbal designates with a variety of reinforcing stimuli (e.g., the word "green" followed by a green light, "music" followed by recorded music, "bell" followed by the sound of a bell, etc.) and recorded GSRs to the visual presentations of the words. At intervals, the unreinforced word "electric shock" was shown. The results showed that the nonsuggestible group, but not the suggestible group, gave larger GSRs to the unreinforced word than the mean GSRs to the reinforced words in the conditioning situation. Yet in the control condition (unreinforced pre-experimental stage) suggestible subjects gave larger GSRs to "electric shock" than to the other words, whereas there was no difference in responsiveness in the nonsuggestible group.

The authors interpret their results as demonstrating "abstract conditioning," while Russian experimenters would call it "semantic conditioning." The Waters and Kodman experiment suggests that the generalization effects of conditioning can overcome a previously well established discrimination, even in nonsuggestible subjects. It remains for others to develop and refine the method and apply it more specifically to the study of meaning. At the least this indicates that a stimulus can acquire meaning from the situation in which it is embedded, or can change its meaning with changes in its context without being itself specifically reinforced.

THE PROBLEM OF AWARENESS

At about the time that Staats and Staats produced their modification of the conditioning method, Branca (1957) published a study based on the classical conditioning paradigm and rearoused mild interest in semantic generalization. He tested for semantic generalization using shock as the unconditioned stimulus (UCS), words and pictures as the conditioned stimuli (CS), and the GSR as the conditioned response (CR). He carried the training trials to the point where GSR had essentially extinguished to everything except the conditioned stimulus. The test for generalization showed the largest amount of generalization when the conditioned stimulus consisted of three synonyms and the test stimulus was the fourth synonym. In descending order, there was less generalization when the conditioned stimulus was a picture and the test stimulus its name; when the conditioned stimulus was a name, and the test stimulus a picture; and when the conditioned stimulus was a single word and the test stimulus its synonym. In all of the five experiments which he conducted, Branca found that the generalization of the conditioned response was 93% predictable on the basis of the subject's expectation of shock. However, he concluded that possibly, since awareness was ascertained after the test for transfer, the subjects had become aware of the connection during the inquiry and after the connection was established, leaving open the question as to whether "true" generalization was involved. The implication here is, of course, that what occurs as a result of awareness cannot be considered generalization. In a replication of an experiment by Volkova (1953),[3] Acker and Edwards (1964) found no differential results with respect to generalization between their instructed ("aware") and noninstructed ("unaware") groups. They discussed this finding in terms of how they might qualify Branca's results, but concluded that since no independent measure of expectation (awareness) was obtained from their own subjects, their results were merely suggestive with respect to generalization without awareness.

A conditioning experiment of Grice and Davis (1958) used a method which seems to rule out awareness as a necessary factor in the generalization of an unconditioned response. Using a puff of air (UCS), they conditioned subjects' eye-blink (UCR) to a tone (CS). Subjects also learned to make a specific motor response (CR) to the conditioned tone. Then two other tones were paired with motor responses, one response being the same as that made to the CS. The unconditioned tone which had a response in common with the CS produced more eye-blinks than did the tone paired with the other response. In this study, there are no verbal aspects, since the variables on the stimulus and response side are nonverbal. Yet it seems not unreasonable to say that here a particular tone acquired the "meaning" of another one, expressed in eye-blinks rather than words.

The questions raised with respect to interpretation by these and other authors illustrate one difference in approach and definition between American and Russian experimenters who are concerned with strikingly similar problems and research methods. To the American experimentalists, the presence of awareness of the meaningful connections involved in the experiment serves to vitiate any results that indicate that generalization has occurred. Thus it would appear that a rather paradoxical conclusion must be reached: that

---

[3] See p. 60.

connections are meaningful, or that meaning can be inferred from connections only if the subject is unaware of the connections; or that meaning exists only at the "unconscious" level. Russian experimenters seem inclined to view the subject's awareness, and the evidence given in his verbal report, not as evidence of a lack of generalization but as a sign of correspondence or consistency between the signalling systems; this in turn would indicate a higher level of integration of the signalling systems than is the case when there is discontinuity or discrepancy between the two systems. The American controversy over the importance of awareness will be discussed again in later sections dealing with other than classical conditioning methods.

THE PROBLEM OF UNKNOWN PARAMETERS

The awareness controversy illustrates in one area the consequences that inadequate data and lack of definition have on both methodology and the interpretation of experimental results. There are many other variables which have been inadequately studied and are thus either uncontrolled in experimental design or ignored in the interpretation of results, especially in generalization studies using classical conditioning methods. Prokasy and Hall (1963), for example, pointed out that the onset characteristics of a stimulus event may affect various response attributes. Sloboda (1964) insisted that latency characteristics of the GSR must be considered when this measure is being used in conditioning experiments. He found that there was no difference in latency of the onset and peak of the GSR accompanying reinforced and unreinforced responses during the conditioning trials in a DRL[4] operant conditioning task using a tone and points as reinforcement. However, during the extinction period, both GSR latencies were significantly different from the corresponding latencies during conditioning. In addition to the cautionary implications of these findings for the interpretation of experiments using GSR as a response measure, these results raise some interesting questions with respect to meaning. How is it that the same unreinforced response produces one GSR latency in the context of the conditioning trials and another in the context of the extinction trials?

White (1964) studied variations in stimulus and response

---

[4]DRL refers to the method of differential reinforcement of a low rate of responding.

modalities. Having determined the subjective intensities of light, tone, and mild shock stimuli, he equated the intensity value of the stimuli used in the experiment. Using the GSR and a plethysmographic record as measures, he found a significantly greater vasomotor responsivity to tone, and a significantly greater GSR reactivity to shock than to tone, although equal to the light stimulus. In a more elaborate experimental design, Kimmel, Hill, & Fowler (1962) matched auditory and visual stimuli for intensity so that they produced, before conditioning, equivalent unconditioned GSRs. Group 1 received 10 shock reinforcements of the light followed by 10 of the tone. Group 2 received 10 shock reinforcements of the tone followed by 10 shock reinforcements of the light. Group 3 received 10 shock reinforcements of each in a balanced order. Group 4 received the CS in the same order as Group 3 but without the shock. The results showed that the light produced significantly greater conditioned GSRs than did the tone, and the tone produced significantly greater conditioned GSRs when it was conditioned following the light-shock pairs than when it was conditioned before the light.

Some other variables which might have some significant bearing on conditioning and generalization have been studied by Maltzman and Raskin in two reported experiments (Maltzman and Raskin, 1964, and Raskin and Maltzman, 1964). In the latter work, they used 30 subjects shock-conditioned to words (CS) by the use of each of two CS-UCS intervals: 0.5 seconds and 10 seconds, and measured both palmar GSR and finger vasoconstriction. As a test, they used words varyingly associated with the CS word. The GSR showed reliably better semantic conditioning and generalization at the 0.5 second interval, while the vasomotor response conditioned and generalized better at the 10-second interval. Thus neither the CS-UCS interval nor the type of response measure used can be ignored when designing experiments, interpreting results, or comparing results of different experiments. If the optimal CS-UCS interval varies with the type of response measure used, we need much more data upon which to base a choice of experimental method. Perhaps some previous results from experiments using autonomic measures should be reevaluated.

The other Maltzman and Raskin (1964) experiment studied the effects of different types of responses to a word stimulus upon generalization of the GSR. Four groups of 30-35 subjects were variously instructed. One group was told to respond to the stimulus word with implicit free association, another to count, one to press a pedal and the fourth, the control group, to listen and do nothing. The experimental groups all showed differential GSR responsiveness to the stimulus word and its associates, whereas the results from the control group were negative.

Another variable of great importance in the interpretation of results in all experiments using GSR as a measure is the initial value effect. It has been assumed that the higher the initial resistance before stimulation, the less the significance of a given GSR measure,[5] since a high initial resistance theoretically allows for greater response latitude. Greenfield, Katz, Alexander, and Roessler (1963) raised a question with respect to this assumption when they performed t-tests of all the means of all the initial GSR levels to 30 tones between high and low responders, and found a significant difference between means but in a direction opposite to that predicted by the Law of Initial Value. Their experiment certainly can not be regarded as a critical test of this law, but it does lend weight to the cautionary statements of such researchers as Franks (1964), Visser (1963), and Martin (1961, 1964) regarding the complexity of conditioning and the variety of parameters involved, especially where physiological measures of response are employed.

THE ORIENTING REFLEX

Another knotty and as yet unresolved problem is the experimental control of the orienting reflex in physiological experiments. Brotsky (1964) pointed out that the orienting reflex is an important individual difference parameter that may account for a large portion of the variance in classical conditioning. In most experiments the assumption is made that habituation of the orienting reflex has occurred when the particular response being measured is extinguished during unreinforced trials prior to the conditioning trials. But an experiment by Unger (1964) raised some interesting questions. He found habituation to a series of auditorily presented numbers. In a series of numbers, each stimulus is acoustically novel, thus ought to elicit an orienting response; on the other hand, each is experientially (meaningfully) expected. Unger showed that dishabituation occurred to numbers which were presented out of order. Furthermore, Kintsch (1964) found that in a learning situation, there was an increase in the GSR on trials where no learning occurred such

---

[5] The GSR measures the lowering of resistance.

that the GSR reached its maximum on the trial of the last error. Habituation of the GSR set in after that trial. He cites these results as indicating, in the light of Sokolov's (1960) theory that the orienting reflex occurs when there is a lack of correspondence between the actual stimulus and the neuronal model (expectation), that the neuronal representation of the subject in a learning task must include a representation of the correct response before habituation of the orienting reflex can occur. This implies that the GSR elicited during conditioning (learning) trials should be regarded as an orienting response. The only conclusion possible at this point would seem to be that there are still so many unidentified variables and parameters involved in classical conditioning that it is impossible to know whether results are due to what an experiment is designed to demonstrate, or whether they are artifacts of one or many unrecognized and thus uncontrolled variables.

Summary

In this section we have attempted to present an overview of the state of the American experimental investigation of meaning within the context of classical conditioning, showing the metamorphosis from the classical conditioning model into the verbal learning model which is more popular in the United States and which will be considered in more detail in a later section. The relationship of this development to the American reluctance to deal with variables outside the realm of experimenter (as opposed to experimental) control was suggested. We have pointed out some of the controversies and confusions which prevail and have tried to relate them to some of the pitfalls inherent in experimental attempts to probe the mysteries of the "black box." Many of these pitfalls are due to inadequate basic data and consequent untested assumptions with regard to some of the physiological measures used.

The only possible conclusion from these experiments seems to be that we are still a long way from identifying, defining, or measuring meaning or understanding how it functions. Much basic work needs to be done in the area of classical conditioning using autonomic measures in order to identify and bring under experimental control the variety of variables which may influence the processes involved. It is to be hoped that this produces a challenge for experimental ingenuity rather than intensified avoidance reactions.

Verbal operant conditioning

The work in verbal conditioning in the United States beginning around 1950 and still gathering momentum, followed from Skinner's work in instrumental conditioning and his view, formally stated in 1957, that verbal responses, like other behavioral responses, are emitted rather than elicited and that the necessary condition for obtaining repeated responses or increased response frequency is reinforcement.

The term "verbal conditioning" is somewhat ambiguous, since it is used to refer to a variety of experimental situations. The original use of the term was in connection with experiments in which stimulus, response, and reinforcing stimulus were all verbal. Gradually the term has been extended to apply to experiments in which the response may be non-verbal and the reinforcer verbal, or the other way around. Strictly speaking, the subject's behavior in such experiments is not "emitted," but rather elicited—at least initially—by some kind of verbal instructions. However, the assumption is made that the behavior is instrumental in that it is continued and increased in frequency by the action of the externally applied reinforcer which can be viewed as a direct consequence of the behavior itself.

The "classical" verbal conditioning experiment was Greenspoon's (1951, 1955) study in which he demonstrated that the emission of plural nouns could be increased in a free operant situation. He instructed his subjects to say words, and reinforced plural nouns by saying, "Ummhumm." A more structured method was devised by Taffel (1952) in which he set a sentence forming task for his subjects who were given a verb and a choice between six pronouns, and were reinforced by the experimenter's "good" when they formed sentences using either "I" or "we." Both authors reported an increase in the frequency of the reinforced responses without the subjects' being aware of the reinforcement contingency. Cohen, Kalish, Thurston, and Cohen (1954) confirmed Greenspoon's and Taffel's findings, and showed that conditioning without awareness occurred when other verbal operants were reinforced.

It should be clearly noted that American verbal conditioning thus refers to experiments using the methods of operant or instrumental conditioning, and must be distinguished from Russian semantic conditioning which to a major extent uses respondent, or classical conditioning methods.

There is nothing in Skinner's view of verbal behavior that takes account of semantic (or mediated) generalization, if there actually is such a phenomenon. Neither does it permit one to say anything about the meaning or significance of signs.[8] Thus the question is not raised as to whether the "reinforcer" might not be regarded by the subject simply as a *signal* that he is performing correctly in the experimental situation. This question has less relevance if it can be shown that conditioning can and does take place without the subject's being aware of the connection between his response and the reinforcement (the reinforcement contingency), in which case it might be argued that the reinforcement could not be functioning as a signal.

Awareness

At the present state of American experimentation in verbal conditioning, perhaps the greatest relevance to the problem of meaning is suggested in the continuing controversy over the importance of awareness of reinforcement contingencies to the conditioning process, and whether awareness, if present, is consequent or antecedent to conditioning. Krasner and Ullmann (1963) contended that the subject's reported awareness should be viewed in the same light as their verbal behavior during the conditioning process itself, since the same variables influencing conditionability influence the level of awareness; yet a possible positive relationship between the two does not necessarily imply that awareness mediates conditionability. Farber (1963) asserted that awareness may be an important though not sufficient condition for conditioning. The human subject, he concluded, does what he thinks he's supposed to do in the experimental situation *if he wants to.* Another way, no less operationally rigorous, of stating this might be to say that he does what he does in the experimental situation depending upon *what it means to him,* which would include both his interpretation of the requirements ("what he thinks he's supposed to do") and his motivation ("if he wants to").

Some American experimenters have shown some impatience with the rather naive assumptions regarding awareness and its supposed effects. Some deal with the problem by making the assumption that awareness is present whether the subject reports it or not. Silverman (1964), for example, has stated flatly that where

---

[8] See the excellent and exhaustive critical review by Chomsky (1959).

awareness does not seem to be a factor in verbal conditioning, its absence is simply an artifact of insensitive interviewing. Krasner and Ullmann (1963) drew attention to factors influencing the *report* of awareness, since the presence or absence and/or level of awareness is ordinarily assessed through the subject's verbal report following the experiment, and elicited in a variety of ways. From a series of experiments focused upon this problem, they concluded 1) that the level of awareness is influenced by informational cues given to the subject; 2) that reporting awareness may itself be conditioned; 3) that the personality of the subject and the atmosphere of the experiment are both relevant variables in reporting awareness; and 4) that the same variables influencing conditionability influence the level of reported awareness.

Farber (1963, p. 196) asserted that

the search for "real" awareness is a chimera. The only important question is whether, by defining awareness in a given way, specifying both the contents of the response and the procedures used to evoke it, one can better account for the variation in the subject's behavior.

One could certainly agree with this statement, but one of the most interesting aspects of the whole awareness controversy is the fact that the term "awareness" has *not* been defined operationally, even when it is used by those experimenters who insist upon rigor and operationalism. It has, rather, been used as loosely as any "soft-headed" clinician might use the term. The consequence of this, as Eriksen (1960) pointed out, is to raise doubts about the adequacy of the operations used to evaluate awareness in investigations of verbal conditioning. Spielberger and DeNike (1962), replicating Greenspoon's experiment, contended that the determination of awareness in such experiments is typically based on the subjects' responses to relatively brief and superficial interviews, often conducted after a series of extinction trials. When more intensive interviewing procedures were used directly following acquisition trials, more subjects were judged to be aware of correct response-reinforcement contingencies[9] or of correlated hypotheses.[10] Furthermore, only subjects who were aware of the contingencies showed any significant increment of responding. Greenspoon (1963) maintained his position in the face of Spielberger and DeNike's (1962) findings and they (Spielberger and DeNike, 1963) replied with

---

[9] Spielberger (1962), Levin (1961), DeNike (1964).
[10] Tatz (1960), Dulany (1961).

a summary of evidence from a number of studies in which it had been consistently observed that:

> a) acquistion of reinforced responses was limited essentially to subjects who were able to verbalize correct or correlated hypotheses; b) the acquisition of subjects (having) correct or correlated hypotheses was specific to the reinforced responses for which these subjects were aware of response-reinforcement contingencies; and c) increments in the conditioning curves for aware subjects tended to correspond to the trial-block on which the subject stated during the post-conditioning interview that he became aware (p. 105).

Furthermore, they asserted that there was evidence[11] that the aware subjects' attitude toward and evaluation of the reinforcing stimulus was related to their performance level.

Spielberger and Levin (1962), using the Taffel method of sentence construction, found that when subjects verbalized awareness of the reinforcement of "I" but not of "we," they showed increments in performance only in "I" sentences, although they were actually reinforced for "we" sentences as well as for "I" sentences.

Spielberger (1962) reviewed and criticized the accumulated body of literature with regard to awareness in verbal conditioning, and reported a series of systematic studies designed to investigate a number of variables not taken into account in the Greenspoon experiment.[12] He concluded that "'what is learned' in verbal conditioning is awareness of a response-reinforcement contingency, and that subjects will act on their awareness provided that they are motivated to receive reinforcement." (Spielberger, 1962, p. 23).[13]

It should be remembered in evaluating the results reported that Spielberger and his group adopted a cognitive learning theory approach to their work in verbal conditioning, whereas the S-R model guided the work of those experimenters who support the direct conditioning, learning-without-awareness hypothesis. In this connection, it is interesting to ponder the results of a verbal conditioning experiment reported by Rosenthal (1963). In this instance, 18 experimenters conducted verbal conditioning trials with subjects who were reinforced for positive ratings of photographs. Of the

---

[11] Mandler and Kaplan (1956), Spielberger, Berger, and Howard (1963), Spielberger, Levin, and Shepard (1962), Crowne and Strickland (1961), Spielberger and DeNike (1962).

[12] Spielberger and DeNike (1962), DeNike and Spielberger (1963), DeNike (1964), Spielberger, Bernstein, and Ratliff (1964).

[13] See also Spielberger (1965).

18 experimenters, nine were told that on the basis of personality test scores their subjects could be expected to be aware of the reinforcement contingency, and the other nine were told not to expect their subjects to be aware. The subject's awareness was estimated from their answers to questionnaires which were scored not by the experimenters involved, but by independent judges (whose reliability was .98). The subjects of the experimenters who expected them to be aware were scored as aware significantly more than the subjects of those experimenters who did not expect their subjects to recognize the reinforcement contingency. Krasner, Ullmann, and Fisher (1964) showed subjects' performance in a research task to be directly influenced by the experimenter's behavioral cues, but Rosenthal would warn that influential behavioral cues may not be readily observable. "The subtlety of (the) communication is such that casual observation of human dyads is unlikely to reveal the nature of this communication process" [Rosenthal (1963) p. 279].

Dixon and Oakes (1965) used cognitive concepts to support the position of Krasner and Ullmann (1962) and Verplanck (1962) that there is no necessary relationship between awareness and conditioning. Between verbal operant conditioning trials, using the Taffel model, they occupied their subjects with a simple color-naming task to prevent them from formulating hypotheses regarding the conditioning task. Although there was no significant difference between the reinforced distracted group and the reinforced undistracted group in the level of awareness of the reinforcement contingency, the degree of awareness was significantly related to conditioning only in the undistracted group. Dixon and Oakes (p. 157) interpret these results as demonstrating that

> when conditions are such that S is not able to formulate hypotheses during acquisition, the same degree of learning may be exhibited as when S does have the opportunity to formulate hypotheses, indicating a direct strengthening effect of the reinforcer, which is not correlated with the degree of S's awareness.

In view of the fact that there was "no difference in level of awareness" in the two groups, it seems untenable to assume that the distraction prevented the formulation of hypotheses in the one group and not the other. This, then, hardly seems to be a definitive answer to the problem of awareness in conditioning, particularly in view of the possible operation of other uncontrolled variables which have been shown to be significant in verbal conditioning, and which will be considered later.

Phelan (1964) pointed out that inadequate verbalization of hypotheses may result in the development of spurious rules which may then be substituted for an unverbalized but efficiently functioning concept. In a sorting task using visual material, 41 of her 60 subjects showed concept acquisition, using perceptual cues of relative difficulty, not only by errorless trials with the original material but also by the subsequent application of the concept with new material. Twenty-eight of the 41 subjects were judged unaware, in that they were unable to verbalize the principle. An unsuccessful attempt to verbalize may destroy a recently formed but functioning concept. This goes a step beyond some of the Russian experimenters' observations that there sometimes exists a discrepancy between the behavior observed in an experimental situation and the subject's report of what he is doing (failure of transfer from first to second signalling system). Phelan found that whereas successful or appropriate verbalization facilitated the subsequent use of the concept (generalization), unsuccessful, contradictory, incomplete, or inadequate attempts at verbalization might commit the subject to nonadjustive behavior in situations requiring a clear concept. Phelan's experiment has demonstrated in the laboratory a common phenomenon observed by every psychotherapist and clinical psychologist: that meaning distortions result in maladaptive and inappropriate behavior.

Ekman, Krasner, and Ullmann (1963) attempted to study the effects of awareness on conditioning by inducing awareness in their subjects through instructions. In addition, they induced a positive or negative "set" by identifying a story-telling task as either a test of empathy or a test of personal problems. During the performance of the task, emotional words were reinforced. Since the frequency of emotional words was increased for the positive-set subjects and decreased for the negative-set subjects, the authors concluded that awareness of the reinforcement contingency might either facilitate or inhibit conditioning, depending upon other variables operating in the experimental situation, and perhaps upon what meaning the reinforcement had for the subject.

Letchworth and Wishner (1962) also used instructions to create a particular "set" in their subjects. One might say that, because of the instructions, the same experimental situation had different meaning for the two experimental groups. One group was told that the purpose of the experiment was to find out how neurotic the subjects were. The other group was told that they were helping the experimenter to satisfy the requirements for the Ph.D degree. According to Wishner's (1955) theory of efficiency and task-centering, the experiment was thus designed to create a self-centered set in one group and a task-centered set in the other. The task involved a pack of cards with three words printed on each, from which the subjects were to choose one. The reinforced choice was a word ending in the letter *s*. The reinforcement was the experimenter's tapping his pencil on the desk. Each group was subdivided for three conditions. These were: 1) relaxed, that is, the subject was told to ignore the pencil tapping; 2) Problem + (P+), that is, the subject was instructed to try to make the experimenter tap his pencil more; and 3) Problem — (P—), that is, the subject was told to try to make the experimenter tap his pencil less. It was predicted that self-centered subjects would show a relatively higher rate of conditioning under relaxed and problem-minus conditions, while other-centered subjects would condition better under the problem-plus condition; the results upheld the prediction. The conclusions were that ". . . self-centered instructions inhibit appropriate learning and reduce the efficiency of behavior" [Letchworth and Wishner (1962) p. 244].

There are a number of interpretive aspects to this experiment which are troublesome, and which a later analysis (Letchworth and Wishner, 1963) fails to clarify. For one thing, it is hard to see how tasks P+ and P— differ except that the first involves positive conditioning, and the second avoidance conditioning. In the first case, the pencil tapping is a positive reinforcement, and in the second it is an aversive stimulus. It is thus hard to understand why, given the efficiency hypothesis, the prediction would be made that self-centered subjects would show a "higher rate of conditioning under P— conditions than under P+ conditions." It is also difficult to see how it is appropriate to speak of "rate of conditioning" in the "relaxed" condition where the subjects were instructed to ignore the reinforcement, which would obviously draw their attention to it, as in the case of the man told to try not to think of "rhinoceros."

The fact that the two groups of subjects responded differently in the identical situations does have some interesting implications with respect to meaning, however. Since the physical situation and the experimental contingencies were the same for both groups, it is clear that the situation had different meanings for the two groups and that their behavior was affected by the meaning attached to the situation. Wishner's (1955) original formulation grew out of an attempt to account for generalization phenomena in other terms than through resorting to undefined concepts of meaning or meaningfulness on the response side. Interestingly enough he overlooked the significance which the Letchworth and Wishner (1962) design and results might have with respect to a definition of meaning that goes beyond simple generalization. According to the usual definition of stimulus, both groups of subjects in the experiment were responding to identical stimuli, yet their responses differed significantly. Thus a logical conclusion would seem to be that either the "functional stimulus" was different for the two groups, or something intervening between the stimulus and response was different for the two groups. In either case, it seems impossible adequately to account for the differences without encountering at some level the problem of meaning.

One experiment is of particular interest because it suggests that the problem of awareness in conditioning is more complicated than any of the above studies has recognized, and because it is relevant to the Russian notions about the discrepancy between first and second signalling system behavior.[14] Hare, Hislop, and Lattey (1964) reinforced subjects for either "like" or "dislike" responses to photographs. They found that conditioning was not related to the response class reinforced, but that only those subjects who were aware of the reinforcement contingency showed an increase in the conditioned response. Furthermore, even though aware of the connection between the response and the reinforcement, the subjects appeared to be unaware that their behavior had been influenced by the reinforcement, even to the extent of stating their intentional resistance to being influenced by the examiner's behavior and their impression that the resistance had been effective.

Williams (1964) in her review article concerning awareness in verbal conditioning suggested that the equivocal and contradictory results appear to be a function of the complexity of the phenomenon and of the difficulty of controlling all the important variables which may influence conditioning and conditionability. Some of these variables are currently under investigation, but so far there have been no systematic attempts to control at once all variables which individual investigations have shown to be influential.

---

[14] See p. 96ff.

The most interesting aspect of the awareness controversy from a theoretical point of view is the operant conditioner's insistence upon the demonstration of "conditioning without awareness." It is hard to understand why, if behavior is maintained by its consequences, the subject's recognition that his behavior produces a consequence (i.e., the subject's being "aware" of the reinforcement contingencies) should invalidate positive results in an operant conditioning experiment, and that "unawareness" should be assumed to support validity. One cannot but wonder whether the fact that the model was carried over from animal to human experimentation may not be the source of a great deal of confused thinking about the problems involved.

Twenty years ago, C. W. Morris wrote (1946, p. 198):

> . . . non-human beings seldom produce the signs which influence their behavior, while human individuals in their language and post-language symbols characteristically do this to a surprising degree. Here is a basic difference between men and animals, and until behavioral theory develops a semiotic adequate to this difference it will remain what it is today: a careful study of animals and a pious hope for a science of the human person.

Present-day operant conditioners might justifiably argue that they have shown that non-human beings indeed *do* produce signs which influence their behavior, so that there is no absolute difference between men and animals in this respect. Perhaps the problem which needs to be tackled is one regarding the *kinds* of signs produced by animals and men: are there differences in kind, and if so, what are the differences? It may be that animal behavior is influenced by self-generated signs belonging to the first signalling system but not by those belonging to the second signalling system—to borrow the Russian terminology. If we were to put our questions in such a form, we could perhaps devise better experimental designs than those patterned upon "classical" animal operant studies.

Current observations of the behavior of dolphins suggest that they may be capable of producing second signalling system signs. It might be more fruitful to design comparative experiments for dolphins and men rather than for rats or pigeons and men.

TRENDS IN VERBAL OPERANT CONDITIONING

The first ten years or so of experimental work in verbal operant conditioning has been reviewed by Adams (1957), Krasner (1958), Salzinger (1959), and Greenspoon (1962), and will therefore not be discussed in detail here. These studies were mostly concerned with demonstrating that certain types of verbal response classes could be conditioned by applying certain types of reinforcers. In addition to showing that the frequency of utterance of certain word classes could be increased, experimenters showed that such verbal phenomena as statement of opinion,[15] expression of "feeling,"[16] complex grammatical constructions,[17] and order of speaking in a group[18] could be conditioned. Other studies examined the effectiveness of substituting nonverbal reinforcers[19] for the usual verbal reinforcers in the conditioning of verbal behavior.

Using variants of method, contemporary work in verbal conditioning assumes that it has been adequately demonstrated that a subject's verbalizations can be operantly controlled and investigators are beginning to move to more refined studies of the possible variables involved in verbal conditioning experiments, including reinforcement variables, response class variables, subject variables, and examiner variables. Reinforcement variables have been examined from the point of view of schedules or patterns of reinforcement,[20] and from the point of view of the nature of the reinforcement.[21] Response class variables have been studied,[22] and subject variables have been investigated from the standpoint of certain personality variables,[23] of the subjects' previous condition of social deprivation or isolation,[24] of their previous reinforcement history,[25] of their level of intelligence,[26] of their social status,[27]

[15] Verplanck (1955), Centers (1963).
[16] Salzinger and Pisoni (1958).
[17] Barik and Lambert (1960).
[18] Levin and Shapiro (1962).
[19] e.g., Sidowski (1954), Southwell (1962), Kilberg (1962), and Simkins (1961).
[20] e.g., Weiss, Krasner and Ullmann (1960, 1963), Bachrach, Candland, and Gibson (1961), Sandler (1962), Craddick and Stern (1964), Craddick and Campitell (1964), Bachrach, Clark, Witters, and Fleming—Holland (1964), Witters and Bachrach (1964), and Dean and Hiesinger (1964).
[21] e.g., Bachrach, Candland and Gibson (1961), Zigler and Kanzer (1962), Marston and Kanfer (1963), Marston (1964), Adams and Frye (1964), Witters (1964), and Spence (1964).
[22] Salzinger, Salzinger, Portnoy, Eckman, Bacon, Deutsch, and Zubin (1962), Salzinger, Portnoy, Zlontogura and Keisner (1963), Ullmann, Krasner and Gelfand (1963), Steinberg and Oakes (1964), and Hickerson (1964).
[23] Krasner, Ullmann, Weiss and Collins (1961).
[24] e.g., Gewirtz and Baer (1958a and b), Stevenson and Fahel (1961), Zigler (1961), Zigler, Hodgden and Stevenson (1958), Simkins (1961).
[25] Shallenberger and Zigler (1961), Stevenson and Snyder (1960).
[26] e.g., Heard, Finley and Staats (1963), Gewirtz and Baer (1958a), Stevenson (1961), Zigler (1958).
[27] e.g., Douvan (1956), Zigler and Kanzer (1962), Zigler (1962).

of their anxiety level,[28] of their need for social approval,[29] and of their psychiatric status.[30] Examiner variables have been considered from the point of view of the examiner's sex,[31] and from the point of view of examiner bias.[32] The interaction between the examiner and the subject has also been investigated.[33]

Some contemporary work has moved toward the study of more complex responding in a verbal operant conditioning situation, such as the conditioning of attitudes and judgments.[34] Particularly notable is the work in progress at Arizona State University by Bachrach and his group since they have demonstrated complexities in operant conditioning which heretofore have to a large extent been obscured. They showed, for example,[35] that conditioning ability varied from subject to subject, and pointed out[36] that the conditions under which conditioned reinforcers operate are still far from being understood. Ayllon and Azrin (1964), for example, found that instructions to psychotic patients had no enduring effect unless accompanied by reinforcement, and reinforcement was ineffectual unless instructions specified the basis for reinforcement.

Such studies as those surveyed above are noted here in order to suggest the trends and directions in research in verbal conditioning. They are not described in detail because their significance with respect to the meaning of meaning is at yet unclear. Indeed, rather than giving us clues to the meaning of meaning, much of the operant conditioning work with human subjects has underscored the importance of and the need for an understanding of meaning. For example, many of the experiments cited have suggested that it is essential to know what the reinforcing stimulus *means* to the subject, for it may be meaning which distinguishes the "functional stimulus" in an experiment from the experimenter-specified stimulus.

---

[28] e.g., Walters and Ray (1960), Walters, Marshall and Shooter (1960).

[29] e.g., Crowne and Strickland (1961), Spielberger, Berger and Howard (1963).

[30] e.g., McGaughran and Moran (1956), Kilberg (1962), Quay and Hunt (1962), Weiss, Krasner and Ullman (1963), Craddick and Campitell (1964), Johannsen and Campbell (1964), Salzinger, Portnoy and Feldman, (1964a and b), and Bryan and Lichtenstein (1964).

[31] e.g., Gewirtz and Baer (1958a), Stevenson (1961), Krasner, Ullmann, Weiss, and Collins (1961), and Cieutat (1964).

[32] Rosenthal (1964).

[33] e.g., Weiss, Krasner and Ullmann (1960), and Ganzer and Sarason (1964).

[34] Krasner, Ullmann, and Fisher (1964), Krasner, Knowles and Ullmann (1964), Le Ny (1963).

[35] Bachrach and Ross (1962).

[36] Verhave and Bachrach (1964).

PRACTICAL IMPLICATIONS OF VERBAL CONDITIONING

The experiments surveyed are interesting to psychologists outside the operant fold mainly in that they suggest that verbal responses can be controlled through verbal reinforcement with such phrases as "good," "right," "umhum," and others which are regularly employed by persons engaged in child rearing, education, and psychotherapy. This finding, of course, has enormous importance with respect to theory and practice in those fields. The impact has been greatest, perhaps, in the field of education, with the development of programmed learning and teaching machines.

There have been some reverberations in the field of psychotherapy, but the problems of research in this area are enormously complex. Aside from the more obvious difficulties, there are problems associated with the therapist as researcher, or the experimenter as therapist. Few experimental psychologists are trained as therapists. Although psychologists who are therapists are usually trained in research, in general the focus of their interest is on therapy rather than research, and the pressure on them to spend their time in practice rather than research is great. In addition, with the current emphasis upon the emotional relationship aspects of the therapeutic communication between therapist and patient as the essential feature in change, many therapists are made uneasy or feel downright repelled by the open emphasis of the operant conditioners upon manipulation and control. With the tendency for increased personal expressiveness on the part of the therapist, there is less and less inclination for him to take toward his client the cooly detached, objective stance of the experimenter. It may be that in actuality the therapist is "nothing but" a reinforcing machine for his client, and that the nearly sanctified "relationship" is "nothing but" the intuitive selection of adequate reinforcement contingencies, but the experimentalists will have to produce much more solid evidence that more than the immediate verbal behavior can be controlled, that alterations in verbal responses can and do generalize to other kinds of behavior, that feelings are conditioned along with words, and that "meanings" can be altered along with verbal behavior, before therapists will take operant methods to their bosoms and scientifically design their therapeutic methods.

However, Adams and Frye (1964) demonstrated the value of operant methods as a research tool in psychotherapy by experimentally investigating the effects of certain types of commonly used psychotherapeutic techniques such as interpretation, minimal social reinforcement (e.g., "umhum" or "good"), hostile statements, and reflection. Their subjects were asked to speak freely about any topic, and the experimenter reinforced personal references by one of four ways on a fixed ratio schedule of 5 :1. Personal reference was increased by interpretation and minimal social reinforcement but hostile statements and reflection decreased personal reference. Effects of interpretation were more resistant to extinction than effects of the other types of reinforcement.

But psychotherapists have long made the claim that behavioral changes must be preceded or accompanied by changes in "feelings," values, and attitudes. The meaning that events and persons have for the patient must be altered before behavior will change. Conditioning methods developed in the laboratory and carried over into the consulting room may teach us that this process is not so long and arduous as it has been thought to be. The work of Wolpe (1958) and others is beginning to lend weight to this hope. As Hefferline (1962) pointed out, a basic claim to be substantiated is that reinforcement can operate just as effectively on the internal receptors as on the exteroceptive. Some of his work,[37] as well as some of the Russian experiments in interoceptive conditioning, is interestingly suggestive of possibilities.

GENERALIZATION OF VERBAL CONDITIONING

A discouraging note was sounded by Zax and Klein (1960) in their review of the literature on behavior changes following psychotherapy when they concluded that there was no adequate evidence to link verbal changes during therapy with behavioral changes in the family and community. However, some experimental attempts have been made to demonstrate generalization of verbally conditioned behavior and/or conditioned verbal behavior. For example, Krasner, Ullmann, and Fisher (1964) showed that the expression of favorable attitudes toward medical scientists was increased by verbal reinforcement, and that performance on a motor task also improved after reinforcement of the favorable attitudes. Gelfand and Singer (1964) studied generalization of judgments of pictures which had been rated on the evaluative Semantic Differential scale. Their ten-year-old female subjects

---

[37] e.g., Hefferline and Keenan (1963).

increased their positive judgments after being verbally reinforced for positive judgments. Negative judgments increased after reinforcement for negative judgments. Both positive and negative judgments generalized without further reinforcement to pictures of male peers, but not to pictures of older women.

Timmons (1962) asked subjects to draw after a session in which they had produced words in a free verbalization situation. Those subjects who had been verbally reinforced for saying words pertaining to building or buildings drew more pictures of buildings than an unreinforced group. In a refinement of this experiment, Embree and Timmons (1964) had their subjects say nouns to determine their operant level. A week later they were asked to draw two pictures. Then they were again asked to say nouns. At this point, the experimental group was reinforced for "people words" on a variable reinforcement schedule in such a way that 75% of the "people words" were reinforced. The control group was not reinforced. Subjects verbalizing awareness of the reinforcement contingency were eliminated from the experiment. Drawings by the groups following the conditioning showed a significantly increased number of pictures of people drawn by the experimental group but not by the control group. Lovaas, in one experiment (1964) increased pre-school children's selection of specific previously not favored foods after verbally conditioning their naming of those foods; in another experiment (1961) he demonstrated an increase in aggressive nonverbal behavior following reinforcement of aggressive verbal behavior. Working with adult subjects, Drennen (1963) conditioned them to use more future tense responses in a sentence-forming task, and showed generalization to a second sentence completion task containing cues present in the original task.

Summary

The experimental analysis of human operant behavior is a neonate, and it is thus difficult to assess its potential. The work that has been done so far has not addressed itself directly to the problem of meaning. There are interesting possibilities to be explored. It is difficult to see how the problem of meaning in operant experiments with human subjects can be avoided, since the question of what constitutes an adequate reinforcement must inevitably arise.

It is not so easy to control experimentally the needs of human subjects since we cannot control their level of deprivation, except perhaps in conditions of total sensory deprivation. Even under these conditions, the problem of what such deprivation *means* to the subject may be a variable which must be reckoned with.

So far, operant work with human subjects has dealt mainly with gross overt behavior. Little has yet been done as regards the significance of instructions as a variable, or in the study of verbal report. Even less has been done with the investigation of physiological variables in an operant setting. The opportunities are vast and exciting, and as unexplored as the moon.

References

ACKER, L. E., & EDWARDS, A. E. Transfer of vasoconstriction over a bipolar meaning dimension. *J. exp. Psychol.*, 1964, *67*, 1–6.

ADAMS, H. E., & FRYE, R. L. Psychotherapeutic techniques as conditioned reinforcers in a structured interview. *Psychol. Rep.*, 1964, *14*, 163–166.

ADAMS, J. Laboratory studies of behavior without awareness. *Psychol. Bull.*, 1957, *54*, 383–405.

ASCH, S. E., & EBENHOLTZ, S. M. The principle of associative symmetry. *Proc. Amer. phil. Soc.*, 1962, *106*, 135–163.

AYLLON, T., & AZRIN, N. H. Reinforcement and instructions with mental patients. *J. exp. Anal. Behav.*, 1964, *7(4)*, 327–331.

BACHRACH, A. J. *Experimental Foundations of Cinical Psychology.* New York: Basic Books, 1962.

——, & ROSS, W. T., JR. Experiments in verbal behavior. II. The reinforcement of linguistic structures using an electronic voice-operated relay. Preliminary results. Contract Nonr. 474(8), ONR & Arizona State Univer., 1962.

——, CANDLAND, D. K., & GIBSON, J. T. Group reinforcement of individual response: Experiments in verbal behavior. *In:* BERG, I. A. & BASS, B. M. 1961.

——, CLARK, J., WITTERS, D. R., & FLEMING-HOLLAND, A. Individual baseline behavior in a small group on a chained schedule of reinforcement. Contract Nonr. 2794(3), ONR & Arizona State Univer., 1964.

BARICK, H. C., & LAMBERT, W. E. Conditioning of complex verbal sequences. *Canadian J. Psychol.*, 1960, *14*, 87–95.

BEIER, E. G. A comparison of differential ratings on three different semantic scales. Unpub. paper, Ref.: *Amer. Psychologist*, 1964, *19(9)*, 709.

BERG, I. A., & BASS, B. M. (Eds.). *Conformity and Deviation.* New York: Harper & Brothers, 1961.

BOUSFIELD, W. A. The problem of meaning in verbal learning. *In:* COFER, C. N. 1961.

——, & COWAN, T. M. Conditioning of motor and verbal responses to non-verbal stimuli. *J. exp. Psychol.,* 1963, *66(1),* 47–52.

BRANCA, A. A. Semantic generalization at the level of the conditioning experiment. *Amer. J. Psychol.,* 1957, *70,* 541–549.

BRAZIER, M. A. B. (Ed.). *The Central Nervous System and Behavior.* (Transactions of the third conference sponsored by the Josiah Macy, Jr., Foundation and the National Science Foundation). New York: Josiah Macy, Jr., Foundation, 1960.

BROTSKY, S. J. The classical conditioning of the galvanic skin response to verbal concepts. Unpub. paper, Ref.: *Amer. Psychologist,* 1964, *19(9),* 712.

BRYAN, J. H., & LICHTENSTEIN, E. Failure to verbally condition socially desirable speech. *Psych. Rep.,* 1964, *14,* 141-142.

CARROLL, J. B. Some cautionary notes on the Semantic Differential. Symposium: *Current Research Methods: II. Semantic Differential.* Cincinnati, APA Convention. Ref.: *Amer. Psychologist,* 1959a, *14,* 382.

——. Review of Osgood, Suci, and Tannenbaum: *The Measurement of Meaning. Language,* 1959b, *35,* 58–77.

CENTERS, R. A laboratory adaptation of the conversational procedure for the conditioning of verbal operants. *J. abnorm. soc. Psychol.,* 1963, *67(4),* 334–339.

CHOMSKY, N. Review of *Verbal Behavior by B. F. Skinner. Language,* 1959, *35,* 26–58.

CIEUTAT, V. J. Sex differences in verbal operant conditioning. *Psychol. Rep.,* 1964, *15,* 259–275.

COFER, C. N. (Ed.). *Verbal Learning and Verbal Behavior.* New York: McGraw-Hill, 1961.

COHEN, B. D., KALISH, H. I., THURSTON, J. R., & COHEN, E. Experimental manipulation of verbal behavior. *J. exp. Psychol.,* 1954, *47,* 106–110.

COHEN, B. H. Role of awareness in meaning established by classical conditioning. *J. exp. Phychol.,* 1964, *67(4),* 373–378.

CORN-BECKER, F., WELCH, L., & FISICHELLI, V. Conditioning factors underlying hypnosis. *J. abnorm. soc. Psychol.,* 1949, *44,* 212–222.

CRADDICK, R. A., & CAMPITELL, J. Verbal conditioning: Resistance to extinction as a function of reinforcement and need for social approval. *Psychol. Rep.,* 1964, *14,* 63–66.

——, & STERN, M. R. Verbal conditioning: The effect of partial reinforcement upon the recall of early memories. *J. abnorm. soc. Psychol.,* 1964, *68(3),* 353–355.

CROWNE, D. P., & STRICKLAND, B. R. The conditioning of verbal behavior as a function of the need for social approval. *J. abnorm. soc. Psychol.,* 1961, *63,* 395–401.

DEAN, S. J., & HIESINGER, L. Operant level, awareness, and the Greenspoon effect. *Psychol. Rep.,* 1964, *15,* 931–938.

DEESE, J. The associative structure of some common English adjectives. *J. verb. Learn. verb. Behav.*, 1964, *3, 347–357*.

DE MONTMOLLIN, G., & LE NY, J. F. Conditionement d'attitude et conditionement verbale. *Psychol. Franc.*, 1962, *7,* 67–74.

DE NIKE, L. D. The temporal relationship between awareness and performance in verbal conditioning. *J. exp. Psychol.*, 1964, *68(6),* 521–529.

——, & SPIELBERGER, C. D. Induced mediating states in verbal conditioning. *J. verb. Learn. verb. Behav.*, 1963, *2, 339–345*.

DIVESTA, F. J., & STOVER, D. O. The semantic mediation of evaluative meaning. *J. exp. Psychol.*, 1962, *64,* 467–475.

DIXON, P. W., & OAKES, W. F. The effect of intertrial activity on the relationship between awareness and verbal operant conditioning. *J. exp. Psychol.*, 1965, *69(2),* 152–157.

DOUVAN, E. Social status and success striving. *J. abnorm. soc. Psychol.*, 1956, *52,* 219–223.

DRENNEN, W. T. Transfer of the effects of verbal conditioning. *J. abnorm. soc. Psychol.*, 1963, *66(6),* 619–622.

DULANY, D. E. Hypotheses and habits in verbal "operant conditioning." *J. abnorm. soc. Psychol.*, 1961, *63,* 251–264.

EKMAN, P., KRASNER, L., & ULLMANN, L. P. Critique and notes. Interaction of set and awareness as determinants of response to verbal conditioning. *J. abnorm. soc. Psychol.*, 1963, *66(4),* 387–389.

EMBREE, E. D., & TIMMONS, E. O. The influence of a conditioned verbal response on a related non-verbal behavior: A replication. Abstr.: *Amer. Psychologist,* 1964, *19(7),* 476.

ERIKSEN, C. W. Discrimination and learning without awareness. *Psychol. Rev.,* 1960, *67,* 279–300.

EYSENCK, H. J. *Handbook of Abnormal Psychology.* New York: Basic Books, 1961.

FARBER, I. E. The things people say to themselves. *Amer. Psychologist,* 1963, *18(4),* 185–197.

FRANKS, C. M. A replication is a replication is not a replication. *Psychol. Rep.,* 1964, *15(2),* 550.

GANZER, V. J., & SARASON, I. G. Interrelationships among hostility, experimental conditions, and verbal behavior. *J. abnorm. soc. Psychol.*, 1964, *68(1),* 79–84.

GELFAND, D. M., & SINGER. R. D. Generalization of children's verbally conditioned personality judgments. Unpub. paper. Ref.: *Amer. Psychologist,* 1964, *19(9),* 713.

GEWIRTZ, J., & BAER, D. The effect of brief social deprivation on behaviors for a social reinforcer. *J. abnorm. soc. Psychol.*, 1958a, *56,* 49–56.

——, ——. Deprivation and satiation of social reinforcers as drive conditions. *J. abnorm. soc. Psychol.*, 1958b, *57,* 165–172.

GREENFIELD, N. S., KATZ, D., ALEXANDER, A. A., & ROESSLER, R. The relationship between physiological and psychological responsivity: Depression and galvanic skin response. *J. nerv. ment. Disease,* 1963, *136(6),* 535–539.

GREENSPOON, J. The effect of verbal and non-verbal stimuli on the frequency of members of two verbal response classes. Unpub. Ph.D. thesis, Indiana Univer., 1951.

——. The reinforcing effect of two spoken sounds on the frequency of two responses. *Amer. J. Psychol.,* 1955, *68,* 409–416.

——. Verbal conditioning and clinical psychology.
In: BACHRACH, A. J. 1962. ,

——. A reply to Spielberger and De Nike: Operant conditioning of plural nouns: A failure to replicate the Greenspoon effect. *Psychol. Rep.,* 1963, *12,* 29–30.

GRICE, G. R., & DAVIS, J. D. Mediated stimulus equivalence and distinctiveness in human conditioning. *J. exp. Psychol.,* 1958, *55,* 565–571.

HARE, R. D. Cognitive factors in transfer of meaning. *Psychol. Rep.,* 1964, *15,* 199–206.

——, HISLOP, M. W., & LATTEY, C. Behavioral change without awareness in a verbal conditioning paradigm. *Psychol. Rep.,* 1964, *15(2),* 542.

HEARD, W. G., FINLEY, J. R., & STAATS, A. W. The relationship of intelligence-test scores to the ease of language conditioning. *J. genet. Psychol.,* 1963, *103,* 227–331.

HEFFERLINE, R. F. Learning theory and clinical psychology—an eventual symbiosis?
In: BACHRACH, A. J. 1962.

——, & KEENAN, B. Amplitude-inducting gradient of a small-scale (covert) operant. *J. exp. Anal. Behav.,* 1963, *6,* 307.

HICKERSON, N. P. Preliminary suggestions on the use of linguistically defined units as variables in verbal conditioning experiments. Contract Nonr. 2974(3), ONR & Arizona State Univer., 1964.

HOROWITZ, L. M., BROWN, Z. M., & WEISSBLUTH, S. Availability and the direction of associations. *J. exp. Psychol.,* 1964, *68(6),* 541–549.

JENKINS, J. J., RUSSELL, W. A., & SUCI, G. J. An atlas of semantic profiles for 360 words. *Tech Rep.* #15, Contract N8onr. 66216, ONR Univer. Minn., 1957.

JOHANNSEN, W. J., & CAMPBELL, S. Y. Verbal conditioning in chronic schizophrenia: Effects of reinforcement class and social responsiveness. *Psychol. Rep.,* 1964, *14,* 567–572.

KILBERG, J. The differential effects of nonverbal and verbal rewards in the modification of verbal behavior of schizophrenic and normal subjects. Unpub. paper, Columbia Univer., 1962.

KIMMEL, H. D., HILL, F. A., & FOWLER, R. L. Intersensory generalization in compound classical conditioning. *Psychol. Rep.,* 1962, *11,* 611–636.

KINTSCH, W. Habituation of the GSR component of the orienting reflex during paired-associate learning before and after learning has taken place. Unpub. paper, Abstr.: *Amer. Psychologist,* 1964, *19(9),* 721.

KRASNER, L. Studies of the conditioning of verbal behavior. *Psychol. Bull.,* 1958, *55,* 148–171.

——, & ULLMANN, L. P. Reported awareness in verbal conditioning as a function of experimental conditions and subject's personality. Unpub. paper, Ref.: *Amer. Psychologist,* 1962, *17(9),* 598.

——, ——. Variables affecting report of awareness in verbal conditioning. *J. Psychol.,* 1963, *56,* 193–202.

——, ——, & FISHER, D. Changes in performance related to verbal conditioning of the subject's attitudes. Unpub. paper, Ref.: *Amer. Psychologist,* 1964, *19(9),* 707.

——, ——, WEISS, R. L., & COLLINS, B. J. Responsivity to verbal conditioning as a function of three different examiners. *J. clin. Psychol.,* 1961, *17(4),* 411–415.

——, KNOWLES, J. B., & ULLMANN, L. P. The effect of verbal conditioning of attitudes on subsequent motor performance. Abstr.: *Amer. Psychologist,* 1964, *19(7),* 584.

LE NY, J. La généralization dans une épreuve de jugement social. (Generalization in a test of social judgment). *Année Psychologique,* 1963, *63(2),* 333–350. *Psychol. Abstr.,* 1964, *38(4),* 795.

LETCHWORTH, G. E., & WISHNER, J. Studies in efficiency: Verbal conditioning as a function of degree of task centering. *J. abnorm. soc. Psychol.,* 1962, *65,* 238–245.

——, ——. Critique and notes: Studies in efficiency: Verbal conditioning as a function of degree of task centering. A replication. *J. abnorm. soc. Psychol.,* 1963, *67(3),* 282–286.

LEVIN, G., & SHAPIRO, D. The operant conditioning of conversation. *J. exp. Anal. Behav.,* 1962, *5,* 309–316.

LEVIN, S. M. The effects of awareness on verbal conditioning. *J. exp. Psychol.,* 1961, *61,* 67–75.

LOVAAS, O. I. Interaction between verbal and nonverbal behavior. *Child Develpm.,* 1961, *32,* 329–336.

——. Control of food intake in children by reinforcement of relevant verbal behavior. *J. abnorm. soc. Psychol.,* 1964, *68(6),* 672–678.

McGAUGHRAN, L. S., & MORAN, L. J. "Conceptual level" versus "conceptual area" analysis of object-sorting behavior of schizophrenic and non-psychiatric groups. *J. abnorm. soc. Psychol.,* 1956, *52,* 43–50.

MALTZMAN, I., & RASKIN, D. C. Semantic generalization of a response-induced GSR. Abstr.: *Amer. Psychologist,* 1964, *19(7),* 561.

MANDLER, G., & KAPLAN, W. K. Subjective evaluation and reinforcing effect on a verbal stimulus. *Science,* 1956, *124,* 582–583.

MARSTON, A. R. Variables in extinction following acquisition with vicarious reinforcement. *J. exp. Psychol.,* 1964, *68(3),* 312–315.

——, & KANFER, F. H. Human reinforcement: Experimenter- and subject-controlled. *J. exp. Psychol.,* 1963, *66(1),* 91–94.

MARTIN, I. Somatic reactivity.

In: Eysenck, H. J. 1961.

——. A physiological approach to conditioning and personality. *Proceedings: 1963 International Congress of Psychol.,* 1964, *17,* 174–175 (Abstr.).

Mordkoff, A. M. An empirical test of the functional autonomy of Semantic Differential scales. *J. verb. Learn. verb. Behav.,* 1963, *2(5–6),* 504–508.

Morris, C. W. *Signs, Language, and Behavior.* New York: Prentice-Hall, 1946.

Phelan, J. G. Replication of effects of verbalization on concept attainment. Unpub. paper, UCLA, 1964.

Phillips, L. W. Mediated verbal similarity as a determinant of the generalization of a conditioned GSR. *J. exp. Psychol.,* 1958, *55,* 56–62.

Platonov, K. *The Word as a Physiological and Therapeutic Factor.* Moscow: Foreign Languages Pub. House, 1959.

Pollio, H. R. Word association as a function of conditioned meaning. *J. exp. Psychol.,* 1963, *66,* 454–460.

Prokasy, W. F., & Hall, J. F. Primary stimulus generalization. *Psychol. Rev.,* 1963, *70,* 310–322.

Quay, H. C., & Hunt, W. A. Psychopathy, neuroticism and verbal conditioning: A replication and extension. Contract Nonr. 7–1228(11), ONR & Northwestern Univer., 1962.

Raskin, D. C., & Maltzman, I. Semantic conditioning and generalization of the GSR and vasomotor responses under different CS-UCS intervals. Abstr.: *Amer. Psychologist,* 1964, *19(7),* 562.

Razran, G. H. S. The observable unconscious and the inferable conscious in current Soviet psychophysiology: Interoceptive conditioning, semantic conditioning, and the orienting reflex. *Psychol. Rev.,* 1961, *68,* 81–147.

Rosenberg, S. (Ed.). *Directions in Psycholinguistics.* New York: MacMillan, 1965 (In press).

Rosenthal, R. On the social psychology of the psychological experiment. The experimenter's hypothesis as unintended determinant of experimental results. *Amer. Scientist,* 1963, *51(2),* 268–283.

——. Experimenter outcome-orientation and the results of the psychological experiment. *Psychol. Bull.,* 1964, *61(6),* 405–412.

Salzinger, K. Experimental manipulation of verbal behavior. *J. gen. Psychol.,* 1959, *61,* 65–74.

——, & Pisoni, S. Reinforcement of affect responses of schizophrenics during the clinical interview. *J. abnorm. soc. Psychol.,* 1958, *57,* 84–90.

——, Portnoy, S., & Feldman, R. S. Verbal behavior in schizophrenics and some comments toward a theory of schizophrenia. Unpub. paper: Symposium on Schizophrenia, American Psychopathological Association, New York, 1964a.

——, ——, ——. Experimental manipulation of continuous speech in schizophrenic patients. *J. abnorm. soc. Psychol.,* 1964b, *68(5),* 508–516.

——, ——, Zlontogura, P., & Keisner, R. The effect of reinforcement on continuous speech and on plural nouns in grammatical context. *J. verb. Learn. verb. Behav.,* 1963, *1(6),* 477–485.

SALZINGER, S., SALZINGER, K., PORTNOY, S., ECKMAN, J., BACON, P. M., DEUTSCH, M., & ZUBIN, J. Operant conditioning of continuous speech in young children. *Child Develpm.,* 1962, *33,* 683-695.

SANDLER, J. The effect of negative verbal cues upon verbal behavior. *J. abnorm. soc. Psychol.,* 1962, *64(4),* 312–316.

SHALLENBERGER, P., & ZIGLER, E. Rigidity, negative reaction tendencies, and cosatiation effects in normal and feeble-minded children. *J. abnorm. soc. Psychol.,* 1961, *63,* 20–26.

SIDOWSKI, J. B. Influence of awareness of reinforcement on verbal conditioning. *J. exp. Psychol.,* 1954, *48,* 355–360.

SILVERMAN, J. Verbal conditioning and the manipulation of anxiety level. Abstr.: *Amer. Psychologist,* 1964, *19(7),* 552-553.

SIMKINS, L. Effects of examiner attitudes and type of reinforcement on the conditioning of hostile verbs. *J. Pers.,* 1961, *29(4),* 380-395.

SKINNER, B. F. *Verbal Behavior.* New York: Appleton-Century Crofts, 1957.

SLOBODA, W. Personal Communication. Research and Training Branch, St. Elizabeths Hospital, Washington, D.C., 1964.

SOKOLOV, E. N. Neuronal models and the orienting reflex. *In:* BRAZIER, M. A. B. 1960.

SOUTHWELL, E. A. Conditioning of hostile and neutral verbs in neurotics and normals. *J. consult. Psychol.,* 1962, *26,* 257–262.

SPENCE, J. T. Verbal discrimination performance under different verbal reinforcement combinations. *J. exp. Psychol.,* 1964, *67(2),* 195–197.

SPIELBERGER, C. D. The role of awareness in verbal conditioning. *J. Pers.,* 1962, *30(Suppl.),* 73–101.

———. Theoretical and epistemological issues in verbal conditioning. Preprint for: ROSENBERG, S. 1965 (In press).

———, & DE NIKE, L. D. Operant conditioning of plural nouns: A failure to replicate the Greenspoon effect. *Psychol. Rep.,* 1962, *11,* 355–366.

———, ———. Implicit epistemological bias and the problem of awareness in verbal conditioning: A reply to Greenspoon. *Psychol. Rep.,* 1963, *12,* 103–106.

———, & LEVIN, S. M. What is learned in verbal conditioning? *J. verb. Learn. verb. Behav.,* 1962, *1(2),* 125–132.

———, ———, & SHEPARD, M. C. The effects of awareness and attitude toward the reinforcement on the operant conditioning of verbal behavior. *J. Pers.,* 1962, *30,* 106–121.

———, BERGER, A. E., & HOWARD, K. The conditioning of verbal behavior as a function of awareness, need for social approval, and motivation. *J. abnorm. soc. Psychol.,* 1963, *67(3),* 241–246.

———, BERNSTEIN, I. H., & RATLIFF, R. G. The information and incentive value of reinforcement in verbal conditioning. Unpub. Paper, 1964.

STAATS, A. W., & STAATS, C. K. Attitudes established by classical conditioning. *J. abnorm. soc. Psychol.,* 1958, *57,* 37–40.

STAATS, C. K., & STAATS, A. W. Meaning established by classical conditioning. *J. exp. Psychol.,* 1957, *54,* 74-80.

STEINBERG, D. D., & OAKES, W. F. Conditioning semantic response classes. *Psychol. Rep.,* 1964, *15,* 802.

STEVENSON, H. Social reinforcement with children as a function of CA, sex of E, and sex of S. *J. abnorm. soc. Psychol.,* 1961, *63,* 147–154.

——, & FAHEL, L. The effect of social reinforcement on the performance of institutionalized and noninstitutionalized normal and feebleminded children. *J. Pers.,* 1961, *29,* 136–147.

——, & SNYDER, L. Performance as a function of the interaction of incentive conditions. *J. Pers.,* 1960, *28,* 1–11.

TAFFEL, C. Conditioning of verbal behavior in an institutionalized population and its relation to "anxiety level." Unpublished Ph.D. thesis, Indiana Univer., 1952.

TANAKA, Y. A cross-culture and cross-concept study of the generality of semantic space. *Proceedings: 1963 International Congress of Psychol.,* 1964, *17,* 126 (Abstr.).

TATZ, S. J. Symbolic activity in "learning without awareness." *Amer. J. Psychol.,* 1960, *73,* 239–247.

THOMPSON, J. W. Language, thinking and electronic machines. *Estratto Rivista Methodos,* 1962, *14,* 147–152.

——. The importance of opposites in human relations. *Human Relations,* 1963, *16(2),* 161–169.

TIMMONS, E. O. The effect of a conditioned verbal response on a related nonverbal behavior. *Psychol. Rec.,* 1962, *12,* 221–271.

TRAPP, E. P., & HIMELSTEIN, P. (Eds.). *Research Readings on the Exceptional Child.* New York: Appleton-Century Crofts, 1962.

TRIANDIS, H. C.
In: Discussions. Proceedings: *1963 International Congress of Psychol.,* 1964, *17,* 193–194 (Abstr.).

ULLMANN, L. P., KRASNER, L., & GELFAND, D. M. Changed content within a reinforced response class. *Psychol. Rep.,* 1963, *12,* 819–829.

UNGER, S. M. Habituation of the vasoconstrictive orienting reaction. *J. exp. Psychol.,* 1964, *67(1),* 11–18.

VERHAVE, T., & BACHRACH, A. J. Social stimuli and provisional reinforcement. Contract Nonr. 2794(03), ONR & Arizona State Univer., 1964.

VERPLANCK, W. S. The control of the content of conversation: Reinforcement of statements of opinion. *J. abnorm. soc. Psychol.,* 1955, *51,* 668–676.

——. Unaware of where's awareness: Some verbal operants . . . notates, monents, and notants. *J. Pers.* (Suppl.), 1962, *30,* 130–150.

VISSER, S. L. Relationships between contingent alpha blocking and conditioned psychogalvanic reflex. *EEG clin. Neurophysiol.,* 1963, *15,* 768–774.

VOLKOVA, V. D. On certain characteristics of the formation of conditioned reflexes to speech stimuli in children. *Fiziol. zh. USSR,* 1953, *39,* 540–548. *From:* RAZRAN, G. H. S. 1961.

WALTERS, R., & RAY, E. Anxiety, isolation, and reinforcer effectiveness. *J. Pers.,* 1960, *28,* 358–367.

——, ——, MARSHALL, W., & SHOOTER, J. Anxiety, isolation and suscepti-bility to social influence. *J. Pers.,* 1960, *28,* 518–529.

WATERS, J. E., & KODMAN, F., JR. Abstract conditioning. *J. Psychol.,* 1962, *53,* 441–452.

WEISS, R. L., KRASNER, L., & ULLMANN, L. P. Responsivity to verbal con-ditioning as a function of emotional atmosphere and pattern of reinforce-ment. *Psychol. Rep.,* 1960, *6,* 415–426.

——, ——, ——. Responsivity of psychiatric patients to verbal conditioning: "Success" and "failure" conditions and pattern of reinforced trials. *Psychol. Rep.,* 1963, *12,* 423–426.

WELCH, L. A behavioristic explanation of the mechanism of suggestion in hypnosis. *J. abnorm. soc. Psychol.,* 1947, *42,* 359-364.

WHITE, E. H. Subjectively equated stimulus intensities and autonomic re-activity. *J. exp. Psychol.,* 1964, *68(3),* 297-300.

WILLIAMS, J. H. Conditioning of verbalization: A review. *Psychol. Bull.,* 1964, *62(6),* 383-393.

WISHNER, J. The concept of efficiency in psychological health and in psy-chopathology. *Psychol. Rev.,* 1955, *62,* 69-80.

——. Studies in efficiency: GSR conditioning as a function of degree of task centering. *J. abnorm. soc. Psychol.,* 1962, *65,* 170-177.

WITTERS, D. R. Fixed ratio performance of psychiatric patients' verbal be-havior in a small group situation. Contract Nonr. 2794(03), ONR & Arizona State Univer., 1964.

——, & BACHRACH, A. J. The effects of competing contingencies upon fixed ratio baselines in a small group situation. Contract Nonr. 2794(03), ONR & Arizona State Univer., 1964.

WOLPE, J. *Psychotherapy by Reciprocal Inhibition.* Stanford, Calif.: Stan-ford Univer. Press, 1958.

ZAX, M., & KLEIN, A. Measurement of personality and behavior changes following psychotherapy. *Psychol. Bull.,* 1960, *57,* 435-448.

ZIGLER, E. The effect of pre-institutional social deprivation on the perform-ance of feebleminded children. Unpub. Ph.D. thesis, Univer. Texas, 1958.

——. Social deprivation and rigidity in the performance of feebleminded children. *J. abnorm. soc. Psychol.,* 1961, *62,* 413-421.

——. Rigidity in the feebleminded. *In:* TRAPP, E. P., & HIMELSTEIN, P. 1962.

——, & KANZER, P. The effectiveness of two classes of verbal reinforcers on the performance of middle- and lower-class children. *J. Pers.,* 1962, *30(2),* 157-163.

——, HODGDEN, L., & STEVENSON, H. The effect of support on the perform-ance of normal and feebleminded children. *J. Pers.,* 1958, *26,* 106-122.

Conditioning Methods, USSR

A word (the living union between sound and meaning) is a microcosm of human consciousness [Vigotsky (1962) p. 153].

Semantic conditioning and the signalling systems

Verbal conditioning as explored by American operant conditioning investigators should not be confused with "semantic conditioning," a term used by Russian experimenters. Both "semantic conditioning" and "verbal regulation of behavior" are Russian phrases referring to experimental studies using classical rather than operant conditioning methods, and to concepts which are more obviously allied to the problem of "meaning," or "semantic generalization," than are present American verbal operant studies. It is clear that the object of study in the Russian laboratories is not meaning *per se*. Yet the nature of the work, dealing as it does with generalization and discrimination, is such that both methods and results are highly relevant to the issue of meaning as a psychological variable. In addition, the fact that physiological measures are so often used helps to broaden the base for conceptions of meaning in that possible "connections" between stimuli and externalized responses, often assumed but seldom demonstrated, can be more or less directly observed. The implications of this for a theory of meaning will be discussed in more detail in a later section.

Russian studies in semantic conditioning or semantic generalization became more sophisticated and complex in the 1950s. Partly this was a function of the emphasis upon elucidation of the theory of signalling systems, and the consequent design of experiments to fit into this theoretical frame of reference. Whereas American experimenters, as we shall show later, in general substituted verbal learning techniques and methods, Russian workers to a large extent maintained the physiologically based, classical conditioning experimental paradigm. Indeed, this method is basic to signalling system theory. There is currently some indication that influences from operant conditioning methodology have begun to seep through the iron curtain. A study by Napalkov and Bobneva (1962) used an instrumental chaining model in a nonverbal concept-formation task with human subjects, for instance. However, there is not enough of this kind of work available in English to assess its value to the problem of meaning.

In Russian experimentation which is relevant to the problem of meaning, the direction of movement appears to be from the simple observation of stimulus and/or response generalization along a meaning dimension toward the use of the generalization phenomenon in the investigation of two major areas of interest: 1) developmental psychology, and 2) the clarification and support of the Russian theoretical position with regard to central nervous system functioning. Actually, this division into two areas is more convenient than real, and has reference to experimental design, methods, and subjects used, rather than to purpose. Russian experimenters never lose sight of the problem of underlying mechanisms even when the major emphasis seems to be focused on developmental aspects. Basic to all Russian semantic experimentation is the concept of the first and second signalling systems and their interactions, and the attempt to anchor these functional processes in the nervous system. Importantly reflected in the Russian experimental method is a concern with problems of the excitation, inhibition, and irradiation of nervous impulse. It is sometimes difficult to know, particularly at the present state of knowledge, whether the latter concepts should be regarded as hypothetical constructs belonging at the same level of abstraction as the concept of the first and second signalling systems, or whether they should be regarded as experimentally demonstrated, neural processes which have certain psychological correlates. The tendency toward reification of concepts presents perennial problems in assessing experimental work and in the interpretation of results.

In any case, basic to the signalling systems is the signalling *process*—the substitution of one stimulus for another by means of connections which are made in some fashion (conditioning). When a connection is made between a stimulus which does not initially elicit a given response and a stimulus which does elicit the response, the originally neutral stimulus comes to elicit the response and it can be said that it has become a signal of the stimulus.

Bridger (1964, pp. 188-189) described the kinds of associations or stimulus substitutions characterizing first signalling system activity as follows:

1. *Primary stimulus generalization:* association through physical similarity.
2. *Generalization based on contiguity* (temporal or spatial).
3. *Stimulus generalization based on identity of affect or activity.*
4. *Generalization based on identity of function.*

First signalling system activity thus closely parallels the Freudian notion of primary process thinking. It is activity which belongs to the first signalling system only when the conditioned stimulus functions *as if* it were the primary (unconditioned) stimulus.

The second signalling system comprises abstractions of reality, and its activity can be described as generalization based on logical or meaningful (semantic) or symbolic (metaphoric) connections. Second signalling system activity parallels secondary process thinking. Thus a word can belong to the first signalling system (when it replaces the concrete object or the single instance) or to the second signalling system (when it becomes a symbol).

SIGNALLING SYSTEM INTERACTION: METHODS OF STUDY

Ivanov-Smolensky (1956) summarized and classified the experimental work devoted to the study of the interrelationships between the first and second signalling systems under three main headings:
1. Studies of dynamic transmission in the first signalling system:
   a. Object $\longrightarrow$ word transfer: replacement of direct positive and inhibitory conditioned stimuli and their dynamic patterns or "stereotypes" by the verbal designates of these stimuli.
   b. Behavior $\longrightarrow$ word transfer: replacement of direct conditioned responses by conditioned verbal responses.
Most of the early work in "semantic generalization" falls within this classification, although some of it belongs under the second.
2. Studies of dynamic transmission from the first to the second signalling system, tracing the spread of excitation in the transfer process from the conditioned connections of the first signalling system to the verbal associations of the second and vice versa:
   a. Word $\longrightarrow$ word transfer: combination of the method of conditioned first signalling system connections with word-association methods (second signalling system).

3. Method of verbal account or subject report: designed

   a. to measure the adequacy of the dynamic reflection in the second signalling system of the first system connections and their dynamic "stereotypes"; and

   b. to clarify the precision and completeness of the verbalization (second signalling system) of the conditioned stimulus, the conditioned response, and the relation between them (in American terms, e.g., "awareness" of experimental contingencies).

Disturbance in the interrelations between first and second signalling systems (Bogachenko, 1956b) might be revealed by such signs as:

1. Absence of, or difficulty with the verbal account.

   a. Complete absence of the reflection of the conditioned response: for example, if the subject actually made a motor response but failed to report having done so in his account of "what happened" in the experiment.

   b. Absence of verbalization of the individual elements of the conditioned response; that is, the subject might report the response, but fail to describe it in accurate detail, or fail to report the conditioned stimulus.

   c. Impeded verbalization of the conditioned response; that is, the subject might be able to report the conditioned response, but only in response to probing or assistance on the part of the examiner.

2. Disturbances in transmission of the elements of the conditioned response from the first to the second signalling systems.

   a. Incorrect verbal description of the stimulus; for example, describing the ringing of a bell as a "crackling light."

   b. Incorrect verbal description (reflection in the second signalling system) of the actual relation between stimulus and response.

Examples of the first class of experimental investigations were covered in a previous chapter. Shvart's (1954 and 1960) work illustrates the shift from the first to the second class of experiments. He conditioned a vasoconstrictive response in nine adult bilingual (Russian and English speaking) subjects to the Russian words дом (house) and доктор (doctor). The response generalized to дым (smoke) and диктор (announcer). Notice that the Russian homonyms are also very close to each other in *visual* structure. The phonetographic generalization, however, disappeared after the conditioned response was well established and was replaced by semantic generalization to *house* and to врач (physician). The homonymic response reappeared 30 minutes after the administration of chloral hydrate, and semantic generalization disappeared. This experiment, in addition to demonstrating the difference and the relationship between the first and second signalling systems, suggests that true semantic conditioning is a higher-level function. It further demonstrates that the lower-level is not lost with the development of the higher, but is held in abeyance and reasserts itself in periods of lower organismic functioning.[1]

Another example is a study by Vinogradova and Eysler (1959) who recorded vasoconstrictive conditioned responses from their subjects, fingers and foreheads to the sound of the word скрипка (violin), using shock as UCS. There was semantic generalization to such words as смычек (violin bow), гитара (guitar), струна (string), мандолина (mandolin), арфа (harp), барабан (drum), оркестр (orchestra), скрытность (reticence), etc. However, it is interesting to note that there was transfer of two sorts: vasoconstriction of both finger and forehead (the typical response to shock, the UCS) to words closely related to the stimulus in *meaning;* and vasoconstriction in the finger with vasodilation in the forehead (the typical *orienting* response), to words distantly related in meaning and to homonyms.

The appearance of the orienting response here points to a phenomenological change in the subjects. Keeping in mind the fact that the orienting response is a response to *novelty,* its appearance in this situation could indicate only that the subject was expecting, or had a "set" for a certain type of input: namely, a succession of conceptually related terms which "signalled" or "meant" shock. Irrelevant terms might safely be ignored, but words related either closely in terms of form or distantly in terms of meaning might require vigilance or alertness, perhaps in order to make a fine distinction. Sokolov (1960) reported that with young children, after the orienting response to a particular word had disappeared, synonyms of the word did not elicit it, but words which were not synonyms did.

The third class of experimental investigations (the method of verbal report) is often combined with other methods, and ex-

---

[1] The Russians term this function "chronogenetic disinhibition." There are many other examples of this process in the literature. It might be thought of as a parallel to the psychoanalytic notion of *regression.* See Bogachenko 1956a.

amples will be noted below in the description of several studies organized to demonstrate a variety of variables in signalling system development and interaction.

The above descriptive classification is helpful in that it summarizes as clearly as possible the various methods used by Russian investigators in their studies of signalling system activity. The fact is, however, that several or all of these methods are often combined in single experiments. For the purpose of examining the Russian contribution to the investigation of meaning we have chosen to look first at the work in developmental psychology along with a few adult experiments which are related to the developmental studies. Luria (1960), who has done a great deal of work with child subjects, emphasized the importance of tracing the "dramatic history" of developmental stages in the verbal regulation of behavior. He considered knowledge of such stages to be crucial to understanding the specificity of the development of the interaction of the signalling systems. Finally we shall turn to some of the very interesting work in proprioceptive conditioning—work that is to date very nearly uniquely Russian.

Developmental studies

Although all developmental studies are concerned with the problems subsumed under the above classifications, and use the methods devised to illuminate these problems, some focus primarily upon determining the ages at which different kinds of transfer from one signalling system to another take place, while others are concerned with both *when* and *how* transfer occurs.

VERBAL REGULATION OF BEHAVIOR

The studies of Luria and his group (Luria, 1960) are the most systematic with respect to the development of the regulatory function of speech. It might be said that in these studies he gives us a picture of how meaning develops in children, or at any rate a notion of what the various stages in the growth of meaning are.

Behavior may be regulated by means of external speech, or by means of internal speech. That is, it may be externally regulated by the verbalizations (speech) of another or by one's own spoken directives; or it may be internally regulated by one's own internalized directives, or subvocal speech. Luria reported that at the age of 14 months, behavior regulation is dominated by the orienting reflex or by what he calls the "inertia of nervous activity." Verbal directives are subordinate in that if they come into conflict with inertia or with the orienting reflex, either of the latter will regulate the child's behavior rather than the verbal command. If, for example, verbal instructions have directed a child's movement two or three times toward the left side, the child needs to have great mobility of the nervous system to be able to change this action to the right in accord with further verbal instruction. It appears that, at this stage, verbal instruction can only initiate behavior, it can not as yet either stop or reverse it. It also fails if it comes into conflict with an immediate perception which arouses the orienting reflex through the relative intensity or other kind of novel aspect of the distracting stimulus.[2] At 28 months, the child's own verbal activity fails to assist in the organization of his own behavior, although effective verbal control can be achieved through training with external verbal commands without using the child's own verbalization.

Inhibitory control, as contrasted with control of excitation, can be most readily effected through the addition of a concrete exteroceptive signal to the verbal signals. Up to the age of about five and a half there is generalization of both the inhibitory and the excitatory functions of speech instructions, so the child is still not ready for the full organization of his behavior through the control of preliminary verbal instructions. At five and a half years of age, this form of organization of motor behavior is completed. The "plasticity" of the nervous system is now well developed, and the child's motor reaction can obey both external and internal verbal command (the second signalling system).

A child of three is unable to respond to positive and negative signals with a stable system of positive and negative reactions unless every signal is individually reinforced by saying "yes" immediately following correct responses and "no" to errors. With such reinforcement, a system of correct reactions is formed in a very short time. At this stage, the controlling function of preliminary instructions is not yet developed. External reinforcement of each response is necessary.

Although a child of three is a slave to the physical properties

---

[2] See also Maslennikova (1956).

of the stimulus (e.g., a long signal evokes a long motor response, a short signal a short one), if the child's own speech is introduced, there is a shift in coordination of the motor response from the physical stimulus to the child's own verbal reaction. For example, if the child says "go" to both signals, regardless of the length of the signal (e.g., a light or auditory signal) the hand movement no longer reflects the length of the signal. This shows a mediating role of meaning, or the semantic aspect of the verbal reaction in the organization of movement.

Speech reactions have two properties, an excitatory one and a semantic one. This is demonstrated by the fact that when the child himself says "press," he presses, and if he says "no" he also presses. In positive motor reactions, saying "press" is positive with respect to both the semantic and the excitatory aspects of the movement. There is motor excitation of both the hand and the speech apparatus and thus both reactions are in the same class. This is not so in the case of negative signals. The child gives a negative semantic reaction ("no") but a positive (excitatory) motor reaction in the speech apparatus (he speaks) and in the hand (he presses).

At this stage of development, then, the child obeys not the semantic content of his own verbal reaction but responds to its excitatory property. The self-regulating influence of speech can be utilized only if there is no conflict between the semantic direction of the word and the innervatory excitation of the movement. If there is conflict, the child, upon receiving the negative stimulus, and upon producing the negative verbal signal, reacts not to the semantic but to the excitatory aspects of the signal.

At the final stage of verbal development, the semantic side of the child's own speech begins to play a really decisive role. At this stage it is not necessary for the child to apply externally vocalized speech, because at the moment when semantic control is developed, the child can use his own internal, subvocal speech. As a result of this internalized process, the child can obey instructions without speaking aloud. He no longer needs the auditory reinforcement of his own speech.

To summarize, the sequence of steps in the child's verbal development are as follows: 1) the child's own verbal activity plays no decisive role in his behavioral organization; 2) the child's verbal activity plays a partial role in organization but only when the semantic and excitatory functions of speech are not in conflict; and

3) the child's own verbal activity is decisive in the organization of his behavior.

Developmental factors in excitation and inhibition

Several investigators in the developmental area have studied negative conditioning (response inhibition) as well as positive conditioning (the establishment of a conditioned response) in an attempt to determine the relative dominance of excitatory and inhibitory processes. Sokolova (1961), using a modification of the old word-association test, studied the effect of age on the inhibition of verbal responses. Following a brief series of verbal stimuli to which the child was to respond with the first word occurring to him, he was instructed *not* to respond, and the series was repeated until three successive stimuli were followed by no response. Extinction was slower with the six-to-eight-year group than with the nine-to-eleven group, and the latter was slower than the thirteen-and-fourteen group. In the younger groups the inhibitory process was also more readily disturbed even after it was established. There was an even sharper differentiation between ages when complex stimuli—such as a combination of a tone, verbal stimulus, and negative reinforcement—were presented interspersed in a series of positive verbal stimuli which called for a verbal response.

Using a similar but more elaborate design, Fuflygina (1956b) established a uniform word-response latency to stimulus words in her child subjects. She then conditioned a motor response (press a rubber balloon) to a number of colored light stimuli such as red, blue, and green lights. When the CR was thoroughly established, with the subject still in position with his hand on the balloon, she readministered the word-association test. Into the list of stimulus words she inserted the verbal designates of the light stimuli to which the motor response had been conditioned (e.g., the words "red," "blue," "green"). She then proceeded to extinguish the subject's word-response to *one* of the verbal designates (e.g., "red") by saying, "Do not answer." The subject was then retested with the light stimuli. Some of the subjects failed to give the conditioned *motor* response to the particular light stimulus (e.g., the red light) to whose verbal designate (red), as stimulus, the *verbal* response had been extinguished. She concluded, thus, that she had demonstrated irradiation, or generalization, of inhibition from the second to the first signalling systems. The results were not uniform for all age groups.

This experiment arouses some interesting speculation. If a child is trained not to respond to certain terms, would this result in a similar lack of response to the objects or events to which the terms refer? In other words, it may be possible for certain kinds of objects and events to be rendered "meaningless" by extinguishing responses to their verbal designates. If this were the case, the existence of "taboo words" might have other than superstitious implications.

In a study of children reported by Pratusevich (1960), positive motor and secretory reactions were conditioned to the sound of a bell and a flash of light (sensory, first signalling system stimuli). When a negative verbal stimulus ("no bell," "no light"—negative second signalling system stimuli) was presented simultaneously with the positive sensory (actual bell or light) stimulus, the responses were inhibited. The author interprets these results as indicating the primacy of the second over the first signalling system. Yet in view of the other evidence of transfer of inhibition and lack of transfer of excitation from the second to the first signalling system in young children, another possible interpretation might be considered: namely, that transfer of inhibiting responses from the second to the first signalling system takes place earlier in ontogenesis than does the transfer of positive responses. It is tantalizing to contemplate how this may be related to the comparative frequency with which positive and negative ("no, no!") commands are used during a child's early training. Can a human organism be trained (conditioned) to respond with a readier conditionability to certain conditioning methods than to others? Or is inhibition of response more readily conditionable than excitation? Or is there a difference with respect to the stimuli used, or the response modality conditioned? These questions can be answered empirically, and their answers could have broad consequences in practical ways as well as with respect to the development of meaning. It must be that meaning develops by means of some combination of generalization of excitation and generalization of inhibition.

SIGNALLING SYSTEM DOMINANCE

It is interesting to compare the foregoing results with some from experiments using adult subjects. Okhnyanskaya (1953) instructed adult subjects to inhale, and when they did so, clear cut vasoconstriction in the arm was registered plethysmographically, and changes in the pneumogram occurred. Then when she told the subject *not* to inhale when the word "inhale" was presented, the vasoconstriction persisted despite an entirely regular pneumogram. In other words, the subject gave a vascular response *as if* he were actually inhaling when he was, in fact, not doing so. The vascular response to the second signalling system stimulus ("inhale") continued. There was no inhibition as a result of the instructions ("do not inhale when I say 'inhale'") at the vascular level, although the motor response was inhibited. The author concluded that positive conditioning to words occurs naturally, in the course of life experiences, and that these conditioned responses may not be deconditioned or inhibited by instructions, or subsequent learning. These results suggest either that children are more plastic in that *any* conditioned response, negative (inhibition) as well as positive, may be more readily disturbed; or that a motor response can be more readily deconditioned or inhibited than an autonomic response; or that as Kapustnik and Faddeeva[3] contended, conditioned reactions formed with the aid of speech reinforcement are not extinguished when the reinforcement is abolished.

It is somewhat difficult to interpret such experimental findings in terms of their significance with regard to the dominance of the first signalling system over the second, or vice versa. It is not entirely clear whether such commands as "press" or "don't press" or "inhale" should be regarded as stimuli belonging to the first or second signalling system, since they refer to specific concrete acts. It seems fairly clear that instructions, such as "when I say 'inhale', don't inhale" belong to the second signalling system, since an abstraction rather than a concrete denotation is involved.

Before speculating further on the basis of these few experiments, let us consider some additional studies. Nikiforova (1956) first extinguished child subjects' vascular orienting response to an indifferent stimulus (a 2700 cycles/second, 75 decibel tone) by presenting it repeatedly for 30 seconds at one-to-two-minute intervals until it ceased to produce changes in the plethysmographic curve. Following extinction, a delayed conditioned motor response to the tone stimulus was established in from 28 to 86 trials, using verbal reinforcement. It was found that the reappearance of the

---

[3] See Gerasimchuk (1956).

vascular response, absent at the beginning of the conditioning trials, preceded the establishment of the delayed conditioned motor response, then finally disappeared again after the delayed response was consolidated. When the verbal designate of the direct signal (the child's own word for the tone) was substituted as the stimulus for the delayed motor response, it produced the same vascular response as did the direct stimulus, even when it failed to produce the conditioned motor response. That is, when the experimenter used a word as stimulus instead of and designating the direct stimulus (the tone), the vascular response occurred even in the absence of the conditioned motor response. Thus, in the Russian terminology, it seems that transfer from the first to the second signalling system occurred at the vegetative response level, even when it failed to occur at the motor response level. In other words, the stimulus word had one meaning at the vegetative level and another, or *no* meaning, at the motor level.

AGES AND STAGES IN DEVELOPMENT

Other kinds of studies with children focused upon generalization phenomena and the ages at which particular kinds of transfer from one signalling system to another took place and under what conditions.

For example, Korbatov (1956) studied the relationship between the degree or amount of conditioning and transfer. Using as subjects 200 children divided into four age groups (4-6, 7-8, 12-13, and 15-16) of 50 each, he found that although a verbally reinforced, conditioned motor response transferred readily from the sound of a bell ringing to the word "ring" (transfer from the first to the second signalling system), the degree of transmission was dependent upon the degree of consolidation of the conditioned response. There seems to be an optimum value for the strength of the conditioned connection with respect to under- or over-conditioning, the optimum value varying with age. However, his attempts to establish the reversal transfer (from second to first signalling system) were unsuccessful with children.

Seredina (1956) attempted to delimit the ages at which different kinds of transfer take place. She trained children to make a simple motor response (press a rubber balloon) to the flash of a yellow light using verbal reinforcement ("press"). After five CRs had been obtained in succession, and following an interval of 30-45 seconds, a test was made of the children's responses to six differently colored lights.

The colored lights were then replaced as stimuli by their verbal counterparts ("yellow light," "green light," etc.), by color names corresponding to the lights ("yellow," "green," etc.), and by control words (adjectives, nouns, verbs unrelated to the stimuli). Children between the ages of 5-6, 8-9, and 11-12, twenty in each age group, were used as subjects. 85% of the 5-6-year olds showed diffuse generalization to all words, but 15% gave differential responses to the words, "yellow light" and "green light"—the verbal designates of the direct stimuli (first signalling system). 55% of the 8-9-year olds gave the diffuse reaction to all words, 20% differentiated the first signalling system words ("yellow light") from other first signalling system words ("green light," etc.). 5% responded to the word "yellow" and no other color words, while 25% responded only to "yellow light" and "yellow" (specialization of the CR in both first and second signalling systems). 70% of the 11-12-year olds gave the specialized CR in both signalling systems, and 30% responded to "yellow" only (the elective form of generalization).

From these results she concluded that the generalization of the conditioned response to verbal stimuli progresses from simple diffuse generalization to specialization and to the elective form, based upon the mutual interaction of the first and second signalling systems.[4] These results call to mind Riess's (1946) findings as well as the work of Luria and Vinogradova (1959) who found less semantic generalization with feebleminded children. Luria and Vinogradova also found, as did Bogachenko (1961), more diffuse generalization in normal children in a state of fatigue. The latter phenomenon is an instance of the kind of "chronogenetic disinhibition" or relapse to an earlier or more primitive level of functioning demonstrated in Shvarts's (1960) adult subjects who were given chloral hydrate.

Chronogenetic disinhibition

Fuflygina (1956a) demonstrated chronogenetic disinhibition in children subjected to the stress of an irrelevant stimulus. Forty-two

---

[4] Diffuse generalization would indicate that a response conditioned to a word generalized to all other words, that "specialized" refers to generalization along the dimension of phonetic or graphic or physical similarity, and "elective" refers to generalization along a meaning dimension.

girls, aged 8, 12, and 16, served as subjects. A word association test was carried out, the subject being instructed to respond with the first word that occurred to her. The experimenter included among other word stimuli such words as "sky," to which children usually reply with stereotypic responses (e.g., "blue"). When some response was stablized to a particular word, the subject was instructed to respond to that specific stimulus word with some *other* word than the word elicited in the first trial. This one specific word stimulus was continuously alternated with the other words. After five new word reactions had been obtained, the experimenter introduced an extraneous stimulus into the situation by flashing lights, sounding a tone, etc., one and a half seconds before the presentation of the particular word stimulus. In addition to chronogenetic disinhibition, observed less often in older than in younger children and more often when the subjects were fatigued, two other types of response were observed: namely, 1) increase in the latency of the response, and 2) complete inhibition of the word response. The three types of changes seemed to be related to the intensity of the competing stimulus. Increase in latency accompanied the least intense extraneous stimuli, inhibition of response accompanied the most intense, and relapse to earlier responses occurred in the middle range of stimulus intensity.

FUNCTIONAL MECHANISMS

In addition to probing the problem of developmental stages, other investigators focused upon underlying functional mechanisms, such as the mechanism of excitation, inhibition, and irradiation. For example, Naroditskaia (1956a), using groups of children aged 5-6, 8-9, 11-12, found that if a motor response was conditioned to a green light ("press") and inhibited to a blue light ("don't press"), not only the words "green" and "blue," but also color-related words such as "grass" and "leaf," "sky" and "sea," produced the identical responses (excitation or inhibition) as the physical stimuli. From this she hypothesized that the conditioned response is elicited not by primary excitation produced by the verbal stimulus, but by secondary excitation which awakened impressions left by past experience.

Gerasimchuk (1956) carried Naroditskaia's hypothesis further and explicated the functional mechanisms involved. He replicated her experiment, then developed an elaboration in which he established new associations between form and color by having the subjects sort and name sets of pictures which were drawings of familiar objects colored in unnatural ways, such as a *blue* chick, a *red* key, etc. Then new conditioned motor responses were established to a blue light, and inhibitions to a red light. When the verbal designates for the unnaturally colored objects (e.g., "chick," and "key") were substituted, the responses generalized to the words designating the objects corresponding to the signal values of the lights. Thus a motor response was given to "chick," and inhibited to "key."

Gerasimchuk concluded that the basis of semantic generalization, or the spontaneous conditioned response to a stimulus never before directly associated with it, is "the elective radiation of the stimulus process," spread through a series of conditioned connections by way of different intermediate stages. In one instance the connecting link is the verbal designate of the conditioned stimulus, in another it is possibly the revival of visual impressions which associate it with the conditioned stimulus. Degtyar', Znanenskaya, and Kol'tsova (1959) suggested that the role of unreinforced temporary connections of an associative type might be the decisive factor in the transfer to a new stimulus of a response developed to another stimulus.

VARIABLES IN CONCEPT ACQUISITION

Razran (1961) reported another series of Russian developmental studies which used as subjects children even younger than Luria's subjects, and different kinds of external verbal stimuli along with a single stimulus object. These experiments demonstrated varying degrees of effectiveness of a variety of stimulus combinations in the verbal regulation of behavior and/or concept formation (transfer from first to second signalling system).

In the first experiment (Kol'tsova, 1958) a doll was shown to ten twenty-month-old children 1,500 times. Five of the children were shown the doll along with the words, "Here is the doll"; "Take the doll"; and "Give me the doll." The other five subjects were shown the doll along with 30 different commands, such as "Look for the doll"; "Rock the doll"; "Find the doll"; etc.—each command used with equal frequency. In the test phase, the experimental doll was presented along with a variety of other toys. Group 1 chose the doll and also other toys, whereas group 2 chose the experimental doll and other dolls, but no other toys, and the latency of their response was four times faster than those of group one.

In a second experiment, Kol'tsova presented a book to nine 19-

month-old children 20 times. Three subjects were shown the single book along with a single verbal command, three were shown the single book along with 20 different commands, and three were shown 20 different books along with a single command, "give me the book." In the test phase, the child was shown a different book along with a variety of other objects and given the command, "Pick a book." Group 2 demonstrated the best grasp of the concept "book." Group 3 displayed rather poor abstraction, and group 1 no generalization at all. From these experiments it would appear that the shift from the verbal representation of a concrete object (first signalling system) to the verbal representation of a class of objects (abstraction, or second signalling system) takes place not so much through exposure to a variety of objects of the same class along with a single verbal designation, which would seem logical, but rather through exposure to a variety of verbalizations regarding the object and/or a variety of motor responses in connection with the object. If the latter, it would appear that the development of meaning is intimately associated with kinesthetic-motor experience, and more dependent on it than upon visual or verbal cues.

In a third experiment using ten children, aged 26 months, Kol'tsova presented 25 small objects. Five children were given 15 of the objects, one at a time, along with the word "thing" and a puff of air to the eyelid, and the remaining ten items with no additional stimulation. The other five children were presented all 25 objects along with the air puff, but only 15 with the word "thing," too. In the test phase, when the objects were placed before the children and the command, "Take something," was given, both eye-blink conditioning and generalization-differentiation were noted. The performance of the first group (where the UCS and the verbal signal occurred together consistently) was superior over the second group, which failed to demonstrate even simple conditioning in spite of the pairing of object and UCS.

These and other experiments demonstrate the part played by compound conditioning in the development of concepts, as well as the superiority of motor-kinesthetic responses over sensory-visual reactions in very young children. In addition, the latter experiment confirms Luria's finding that the addition of exteroceptive stimuli facilitates transfer. A further experiment with two-year olds (wherein geometric figures were presented with the word "thing" and an air puff, and objects were presented with the word "nothing" and no air puff) seems to support Luria's contention that there must be congruence between positive (excitatory) and negative (inhibitory) aspects for differentiation to be established.

Naroditskaia (1956b) carried out experiments with four groups of older children: 30 each of 5-6, 8, 10, and 12 years. The child subject sat in a booth isolated from the experimenter, with his hands on a rubber balloon. He was shown the picture of a jackdaw along with the verbal command, "Press." After four or five showings, the children in general anticipated the verbal reinforcement and pressed before the command was voiced. Then the subject was shown the picture of an animal (tiger, e.g.) along with the command, "Don't press." Conditioned positive responses to pictures of six different kinds of birds and negative responses (inhibitory) to pictures of six different animals were established. Then the words "bird" or "beast" were substituted for the pictures of the concrete objects, without further reinforcement, and the responses were recorded. In a second experiment, the procedure was reversed, the conditioning being established to the words "bird" and "beast" and generalization tested to the pictures of all the varieties of both. She found that generalization of the motor reaction and its inhibition occurred in both directions, from the specific to the generic, or categorical, and from the generic to the specific. However, only a small percentage of the five-year olds immediately transferred from the specific to the generic stimuli, and none from the generic to the specific. The 12-year olds displayed nearly 100% immediate transfer in both directions. About half the eight-year olds, and 60% of the ten-year olds showed immediate generalization of the motor reaction to the generic term, but only about 25% of eight-year olds, and 40% of ten-year olds displayed immediate transfer in the opposite direction.

Faddeeva (1956) in a replication and extension of Naroditskaia's work, found that in some cases the subject was unable to supply the generic word when questioned about what was happening in the experiment, although there was an immediate transfer of the motor response. Although the subject, let us say, would press when shown pictures of birds, and not press in response to pictures of animals, he or she would respond to the question, "When did you press?" by an enumeration of the specific birds rather than by answering: "To pictures of birds." Further investigation disclosed that the generalized conditioned reactions were unstable. The children, for example, were unable to encompass additions of specific instances of the conditioned class: that is, they failed to respond to pictures of varieties other than those that had been reinforced. When the generic word was available, however, even implicitly, the generalized conditioning was immediate and stable.

VARIABLES IN LEARNED (CONDITIONED) DISCRIMINATION

In order to answer the question: "Does a differentiation established in combination with verbal conditioning remain intact upon switching over to responses provoked by the same stimulus elaborated in combination with unconditioned conditioning?", Alekseenko (1956) used the blink reflex as the response, an air puff and the word "blink" as the unconditioned stimuli, and pure sounds as the conditioned (discriminative) stimuli. The seven subjects ranged in age from 19 to 25. The subject was placed in a screened, soundproof chamber, with all the apparatus outside; contact with the experimenter was by telephone only. The conditioned stimulus, a 700 cycles/second, 40 decibels pure sound was delivered through earphones. The unconditioned stimulus, a puff of air, was delivered to the subject's cornea through a tube fixed in front of his eye and mounted on a loop which encircled his head. Blinks were recorded by a photoelectric method which registered the intensity of the movement. 40 to 50 applications of the CS were delivered at intervals of from 15 to 25 seconds, with a duration of 7 seconds.

Following stabilization of the conditioned response, it was temporarily extinguished immediately by the experimenter's saying, "Now you'll feel no more blowing." Then the same CR was established to the same CS (the 700 cycle tone) by means of verbal conditioning: the experimenter's either saying "Blink!", or giving preliminary instructions, "When you hear the sound, blink." When this CR was stabilized, differentations were established to sounds of 800, 770, and 750 cycles/second by means of pairing these sounds with the command: "Don't blink." Differentiated stimuli were applied once for every 2 to 4 positive stimuli (700 cycles/second tone), and the discrimination was established in from 5-19 applications. The subject was then told, "Now we'll repeat the experiment with blowing." The verbally conditioned CR was immediately extinguished, and the CR established earlier by using the UCS was at once restored. The two blinking responses were distinguishable since they differed in their nature and latency. The discrimination previously established failed to remain intact.

Here the subject has demonstrated his ability to make a fine auditory discrimination, established with the aid of verbal rein-forcement. 700 cycles/second now "means" respond, 750 means don't respond. But when the UCS is reintroduced, the meaning of 750, and even 800, changes, and now means the same as 700. According to the author then, in this instance, transfer of an inhibitory response established in the second signalling system failed to transfer to the situation where direct (first signalling sys-tem) stimulation was used, although the whole (second signalling system) discrimination remained intact.

Further experiments (Alekseenko 1964) were designed to in-vestigate the coordination of simultaneous conditioned reactions (finger withdrawal and eye-blink) to the same conditional stimulus (a 700 cycle tone), using verbal reinforcement (second signalling system stimuli) and unconditional reinforcement (shock and air puffs). His results suggested extremely complex interrelationships, even in such a relatively simple experimental situation, which have not even begun to be experimentally investigated. The author con-cluded that the conceptions of the interaction, as a complex unity, of the first and second signalling systems are not adequate to de-scribe the experimental results.

Experimenting in visual rather than auditory discrimination,[5] Samsonova (1956) found that with a simple motor conditioned reaction much finer visual differentations could be formed than with a simple verbal reaction.

As stimuli, she used two 5 mm. white, horizontal strips against a black background, mounted 10 mm. apart one above the other in an apparatus in such a way that the lower strip was fixed at a dis-tance of 130 cm. from the subject, while the upper strip was mov-able and could be advanced 40 cm. toward the subject. The ap-paratus was supplied with diaphragms which screened the marginal portions of the strips and exposed only the central portions.

The subjects' motor responses were recorded, also their reaction times and electromyographic tracings from the arm muscles. The command: "Press" was given when the two strips were equidistant. Then the top strip was moved 40 cm. closer to the subject and the command: "Don't press" was given. Four or five positive stimuli were given for every inhibitory one, and finer and finer differenti-ations were established by repeated trials showing the strips at varying distances from each other.

Prior to the acquisition of the differentiation there was rapid

---

[5] See also Samsonova (1955a, b and c).

acquisition of the positive conditioned response and rapid decrease of latency of the motor responses. In some subjects the positive CR manifested itself first in a change in the electrical activity of the muscle, and it was only later that a readily verbalizable motor response occurred.

Discrimination developed slowly, and was accompanied by marked increases in latency. Fluctuations in the duration of latent periods are regarded as "a reflection of the dynamics of the nervous processes in the course of [the] elaboration of positive and inhibited conditioned reactions."[6] What is interesting from the point of view of the study of meaning is that the verbalizations of the subjects prior and subsequent to the establishment of the differentiation (e.g., "I don't know what you want me to do," and "Now I understand—the strips are placed at different distances") suggest that the motor differentiation is established *before* the verbal differentiation—that is, the differentiation, or the *meaning* of the stimulus, is established in the first signalling system before it is established in the second signalling system, and not the other way around. One might say the sequence is: "I do it, thus I understand what it means," rather than "I understand what it means, thus I can do it." This interpretation is supported by the findings from the developmental studies with very young children; namely, that generalized concepts (meanings) such as "book" and "doll" are more readily formed through motor activity connected with the objects to be discriminated.

In further elaborations of this experimental method, Samsonova (1955b) demonstrated that visual differentiations established by one kind of simple motor response (pressing a balloon with the right hand) remains undisturbed when other simple motor responses are substituted, even when they have different motor characteristics (for example, press with the left hand and raise the right hand). When these simple motor responses were replaced with one requiring special skill (raise the fourth finger), in most subjects the latency of response decreased and finer differentiations were made. In still further elaborations, using the same apparatus and recording procedures, Samsonova (1955c) found that when the motor response was replaced by a verbal response (the subject's saying "equal") the differentiation became impaired, although when the verbal response was introduced at the beginning of the conditioning process, the differentiation became precise very quickly. However,

---

[6] Samsonova (1955a, p. 231).

in the latter case, the maximum differentiation achieved early changed very little with subsequent trials, and remained much less fine than that achieved with motor responses. To summarize, whereas with the conditioned verbal reaction differentiation proceeded more rapidly, *limits* of differentiation were reached more quickly. With the motor reaction, discrimination was achieved more slowly, but reached a higher level of differentiation. If one motor reaction was substituted for another, no change in the discrimination level occurred, but if a verbal response was substituted, then the limit of differentiation was reduced.

ELECTIVE GENERALIZATION

Ivanov-Smolensky (1956) pointed out that one of the peculiarities of the elective generalization from the first to the second signalling system is the instantaneous, dynamic transmission of a conditioned response to a voiced or written verbal designate of a conditioned stimulus without any previous elaboration ("one-shot learning"). He quoted (p. 372) Korbatov's[7] findings that this transmission is transient, that it is related to the age of the individual, to the stability of the conditioned connection, and to the amount and intensity of external inhibition (the effect of distraction or the interference of the orienting response). In addition, he tells us that elective irradiation of both excitatory and inhibitory processes interlinking the two signalling systems have been observed for both conditioned motor and visceral responses which are constantly acting upon each other. Thus if a conditioned response is established on an unconditioned vegetative reflex, the same conditioned response can be elicited by replacing the conditioned stimulus by its verbal designate.

For example, electric shock reduces blood coagulation time. Markosyan (1958), using shock as UCS and the sound of a metronome as the CS, found transfer to the word *metronome* as well as to phonetographically related words. Then he used the flash of an electric lamp as CS, and found transfer to words meaning lamp, lantern, and light *(svet)* but not to *svist* (whistle). After a while, the subjects manifested clear-cut reductions in time of blood coagulation when, in the absence of shock, he merely said, "You're getting a shock"; or, "It's going to hurt." Here, it would seem, is a

---

[7] Translations of Russian sources give alternate spellings of this name (e.g., Kurbatov).

true "meaning" response which it would be difficult to rationalize in terms of simple association. One is reminded of a Spence and Goldstein (1961) experiment in the United States in which the verbal threat of punishment produced more rapid conditioning of the eye-blink response than did the actual noxious stimulus, and also of the Waters and Kodman (1962) experiment,[8] where the subjects gave larger GSRs to the unreinforced words, "electric shock," than they gave to words which had been repeatedly reinforced.

Elkin (1955), using shock as UCS, conditioned a hand-withdrawal response in 30 university students to three short sentences of two or three words each: 1) "I am switching on / the shock." 2) "The manuscript / was read." and 3) "The student / passed / the examination."[9] In testing for transfer to individual words, there was generalization to both words of sentence one, in which the whole meaning of the sentence is implied in each word. However, there was no transfer to either word in sentence two in which the meaning of the sentence was implied in neither word. With the third group of words the transfer was differentially distributed: 87% to *passed*, 50% to *examination*, and only 10% to *student*. As Miller (1965) reminded us (p. 18): "The meaning of an utterance is not a linear sum of the meanings of the words that comprise it." Razran (1952) alerted us long ago to the complications and contributions of syntax to verbal meaning.

Elaborations of the earliest model[10] of transfer from first to second signalling systems to include explicitly in the experimental design the primitive reflex system, have led to some of the most interesting developments (in Russian experimentation) with respect to the understanding of meaning in a general sense: namely, the studies in proprioceptive conditioning.[11] An example of a sort of transitional study is one by Korbatov (1961) using 7- and 9-year-old children as subjects. He conditioned two types of responses: 1) autonomic (vasodilation reinforced by warmth and recorded plethysmographically), and 2) motor (compression of a rubber balloon). The orienting response of turning the head toward the stimulus inhibited the motor CR. Once the conditioned vasomotor

---

[8] See p. 63-64 above.
[9] Groups of words marked off by a divider (/) are rendered in Russian by a single word.
[10] Such as Kapustnik's (1930).
[11] Reported by Razran (1961).

CR to the sensory stimulus was well established (requiring a large number of UCS-CS combinations), it persisted in spite of the orienting response—it was not inhibited by the turning response. This and other experiments in proprioceptive conditioning present a challenge to American association (S-R) theorists that will be hard to ignore, for the implications with respect to the role of meaning in learning, especially emotional learning—in personality development, and in the control or modification of behavior (e.g., education and psychotherapy)—are vast and fascinating.

Proprioceptive-semantic conditioning

Proprioceptive conditioning[12] is defined as classical conditioning in which either the conditioned stimuli or the unconditioned stimuli or both are delivered directly to the mucosa or some specific viscus. Four classes of proprioceptive conditioning can be distinguished: 1) interoceptive, in which both the conditioned and unconditioned stimuli are interoceptive; 2) interoexteroceptive, in which the UCS is exteroceptive and the CS is interoceptive; 3) exterointeroceptive, in which the UCS is interoceptive and the CS is exteroceptive, and 4) exteroexteroceptive, which is classical conditioning. Only classes 1 and 2 are true cases of interoceptive signalization in which the signalizers, initiators, or conveyors of acquired conditioned information are entirely internal (within the "black box"). A more elaborate classification scheme within the 1 and 2 categories would take account of the type of response conditioned (e.g., visceral, coordinated-motor, sensory-verbal) as well as the type of stimulus.

INTEROCEPTIVE CONDITIONING

It is known that conditioning to interoceptive stimuli conflicts with conditioning to exteroceptive stimuli in a way that conditioning to exteroceptive stimulation of different sense modalities does not (Razran, 1961). When two types of conditioned stimuli are presented in close succession, interoceptive conditioned stimuli *decrease* the conditioned response to subsequent exteroceptive conditioned stimuli while exteroceptive conditioned stimuli *increase* the conditioned response to subsequent interoceptive stimuli. Another way of saying this is that the response to the interoceptive stimulus be-

---

[12] See Razran (1961) for an extensive discussion of which this is a summary.

comes dominant over the response to the exteroceptive stimulus, to the extent that the latter tends to drop out or extinguish. The following experimental work makes this difference clear.[13]

Experiments with human subjects having stomach fistulas were conducted according to the following schedules:

1. The inside of the stomach was cooled, followed 10 or 15 seconds later by warming of the epigastric region.
2. The inside of the stomach was warmed, followed by cooling of the epigastric region.

Vasoconstriction accompanied cooling; vasodilation, warming. In both these interoceptive series, the first response (constriction in the first case, dilation in the second) suppressed the opposing succeeding reaction and became strengthened at the latter's expense.

3. The outside of the stomach was cooled, followed by warming of the inside.
4. The outside was warmed, followed by cooling of the inside.

In these exteroceptive series, the preceding response was clearly weakened, the succeeding response strengthened. In all instances the exteroceptive stimuli lost their original function and the response to the interoceptive stimulus became dominant.

What is even more startling and interesting from the point of view of the meaning of meaning, and significant with regard to the verbal control of behavior, is the fact that when the response (constriction) was elicited by a *verbal* conditioned stimulus (the spoken words, "I am cooling your stomach on the inside," in the absence of any actual cooling), it was dominant over the response to the exteroceptive stimulus even when the *actual* UCS (warming on the outside) was being applied.

Experiments such as this raise some interesting theoretical questions and implications with respect to the problems of conditioning theory (learning).[14] With respect to the question of meaning, some implications seem clear. If we are to define meaning in behavioral terms, then not only external, voluntary behavior, but also internal involuntary behavior must be included. The Russian experimenters have opened up the "black box" and made the formerly unobservable observable. What this involves with respect to the problem of meaning is that if we are going to define meaning in terms of a mediating response, then we must revise our notions as to what the mediation category contains. Some of the variables

---

13 See Razran (1961) for detailed discussion.
14 See Razran (1961) for a discussion of these implications.

which American investigators have assigned to the mediation category, because they could be dealt with only on an inferential basis, have been studied directly by Russian experimenters, and as a result emerge from the category of intervening variable or hypothetical construct, become validly classifiable in the stimulus or response categories, and become manipulable as such.

In a further experiment,[15] using a method of successive trials, on odd trials a flash of blue light preceded warming of the epigastric region, giving rise to stereotypic vasodilation; on even trials, the blue light was followed by cooling the mucosa with the characteristic vasoconstrictive response. Vasodilation was then produced on odd trials when either the blue light was flashed or the words "I am flashing a blue light," were spoken. Vasoconstriction occurred on even trials to the same stimuli. Then a conditioning series was presented in which on odd trials a red light was flashed preceding cooling of the epigastric region (constriction), while the mucosa was warmed on even trials, resulting in characteristic responses being given on odd (constriction) and even (dilation) test trials to the *red* light in the test series. Following the conditioning and test trials for both series, when the red and blue lights were flashed without regard for the trial sequences, the subjects responded with irregular and conflicting vasomotion accompanied by vomiting, sensory distortions, and headache.

This experiment demonstrates the profoundly disturbing effects of conflicting meanings. In this case, the "meaning" of the stimulus with respect to the response was a function not only of the color cue, but also of the temporal sequence. Thus, although a given stimulus may have a perfectly clear meaning (signal a specific, appropriate response) in one context, it may become confused in another context (where other stimuli neither support, nor confirm, but rather conflict with it).[16]

The problem of the stimulus and response properties and conditionability of certain internal processes becomes crucial with the shift of such processes from the ranks of the inferred to the observable. With the development of techniques for studying such processes directly, experimental results may make it possible to

---

15 See Razran (1961).

16 Perhaps this gives us an operational definition and a way of experimentally studying *ambivalence*: responses conditioned to two or more different signal values (meanings) of the same conditioned stimulus such that the different conditioned responses are incompatible with each other and have equal probability of occurring to the CS.

generate testable hypotheses with respect to more highly elaborated and complex definitions of meaning without necessarily removing the concept from the realm of the S-R model.

CLASSICAL AND INSTRUMENTAL METHODS

Although Russian experimentation typically employs the classical conditioning paradigm, the operant model is beginning to appear in some laboratories in the USSR. Russian application of the operant method suggests new possibilities for the study of instrumental conditioning with human subjects, for the application of the method in verbal conditioning, and for the elaboration of the S-R definition of meaning. An example of the Russian use of the instrumental paradigm is an experiment in which Lisina (1958) subjected five adult subjects to prolonged and moderately painful electrical stimuli, which characteristically produce vasoconstriction. Continuous plethysmographic records were made of changes in the volume of the blood vessels in the subjects' arms. Occasional and infrequent instances of spontaneous vasodilation occurred, at which point shock was terminated. There was no change in the records (no conditioning of the dilation R) even after 80 reinforcements (termination of shock). However, when the subjects were permitted to observe the simultaneous recording of their own vasomotor responses, the transformation from constriction to dilatation was rapidly achieved.

This and some other Russian studies seem to contradict Kimble's (1961) assertion that the evidence points unequivocally to the conclusion that autonomically mediated responses (such as vasoconstriction, GSR, etc.) can be modified by classical but not by instrumental conditioning methods. It would appear that autonomic reactions *can* be modified operantly, but only when the subject is aware of the reinforcement contingencies or when meaning is present.

One is reminded here of an American study by Hefferline and Perera (1963). In this experiment the subject received a tone as a signal to press a key whenever the experimenter observed, on an electromyographic record, that the subject had emitted an infinitesimal muscle twitch (of which he was unaware) in this thumb. After several conditioning sessions, the tone was progressively diminished to zero, yet the subject continued to press the key in response to every twitch, and reported hearing the tone. In addition, the frequency of the muscle twitch was increased. In this case the subject was not aware of the reinforcement contingency, yet conditioning occurred, and the subject even rationalized his response (press) by hallucinating the nonexistent CS (tone). It should be noted, however, that Lisina's experiment uses a simple, straightforward instrumental conditioning model in which a vegetative response is conditioned, dilatation being the reinforcement contingency, and the reinforcement being avoidance of shock. Hefferline's is a more complicated model wherein the conditioned instrumental response is an involuntary motor response (muscle twitch) which produces and is reinforced by a voluntary motor response (press).

Actually the Hefferline experiment could perhaps better be viewed in terms of a classical model in which the CS (muscle twitch) replaces the UCS (tone) as the evoking stimulus for the CR (press), conditioned by the instruction: "When you hear a tone, press." Thus the two experiments are not strictly comparable with respect to illuminating the problem of awareness of reinforcement contingencies. However, comparing the two in terms of transmission from one signalling system to another is interesting and instructive. In Lisina's experiment, the transfer is from the reflex system into the second signalling system.[17] In Hefferline's experiment, the transfer is from the second signalling system (verbal instruction: "Press") to the reflex system (muscle twitch), with respect to the reinforcing stimulus, although the transfer is not accurately reflected in the second signalling system: that is, the subject reports that his motor response is to the tone stimulus, even though there is no tone.

This illustrates the complexity of the interaction of the signalling systems with each other and with the reflex system although this particular experiment is an American experiment and thus not designed to do so. Consequently, it has many fascinating implications for a theory of meaning, as well as for questions regarding differences and similarities in operant and classical conditioning.[18]

With respect to what meaning is, and how meanings come to be formed, and how meaning influences behavior, the Russian interoceptive conditioning experiments designed to investigate signalling system transfer, interaction, and dominance have most fas-

---

[17] This is an instance of a nonverbal second signalling system stimulus: the plethysmographic record.

[18] See Kimble (1961) pp. 78-109.

cinating implications and cry out for replication. It seems abundantly clear from both experimental evidence and common-sense observation that established autonomic (emotional) responses to both first and second system stimuli are highly resistant to extinction or deconditioning or reconditioning. The plaint, "I *know* such and such, but I *feel* this and that!" is repeated hundreds of times a week in every psychotherapist's office, as well as frequently in everyday life. If this were not so, psychotherapy and other procedures to induce change would certainly be speedier, less costly, and more reliable than they are.

However, a fascinating series of studies (Ayrapetyants, 1952), reported by Razran (1961), suggests that "knowing about" may, under certain circumstances, take precedence over "feeling directly" (sensation), or that signals of the second system may be responded to in preference to those of the first, as in Lisina's study.

Three patients with primary bladder fistulas were subjects for an experiment in which their bladders were distended by inflow of air or of a physiological solution. Conspicuously displayed to the subjects were the devices recording amount of inflow; bladder compression; rate and amount of urine secretion; accompanying respiratory, vascular, and psychogalvanic changes; and the subjects' signal of the time and intensity of urinary urges. The apparatus was so arranged that the experimenter could display to the subjects sham readings of the inflow, showing high readings where the actual inflow was low, and vice versa. The subjects' reactions were appropriate to the inflow readings on the scale rather than to the actual interoceptive condition or degree of distention. That is, not only were the physiological responses appropriate to the sham readings rather than to the actual state of distention, but also the subjects' reported sensations. A nonverbal second signalling system stimulus (the recording) was dominant over first signalling system stimuli (sensations) in evoking both reflex and second signalling system responses.

Thus it seems that a simple explanation of orderly development from one (lower) system to another (higher) is not sufficient to account for the experimental evidence. It is more likely that we are here (as usual) dealing with an organization of interacting systems, one perhaps being phylogenetically and ontogenetically "higher" than another, not necessarily taking precedence over the other by virtue of its being higher or lower in the scale, but rather by virtue of the interaction of complex and as yet unknown variables.

Summary

In spite of, or perhaps because of the Russian experimenters' primary interest in physiological, and especially neurological processes, their investigations of semantic processes often seem to have more interesting psychological implications than most American experimentation in the field of verbal behavior. Soviet experimentation is not directly and explicitly concerned with meaning *qua* meaning, but it has been very much concerned with the developmental aspects of semantic conditioning. As a consequence, this work suggests ways in which meaning is acquired from infancy through childhood and methods by which more information might be experimentally obtained.

Soviet experimental work has also concerned itself with how connections are formed and elaborated, and how they operate in adults. Soviet scientists are just as insistent as the strictest American S-R theorist that all behavior is the consequence of a stimulus, but stimuli may be "external or internal, physical, chemical, verbal, or psychological" [Ban (1964) p. 53]. Verbal instructions and verbal reports are combined with vegetative, motor, and verbal responses to varieties of stimuli ranging from interoceptive to verbal in painstaking and minute investigations of the smallest variations in already simplified operations. Soviet experimenters are very much interested in the interaction of psychological systems, and they rely upon their experimental methods and designs to ferret these out rather than upon statistical designs to discover relationships and interactions between and among variables.

Russian experimenters tend to observe small bits of their subjects' behavior, and to state their interpretations and conclusions in terms of inner processes, and of constructs referring to internal systems. Although some of the Russian hypothetical constructs, such as the signalling systems, are finding their way into the American literature, at the present time their methods and data are perhaps of more interest to American psychologists than their theoretical formulations.

In general, Russian studies present many difficulties with respect to interpretation of the results. The more obvious problems have to do with the relative unavailability of the work in English. It is hard to know whether or not the translated articles are representative or selective, and thus whether the gaps are due to selectivity in translation or report, or to real omissions in experimentation. Consequently, one is forced to rely a great deal upon secondary sources for information, and in many instances, however thorough the report may be, the particular, critical bit of information that is needed is omitted. Furthermore, the author reporting frequently has some bias, and his summary will include only those data which give support to or illuminate his point of view. This is not to imply that there is anything wrong with this, but simply to note that information crucial to other investigations may be, and probably is, left out. This renders the secondary sources considerably less useful than they would be if the primary source material were readily available for reference.

Another problem is that the Russian writers sometimes omit detail about the experimental design and the experimental procedures used, although they tend to report their actual raw data far more fully than American writers do. But the omissions make interpretations and evaluation difficult and tenuous, and replication well nigh impossible.

Finally, Russian experimenters tend to present their work as rather factual, empirical reportage. Each experiment, by and large, is a discrete empirical event. There seems to be little attempt to relate results from one experiment, or a series of experiments to others, or to discuss the significance of differences or discrepancies where they occur in seemingly related work. The reader is left with the facts, often incomplete, to relate, evaluate, and interpret as he will, with insufficient background or correlative information to do so. What interpretation or discussion is made by the authors is usually in terms of the significance of the findings with respect to physiological constructs which are often unclear to American readers.

Such differences in interest, orientation, and procedure create difficulties for the comparison of Russian with American work, especially with regard to interpretation and conclusions from the results. With respect to the problem of the definition of meaning, however, it may be possible to look beyond the specific interpretations which reflect experimenter bias in the theoretical realm to the elements revealed in the results themselves for significant variables needing further elucidation and investigation. In spite of the difficulties, a familiarity with Russian experimentation and conceptualization on the part of more American experimental psychologists might be very salutary for the development of experimental psychology in the United States. One would certainly not advocate copying Russian techniques or adopting their theoretical orientation, but a marriage of the Russian physiological approach with the American behavioristic rigor might produce a hybrid offspring more vigorous and powerful than either parent.

References

ALEKSEENKO, N. Y. Differentiations following replacement of speech conditioning by unconditioned conditioning in adult man.
In: RUSINOV, V. S., et al. II. 1956.

——. Interaction of simultaneous reaction conditions of humans. Foreign Tech. Div., Air Force Systems Command, Wright-Patterson AFB, Ohio: 1964.

AYRAPETYANTS, E. S. Higher nervous function and the receptors of internal organs. Moscow: Akad. Nauk USSR, 1952.
From: RAZRAN, G. H. S. 1961.

BAN, T. *Conditioning and Psychiatry.* Chicago: Aldine, 1964.

BOGACHENKO, L. S. The phenomena of chronogenetic disinhibition of conditioned reactions. (a)
In: IVANOV-SMOLENSKY, A. G., et al. II. 1956.

——. Experimental study of the derangements of the higher nervous activity, particularly the interrelations in the first and second signalling systems, in children during acute stages of rheumatic fever. (b)
In: IVANOV-SMOLENSKY, A. G., et al. II. 1956.

——. Some characteristics of the formation of conditioned reactions to complex sensory and verbal stimuli in children at the end of the school days.
In: GARTSSHTEIN, N. G., & BOGACHENKO, L. S. 1961.

BRAZIER, M. A. B. (Ed.). *The Central Nervous System and Behavior.* (Transactions of the third conference sponsored by Josiah Macy, Jr., Foundation and National Sci. Foundation). New York: Josiah Macy, Jr., Foundation, 1960.

BRIDGER, W. H. Contributions of conditioning principles to psychiatry.
In: LEBENSOHN. Z. M., et al. 1964.

BROZEK, J. Recent developments in Soviet psychology.
In: FARNSWORTH, P. R., et al. XV. 1964.

DEGTYAR, YE. N., ZNANENSKAYA, A. M., & KOL'TSOVA, M. M. Physiological mechanisms of certain forms of generalization in young children.
In: Works of the Institute of Physiology. VIII. (Trans. from Russian). Foreign Tech. Div., Air Force Systems Command, Wright-Patterson AFB; Ohio: 1959.

ELKIN, D. G. The characteristics of conditioned reflexes to a complex verbal stimulus. *Vop. Psikhol.*, 1955, *1(4)*, 79–89.
From: RAZRAN, G. H. S. 1961.

FADDEEVA, V. K. On the role of elective irradiation and induction in certain complex forms of joint activity by the two signalling systems. *In:* IVANOV-SMOLENSKY, A. G., et al. II. 1956.

FARNSWORTH, P. R., et al. (Eds.). Annual Review of Psychology. XV. Palo Alto, Calif.: Annual Reviews, Inc., 1964.

FUFLYGINA, T. P. On the change of word reactions to word stimuli in children under influence of external inhibition. (a) *In:* IVANOV-SMOLENSKY, A. G., et al. II. 1956.

——. On the irradiation of the inhibitory process from the second signalling system into the first. (b) *In:* IVANOV-SMOLENSKY, A. G., et al. II. 1956.

GARTSSHTEIN, N. G., & BOGACHENKO, L. S. (Eds.). *(Higher Nervous Activity in Healthy and Ill Children).* Moscow: Academy of Sciences of the USSR, 1961. *From:* BROZEK, J. 1964.

GERASIMCHUK, V. A. Certain new data on serial conditioned connections in the cerebral cortex of a child. *In:* IVANOV-SMOLENSKY, A. G., et al. II. 1956.

HEFFERLINE, R. F., & PERERA, T. B. Proprioceptive discrimination of a covert operant without its observation by the subject. *Science,* 1963, *139,* 834-835.

IVANOV-SMOLENSKY, A. G. Certain new data from the study of neural mechanisms of the interaction of the cortical signalling systems. *In:* IVANOV-SMOLENSKY, A. G., et al. II. 1956.

——, et al. (Eds.). *(Works of the Institute of Higher Nervous Activity: Pathophysiological Series.* II.) Moscow: Academy of Sciences of the USSR, 1956. Jerusalem: Israel Program for Scientific Translations, 1960. (Office of Tech. Serv., U.S. Dept. Commerce, Washington, D.C. 20025; PST Catalogue #72).

KAPUSTNIK, O. P. The interrelationship between direct conditioned stimuli and their verbal symbols. (Trans. from Russian). *Psych. Abstr.,* 1930, *8,* 152.

KIMBLE, G. A. (Ed.). *Hilgard and Marquis' Conditioning and Learning.* New York: Appleton-Century-Crofts, revision, 1961.

KOL'TSOVA, M. M. *The Formation of Higher Nervous Activity in the Child.* Moscow: Medgiz, 1958. *From:* RAZRAN, G. H. S., 1961.

KORBATOV, B. M. Study of the dynamic transmission of a conditioned connection from one cortical signalling system into the other. *In:* IVANOV-SMOLENSKY, A. G., et al. II. 1956.

——. Further studies on the interaction between the signal systems in school children. *In:* GARTSSHTEIN, N. G., & BOGACHENKO, L. S. 1961.

LEBENSOHN, Z. M., et al. *Pavlovian Conditioning and American Psychiatry.* New York: Group for the Advancement of Psychiatry, 1964.

LISINA, M. I. The role of orientation in the transformation of involuntary into voluntary reactions.
In: VORONIN, L. G., et al. 1958.

LURIA, A. R. Verbal regulation of behavior.
In: BRAZIER, M. A. B. 1960.

——, & VINOGRADOVA, O. S. An objective investigation of the dynamics of semantic systems. *Brit. J. gen. Psychol.,* 1959, *50,* 89-105.

MARKOSYAN, A. A. The interaction of signal systems in the process of blood coagulation. *Zh. vyssh. nervn. Deyatel.,* 1958, *8,* 161-167.
From: RAZRAN, G. H. S. 1961.

MASLENNIKOVA, V. M. On the influence of external inhibition on the joint activity of the first and second signalling systems.
In: IVANOV-SMOLENSKY, A. G., et al. II. 1956.

MILLER, G. A. Some preliminaries to psycholinguistics. *Amer. Psychologist,* 1965, *20(1),* 15-20.

NAPALKOV, A. V., & BOBNEVA, N. L. An analysis of conditioned reflexes and of the thought processes of the human brain. (Trans. from Russian). Foreign Tech. Div., Air Force Systems Command, Wright-Patterson AFB, Ohio: 1962.

NARODITSKAIA, G. D. A study of the question of the phenomenon of the so-called secondary excitation in the cerebral cortex of children. (a)
In: IVANOV-SMOLENSKY, A. G., et al. II. 1956.

——. The compound dynamic pattern in children of different ages. (b)
In: IVANOV-SMOLENSKY, A. G., et al. II. 1956.

NIKIFOROVA, E. M. On the influence of delaying inhibition of the conditioned motor reaction on the cardio-vascular system (preliminary note).
In: IVANOV-SMOLENSKY, A. G., et al. II. 1956.

OKHNYANSKAYA, L. G. A study of the conditioned respiratory-vasomotor reflexes: Respiration as the stimulus of vaso-motion. *Fiziol. Zh. SSSR,* 1953, *39,* 610-613.
From: RAZRAN, G. H. S. 1961.

PRATUSEVICH, YU. M. *(Verbal Stimuli Used with Children).* Medgiz, Moscow: 1960.
From: BROZEK, J. 1964.

RAZRAN, G. H. S. Experimental semantics. *Trans. N.Y. Acad. Sci.,* 1952, *14,* 171-177.

——. The observable unconscious and the inferable conscious in current Soviet psychophysiology: Interoceptive conditioning, semantic conditioning, and the orienting reflex. *Psychol. Rev.,* 1961, *68,* 81-147.

RIESS, B. F. Genetic changes in semantic conditioning. *J. exp. Psychol.,* 1946, *36,* 143-152.

Rusinov, V. S., et al. (Eds.). *Works of the Institute of Higher Nervous Activity: Physiological Series.* II. Moscow: Academy of Sciences of the USSR, 1956. Jerusalem, Israel Program for Scientific Translations, 1960. (Office Tech. Serv., U.S. Dept. Commerce, Washington, D.C., 20025; PST Catalogue #71).

Samsonova, V. G. Elaboration of visual differentiations in response to stimuli at varying distances. (a)
In: Usievich, M. A., et al. I. 1955.

———. Fluctuations in fine visual differentiations as a function of the characteristics of the conditioned motor response. (b)
In: Usievich, M. A., et al. I. 1955.

———. Differentiation limits in verbally reinforced motor reactions and certain functional and correlational characteristics of the first and second signalling systems under various conditions of interaction. (c)
In: Usievich, M. A., et al. I. 1955.

———. The influence of reconditioning the stimulus value of light stimuli on the optic analysis of adult man.
In: Rusinov, V. S., et al. II. 1956.

Seredina, M. I. Age characteristics involved in the generalization of conditioned word stimuli.
In: Ivanov-Smolensky, A. G., et al. II. 1956.

Shvarts, L. A. The problems of words as conditioned stimuli. *Byull. eksp. Viol. Med.,* 1954, *38(12),* 15-18.
From: Razran, G. H. S. 1961.

———. Conditioned reflexes to verbal stimuli. *Vop. Psikhol.,* 1960, *6(1),* 86-98.
From: Razran, G. H. S. 1961.

Sokolov, E. N. Neuronal models and the orienting reflex.
In: Brazier, M. A. B. 1960.

Sokolova, M. V. Developmental characteristics of inhibition of verbal reactions in children.
In: Gartsshtein, N. G. & Bogachenko, L. S. 1961.

Spence, K. W., & Goldstein, H. Eyelid conditioning performance as a function of emotion producing instructions. *J. exp. Psychol.,* 1961, *62,* 291-294.

Usievich, M. A., et al. (Eds.). *Works of the Institute of Higher Nervous Activity: Physiological Series.* I. Moscow: Academy of Sciences of the USSR, 1955. Jerusalem: Israel Program for Scientific Translations, 1960. (Office Tech. Serv., U.S. Dept. Commerce, Washington, D.C., 20025, PST Catalogue #69).

Vigotsky, L. S. *Thought and Language.* Cambridge, Mass.: The M. I. T. Press, 1962.

VINOGRADOVA, O. S., & EYSLER, N. A. The manifestations of verbal connections in recording vascular reactions. *Vop. Psikhol.*, 1959, *2*, 101–116.
From: RAZRAN, G. H. S. 1961.

VORONIN, L. G., et al. (Eds.). The orienting reflex and orienting-investigatory activity. Trans. from Russian. Moscow: *Aked. Pedag. Nauk.* RSFSR, 1958.
From: RAZRAN, G. H. S. 1961.

WATERS, J. E., & KODMAN, F., JR. Abstract conditioning. *J. Psychol.*, 1962, *53*, 441-452.

Word Association and Verbal
Learning Methods, USA

I am convinced that meaning is the single most important variable in human learning, verbal or otherwise . . . that human adjustment is mainly a matter of acquiring and modifying the significances of signs and learning how to behave in ways appropriate to these significances [Osgood (1961) p. 91].

Introduction

Many experimental studies employ meaningful materials, but it is relatively rarely that meaning itself has been an independent variable in learning experiments. Even when meaning has been deliberately varied in some way, interest has been focused primarily on the learning process. The use of the learning process as a means of studying the phenomenon of meaning, or as a means of measuring meaning, or as a means of arriving at a definition of meaning, reflects rather recent developments in both interest and method.

Learning methods in the study of "meaning" have taken two major forms, one based upon and derived from the classical conditioning paradigm, the other based upon word association methods and derived from classical associationistic theory. Classical associationism adopted an activist notion of the acquisition of meaning (Ehrlich, 1964). Relevant contemporaneous psychological events become associated with a word from its first exposure. With repetition of the word, a pattern becomes established linking the word with other events. After a general semantic structure becomes established, the presentation of a stimulus word will trigger the activation of at least some part of that structure. Thus, in such a frame of reference, meaning might be defined as a structural set of associations elicited by the presentation of a word.

Drever (1964, p. 180) wrote: ". . . by 1900 associationism was dead in Britain and on the continent. There are signs that before the end of the present century it will have been allowed to lie down." It would appear that in America it is being kept on its feet, at least in the area of verbal learning and verbal behavior.

Association studies of meaning have focused primarily upon attempts to discover effective measures of word relatedness, or upon the effects of associative bonds in the recall or recognition of learned material. Measures of word relatedness usually have taken the form of some kind of numerical index of association, based upon frequency counts derived from word association tests. The effects of associative bonds in recall and recognition are generally studied by means of associative clustering or through paired-associate learning methods.

Meaningfulness: measures of word relatedness

Measures of word relatedness have been either empirically derived (e.g., Bousfield, Jenkins et al.), or have been arrived at by inductive methods (e.g., Noble, Deese). All are based on associative frequency measures of some kind, some using the old Kent-Rosanoff frequency tables or modifications thereof (e.g., the Minnesota norms[1]), others developing their own frequency norms. Some have provided a basis for elaboration into theories of mediation (e.g., Bousfield's theory of Response Identities) or of associative structure (e.g., Deese), others have been tested for their predictive effectiveness in a few scattered experiments and have more or less faded from sight.

In 1957, Cofer (1957) used a variety of words from Haagen's (1949) synonym list to compose a free association test. The words were chosen so that associations to each of a number of words, between which the degree of synonymity was known to vary, would be obtained. The associative responses to each word were then compared for overlap, and it was demonstrated that as the degree of synonymity declined, the associative overlap declined (see also Cofer and Yarczower, 1957). If synonymity is one way of defining meaning, then it would seem from this evidence that associative overlap is probably no more nor less effective as a meaning indicator than synonymity, at least so far as this aspect of meaning is concerned.

In spite of this finding, though, or perhaps because of it, attempts

---

[1] Russell and Jenkins (1954).

to develop methods of measuring relatedness between and among words, using associative frequencies and associative overlap, have continued unabated. The proliferation of measurement formulas has produced considerable controversy, but little systematic investigation of the manner and extent of the interrelationships between and among the various measures.[2] However, the development of some of the indices has led to much research focused upon the relationship between the association value or associative strength of words and other variables. Cofer, Deese, Jenkins, Mandler, Underwood, Schulz and others have continued to work systematically with certain of the indices in their attempts to elucidate the contribution of a variety of variables to the learning process. Again the interest is focused upon learning rather than meaning, as if the meaning problem, at least for these purposes, had been solved.

Since Marshall and Cofer (1963) reviewed in detail the literature with respect to measures of word relatedness,[3] or indices of meaningfulness, they will merely be summarized briefly here. The authors reported ten different measures, based on associative norms, which are summarized in Table 1 (next page), from their review paper.

1. *Frequency of Association Index* $= \dfrac{\Sigma \, Ra}{N}$

where: Ra = a particular response to a given word S
 Σ Ra = number of subjects giving Ra to S
  N = total number of subjects, each giving any single R to S *or*
   = total number of different responses given by a single subject to S in continuous associations [e.g., Noble (1952), Mandler (1955)]
[Jenkins and Russell (1952); Jenkins, Mink, and Russell (1958)]

O'Neil (1953) used this index to select associates to words and found that tachistoscopic recognition of the words was facilitated by their being exposed in the context of an associate. Russell and Storms (1955) showed that chains of associations could mediate the learning of a given list after learning another. Mink (1957) found that the amount of generalization between word pairs, as

---

[2] An exception can be found in Bousfield, Steward, and Cowan (1961).
[3] See also Marshall and Cofer (1962) for more detail.

TABLE 1. MEASURES OF WORD RELATEDNESS BASED ON ASSOCIATIVE NORMS[4]

Name of index	No. of words related	Base norms	Investigations
1. Frequency of Associations	2	Primaries in free association	Jenkins & Russell (1952) Jenkins, Mink, & Russell (1958)
2. Mutual Frequency or Measure of Relatedness	2	Free associations	Jenkins & Cofer (1957) Bousfield, Whitmarsh & Berkowitz (1958)
3. Index of Generalization	2	Free associations	Bousfield, Whitmarsh, & Danick (1958)
4. Inter-Item Associative Strength	2 or more	Free associations	Deese (1959a)
5. Index of Total Association	2 or more	Free associations	Marshall & Cofer (1962)
6. Index of Concept Cohesiveness	2 or more	Free associations	Marshall & Cofer (1962)
7. Measure of Stimulus Equivalence	2 or more	Free associations	Bousfield, Steward, & Cowan (1961)
8. Index of Dominance Level	2 or more	Sensory associations	Underwood & Richardson (1956a & 1956b)
9. Taxonomic Index	2 or more	Restricted associations	Cohen, Bousfield, & Whitmarsh (1957)
10. Cue Number	?	Free associations	Rothkopf & Coke (1961a & 1961b)

measured by an instrumental motor response, was related to both the direction and strength of the association between the members.

2. *Mutual Frequency* (MF) *or*

Measure of Relatedness (MR) $= \dfrac{R_c}{R_t}$

---

[4] From Marshall and Cofer (1962 and 1963).

where: $R_c = \Sigma$ Rs common to S_1 and S_2

$R_t = \Sigma$ *all* Rs to S_1 and S_2.[5]

[Jenkins and Cofer (1957); Cofer (1957)]

Jenkins and Cofer (1957) used this index to assess overlap between response distributions to compound verbal stimuli, as well as to the elements of the compound. Cofer (1957) demonstrated that associate overlap between pairs decreased as their rated synonymity decreased. Deese (1962b) used the MR in a factor analysis of associative interrelations among responses to the word "butterfly," from which six factors emerged.

3. *Index of Generalization* (IG) $= \dfrac{R_c}{R_t}$

where: $R_c = \Sigma$ responses common to trained (conditioned) word and test word

$R_t =$ Sum of all responses to test word.[6]

[Bousfield, Whitmarsh, and Danick (1958)]

✗ In a variation of the Index of Generalization, Bousfield, Cohen, and Whitmarsh (1958b) using word-association norms, first stated the partial response identities hypothesis which assumes that any word implicitly elicits itself as a response 100% of the time (R_{rep}). This index is the ratio of the composite sum of the cultural frequencies of the responses to a test word which are the same as responses to the trial word, to the total response frequency to the tested word, or

$$IG = \frac{R_{c[t+t]}}{N}$$

where: $R_{c[t+t]} =$ shared composite responses to trial (t) and test (*t*) word

N = number of subjects giving responses to stimulus words.

For example, the word "hard" is assumed to elicit itself 1,008 times out of 1,008 responses. It elicits "soft" 674 times, "smooth" 12 times, and "easy" 24 times. The word "soft" is assumed to elicit

---

[5] It is important to keep in mind that there is an assumption made here that every S word elicits itself as a first response, and the S word itself is therefore counted as an R to itself.

[6] Note that the amount of predicted generalization will differ for two words depending upon which one is the conditioned word and which is the test word: that is, whether association is "backward" or "forward."

"soft" 1,008 times. It elicits "hard" 445 times, "smooth" 28 times, and "easy" 6 times. Thus the composite of responses to "soft" which are shared with "hard" are, "hard," "smooth," and "easy," and the index would be the ratio of the sum of these frequencies (478) to the total frequency (1,008), or .48. The correlation between this index and empirically obtained generalization frequencies was significant. Using this index of predicted generalization for each of the word pairs used by Razran (1949) in his experiment on the generalization of salivary conditioning, Whitmarsh and Bousfield (1961) correlated IG with the obtained generalization in Razran's study. Using the rank order method, they obtained a *Rho* of .83. Using sum of squares, they obtained an *r* of .70 with a P value of less than .001.

Some evidence in support of Bousfield's theory of response identities may be adduced from Astrup's (1962) finding that in mental patients the associative reaction to a word is often preceded by the repetition, aloud, of the stimulus word. Flavell (1961a and 1961b) also produced experimental support for the assumptions regarding the representational response, and Deese put the assumption to work in his own index, as follows: x

$$4.\ \textit{Index of Inter-Item Associative Strength} = \frac{DR_{c1}+DR_{c2}+DR_{c3}+DR_{c4}}{R_{ct}}$$

where: DR = frequency with which a given R word is a response to another word

    c = "list name" or S word (thus c_1 refers to column 1, c_2 to column 2, etc.)

    R_{ct} = total number of columns, or stimulus words.

[Deese (1959a)]

The matrix of columns and rows, obtained from free association to each word of a list of words, showed all the stimulus words across the top row and also down the left column, the intersecting cells containing the frequency with which a word in the column is a response to the word at the top of the column. This index, the mean extent to which words elicit each other, reflects the extent of direct association in a group of words.

To test the efficiency of this index, Deese constructed two lists of 45 words, each containing 15 high- and 15 low-frequency responses to a Kent-Rosanoff stimulus word, and 15 unrelated words. Following presentation of a list, his subjects were asked to list the words which they recalled. Half of the subjects were given the Kent-Rosanoff stimulus word as a "list name," the other half an irrelevant "list name." Free associations to all the list words were then obtained to determine their associative frequency. Deese found the inter-item associative strength to be positively correlated (.88) with the number of words recalled per list, and negatively correlated (—.48) with the number of extra-list intrusions in recall, although positively correlated (.55) with the *commonality* of the extra-list intrusions which occurred. In another experiment (Deese, 1959b) he found that the probability of occurrence of a particular word as an intrusion in recall was proportional to the average associative strength of that word to the words on the list. Cofer (1961a) verified Deese's results.

This index is a measure of direct association within a *group* of words. Deese (1962b) later revised and elaborated the method on the basis of his contention that

the meaningfulness of words refers to organized relations among the words and among words and objects in the natural world. Associations are related to one another in some organized fashion and also related in some way to perceived properties in the natural world. The only conclusion is that . . . the way to discover the associative meaning of words is not to classify associations according to other senses of meaning but to discover the relationships associations have with one another. [p. 162]

In this statement, Deese implies a distinction between meaning as association and other kinds of meaning, and implicitly recognizes that the problem of definition and measurement of meaning is larger than the mere measurement of association. Leaving for the time the larger problem of meaning, he devoted his efforts to the refinement of measures which would at least define the *associative* meaning of words.

He contended that relationships between free associations can be discovered only from *all* the responses that are common to given word stimuli. Thus any two stimuli

. . . may be said to have the same associative meaning when the distribution of associates to them is *identical.* Two stimuli overlap or resemble one another in associative meaning to the extent that they have the same distribution of associates [Deese (1962b) p. 163].

On the basis of this assumption, Deese developed a matrix showing the frequency of responses common to any two stimuli, with the frequency of the stimulus word as a response to itself entered with 100% frequency (Bousfield's notion that any word elicits itself as an implicit response 100% of the time = the representational response = R_{rep}). Thus the stimulus words of any group of stimuli define both columns and rows of the matrix, and in the intersections are entered the total frequency of common responses to the two stimulus words expressed as a percentage of the total responses to the two stimulus words. From such a matrix it is then possible, through factor analysis, to extract associative weightings for the various associates, and to arrive at a closer approximation of the significant psychological "meaning" of words as opposed to, for example, the predictive capacity of associative frequencies in learning experiments. It remains, however, for future data collection and analysis to discover the full value of this approach as a measure of association, and to evaluate its contribution to an enhanced understanding of meaning in a larger sense.

5. *Index of Total Association* $= \dfrac{R_{c1} + R_{c2} \ldots + R_{cn}}{(R_t)(N)} \times 100$

where: $R_{c1} = \Sigma$ of responses, direct and indirect to S word of list 1, etc.

R_t = total number of responses

N = number of list members.

[Marshall and Cofer (1962)]

This index is an elaboration of the original Deese (1959a) formulation, takes account of other than direct associations, and gives the mean extent to which the stimulus items in a list of words elicit each other as direct associates as well as the extent to which they *all* also elicit other responses in common. Although this goes beyond the original Deese formulation, it does not, as Deese's later formulation does, take account of the responses shared by any *two* stimulus words. This is done by the following index:

6. *Index of Concept Cohesiveness* $= \dfrac{R_{ct}}{R_{cn}}$

where: $R_{ct} = \Sigma$ responses common to all stimuli in a set of word stimuli

$R_{cn} = \Sigma$ responses common to any two or more stimuli.

[Marshall and Cofer (1962)]

This index, untested with respect to its usefulness, differs from both Deese formulations, and from the authors' own previous elaboration. To what extent it differs, and to what extent it may add to the efficiency of prediction or to the understanding of meaning, remains to be seen.

7. *Measure of Stimulus Equivalence* $= \Sigma R_c$ to $S_2 \ldots _n$
   where: $R_c =$ common responses to
   $\quad\quad\quad S_2 \ldots _n =$ any two or more stimuli.
[Bousfield, Steward, and Cowan (1961)]
   There is some relationship between this index and Deese's measure, and some experimental comparisons will be considered in later sections.

8. *Index of Dominance Level* $= \dfrac{\Sigma C_r}{R_t}$

   where: $C_r =$ category response (e.g., "fruit" as R to S word "apple")
   $\quad\quad\quad R_t =$ total responses.
[Underwood and Richardson (1956a)]
This index is similar to the Index of Frequency of Associations, with the addition that response restrictions were imposed and responses categorized. Using sets of four words, the same authors (1956b) found that the higher the dominance level of the set, the greater the number of concepts (meanings) discovered and correct (category) responses given in 20 trials. In addition, frequency of interfering responses varied inversely with the index. Bousfield and Puff (1964), using word lists containing words of high and low dominance level, found significant associative clustering in recall for only the high dominance words.

9. *Taxonomic Index* $= \Sigma R$ to category name (simple response-restricted association).
[Cohen, Bousfield, and Whitmarsh (1957)]

10. *Cue Number* (N_c) = The number of stimuli in the Kent-Rosanoff set which elicit a word as a response twelve or more times, or as one of the ten most common associates of the stimulus, whichever yields the larger R frequency.
[Rothkopf and Coke (1961a and 1961b)]

The authors had subjects study each of 99 Kent-Rosanoff stimulus words for five seconds and then attempt recall. The correlation between N_c and recall frequency was .62. In addition, the probability of a word's following in recall immediately after one of its cues was directly proportional to the frequency of its cues in the list.

It is interesting to note that terms such as "word relatedness," "generalization," and "associative strength" are used in these studies, and that, except for Deese, the authors generally avoid the terms "meaning" or "meaningfulness." It is not clear why Noble's[7] index (m) was omitted from this summary, since it had been and still is used in some association studies, and has been correlated with various other measures of meaningfulness, association, or meaning. For example, Rosen and Russell (1957) supported the value of m when their study demonstrated that the hierarchy of responses obtained from individuals' giving successive associations to the same word is similar to the hierarchy obtained from single responses to the same word given by a group. Laffal and Feldman (1962) found in addition that the word category structure obtained by the two methods was substantially similar. Jenkins and Russell (1956) furthermore found a correlation of .71 between Noble's m and Osgood's index of meaning obtained on the basis of the Semantic Differential. Goodale (1964) confirmed the Jenkins and Russell finding when he correlated the mean D values (distance scores from the Semantic Differential) for all 58 of his subjects with the m value of each stimulus noun, although individual correlations failed to reach significance.

Kimbrough and Cofer (1957) elaborated on Noble's method for evaluating discrete continuous associations by having subjects record their associations over a five-minute period on 3 x 5 cards. A weighted frequency score was obtained by summing the frequencies over the five-minute period after multiplying frequencies in the first minute by five, in the second minute by four, in the third minute by three and so on, then extracting the square root of the sum according to the formula:

weighted score $= \sqrt{5f_1 + 4f_2 + 3f_3 + 2f_4 + f_5}$

where: f = frequency of associates

In the present state of development, the various indices of word relatedness themselves seem to be of doubtful, or at least severely limited, value with regard to their contribution to the understanding

---

[7] See Noble (1952).

of meaning. Their contribution as predictive aids in learning and other kinds of verbal situations still remains to be thoroughly tested, although their value here seems clearer than their value in the explication of meaning. Underwood and Schulz (1960) reminded us that even the dimension of meaningfulness in the associative sense is not unitary but complex, and asserted that in their opinion no hint of this complexity is given by such simple defining operations as associative indices.

Variables affecting association

Wicklund, Palermo, and Jenkins (1964a) pointed out that the relative rates of growth of associative habits are determined by such factors as broad and specific cultural determinants and semantic and syntactic determinants, the relative importance of which may vary with age. They concluded that (p. 418)

> ... because of the forced frequency aspect of the type of norms used in (these) experiments, the constant increases in absolute strength of associative habits cannot be linearly reflected in the normative data. ... all associative habits tend to increase as a function of the frequency of occurrence of the context necessary for the formation of the associates.

Deese (1964) agreed that "the extent to which words share associative distributions is determined by the extent to which they share contexts in ordinary discourse." (p. 351).

LINGUISTIC CONTEXT

Context is important not only in the formation of associations, but also contributes to the meaning of the words used in verbal experiments as well as in ordinary discourse. The relationship between linguistic (syntactic) context and meaning has received some experimental attention, but has not yet been adequately explored. Deese (1962a) found a close relationship between the distributions of associations and the form-class of words used as stimuli. He thus concluded that associative meaning is determined by the structures which are similar to the conceptual schemes which define form-class and which make it possible for English speakers to use words of different classes in appropriate positions in sentences. It is possible, therefore, that there is some kind of continuity between grammar and meaning. Deese's work (1964) has indicated, for example, that uncommon adjectives are likely to elicit words making ordinary sequences in language, whereas common adjectives elicit other adjectives which are overwhelmingly antonymic.

Cofer has for some time been interested in the effects of context upon a variety of variables. Cofer and Shepp (1957) found that the recognition of a word was facilitated by its relationship to the preceding word in the context in which it was presented. In a study of noun-clustering in recall, Cofer (1961b and 1965) found a suppression of category-clustering of nouns which had been embedded in sentences.[8] In another study, he (Cofer 1962) was concerned with some of the mechanisms involved in contextual effects. Mandler,[9] too, has been consistently interested in context.[10]

Howe (1964) tested such variables as verb tense, negatives, and other determinants as to their effect upon the intensity of evaluative meaning and found significant effects. Howes and Osgood (1954) and Howes (1957) viewed association as a function of the combination of probabilities of a particular word's appearing in various linguistic contexts. Flavell and Flavell (1959) essentially substantiated Howes' contention in an experiment in which subjects were asked to match pairs of words for similarity of meaning, relatedness, and associative strength. For similarity and relatedness, the judgment bearing on two words was roughly predictable from the logico-grammatical relationships involved. However, associative judgments yielded a different (and unexplained) relationship hierarchy.

"MEANING" CONTEXT

Later work of Flavell (1961a and b) led him to the conclusion that the meaning of a sign (word) has at least two components: a representational process reflecting the attributes of the referent itself (a) and a representational process reflecting the attributes of nonreferents frequently associated with the sign (b). Using the judged concurrence in experience as an index (c) of the second type of representational process (b), he demonstrated that a combination of a Semantic Differential similarity index with c predicted

---

[8] See also Underwood and Postman (1963), Cofer (1960).

[9] See Underwood and Postman (1963).

[10] See also studies by Jensen and Rohwer (1963) and Newman and Taylor (1963).

judged semantic similarity better than either index alone. On the other hand, Staats (1961) found a correlation of .90 (p < .01) between the Semantic Differential rating of a stimulus word and the mean evaluative SD ratings of the first 20 associates to the stimulus word, and Pollio (1962) obtained a significant correlation between Semantic Differential ratings of 50 Kent-Rosanoff words and the SD ratings of their primary associates on all three SD meaning dimensions.

Kincaid, Bousfield, and Whitmarsh (1962) proposed the notion of "parasitic reinforcement" to account for something like the second representational component (b) hypothesized by Flavell. They suggested that the verbal conditioning of a response to a stimulus word involves not only the conditioning to the stimulus word, but also a simultaneous conditioning to the composite of verbal responses to that word. One is reminded of Miller's (1935), and later Osgood's (1956a) conclusion about previous associations and their influence upon the generalization of subsequent conditioning.

Bettinghaus (1963) had 42 subjects rate first a list of 10 nouns, then a list of 10 adjectives on three Semantic Differential scales. A week later each subject was asked to make 10 noun-adjective pairs, using each word only once. After another week each subject was asked to rate his own pairings on the same Semantic Differential scales, and three days following this to rate the nouns and adjectives individually. He found a high degree of attitudinal congruence between the word pairs, which were judged in a manner that balanced the initial meanings of the two words. Thus changes in meaning for adjectives and nouns depend upon the meaning of the words with which they have been associated as well as upon their initial meanings.[11] An extensive series of experiments by Gonzales and Cofer (1956a and b, 1957, 1959) also are devoted to the study of the interaction of nouns and adjectives.[12]

SITUATIONAL CONTEXT

Such studies as these have interesting implications for meaning, since they seem to show the operation of some variable other than direct association, or synonymic relationships. The effects of context on a variety of processes, such as conditioning, generalization, association, recognition, and recall, are sufficiently noticeable

[11] See also Deese (1964).
[12] See Cofer (1965).

that a reasonable conclusion seems to be that simple results and simple explanations obtain only when experiments are so simply designed that generalization from their results to more complex situations is not tenable. Studies of another kind of context tend to support this contention. This type of context which, for lack of a better term, might be called situational context—as opposed to linguistic context—has obvious effects upon the association value and meaning of words or other stimuli or events. This embraces a vast area which seems to have been almost untouched experimentally.

Underwood, Ham, and Ekstrand (1962) attempted to study the effects of context changes upon retention. Portnoy, Portnoy, and Salzinger (1964) reported a study of the relationship between stimulus discriminability and contextual variables using a search-time technique. Fluckiger (1962) found changes in the meaning of stimulus signs and their assigns (as indicated by their Semantic Differential ratings) as a result of associating them within a story context.

Sundberg's (1964) results are suggestive of some other complexities in the investigation of meaning, and perhaps of the source of some inconsistencies in experimental results. In developing a test of implied meanings, he showed that meaning inferred from spoken statements was not independent of such variables as voice quality and emphasis. Meanings selected on a multiple-choice questionnaire when the stimulus words were spoken were different from the meanings selected when the words were presented in written form. Furthermore, these choices differed from the modal choices made by the group when they were given the statements in written form and were asked to choose the "logical" or "natural" implication.

Summary

It is fairly certain that only the first few words, and not the last, have been said on the subject of the word association method and its contribution to the understanding of meaning. Surely associations between and among words must play a large and important role in any adequate definition of meaning. It is somewhat discouraging, however, to juxtapose the formulation of Noble, Bousfield and others that meaning is determined by associations, with Pollio's (1963) statement that association is determined by meaning.

Tautological definitions are unlikely to advance understanding to any significant extent.

One thing that characterizes nearly all the work in the area of learning experiments in verbal behavior is the way in which the authors talk about their results. Their discussions are invariably in terms of the characteristic ways in which verbal responses to verbal stimuli "behave,"[13] not in terms of the characteristics of the persons who perceive the stimuli and make the responses. The consequence of the "empty organism" or "black box" approach which their way of speaking reflects, is substantially to rule out of consideration and study those variables which, it would seem, must be involved in meaning. As Miller[14] pointed out,

> . . . the formal description of a language is clearly different from a description of the people who use that language; even after the linguist solves his problems, therefore, the psychologist is faced with the task of understanding how the rules are actually acquired and used.

Exactly what may be the role in the understanding of meaning, then, of association in general and word-association in particular, is still far from clear. It will probably not be clarified by the experimenters' narrowly focusing upon word-association phenomena themselves. However, this focus might produce methods to organize observations from such studies which then might be used in more inclusive research models. This remains for the future. Some of the measuring indices, however, have been used in studies of clustering and in paired-associate learning experiments which will be examined in later sections for their contributions to the search for meaning.

Semantic satiation

A small area of study related to association is one which looks at the interference side of the associative process rather than at the facilitative side. It seems fairly obvious that both interference and facilitative factors must be understood in order clearly to define the associative process and its effects upon other processes. Not only generalization but also discrimination and differentiation are

---

[13] Mandler and Miller are notable exceptions to this generalized observation.
[14] Underwood and Postman (1963 p. 209); see also Miller (1965).

involved in the development of meaning. Thus inhibitory as well as excitatory factors must be involved.

Only a few authors have reported experimental demonstrations of the kind of satiation effects which everyone has experienced after repeating a word over and over. Upon repetition, a word seems to "lose meaning." Experimental satiation is usually defined as a situation in which a subject is asked to repeat, for some specified time at some specified rate, a word presented to him. The effect of the repetition is conceived of as an alteration of associational structures (Ehrlich, 1964).

Smith and Raygor (1956) found that if they required subjects to observe a stimulus word for a period of time before associating to it, the associations given to it were of a lower commonality than would be expected. Although this was intended as an experiment in satiation, what seems likely to have occurred is that the common associates were produced silently or implicitly during the period of contemplation, so that when the subject was asked for his associations, he might have arrived at the point in his own "list" of associates which contained the more personal and idiosyncratic associations to the stimulus word. Some preliminary pilot work of this book's author suggests that in continuous association to a stimulus word (in this case, for five minutes), the more common associates are given earlier in the period of association and the more personal ones later. Contrary to the Smith and Raygor findings, Wolfensberger (1963) found no effect upon either the latency or the associative commonness of the response from verbal satiation in either normals or retardates.

Wertheimer and Gillis (1958) found that short words and words having concrete rather than abstract referents have more resistance to satiation (extinction) than longer or more abstract words. Using as a criterion the subjects' judgments of "meaninglessness," Wertheimer (1958) found that words high in phonetic symbolism were more resistant to satiation effects than were those low in phonetic symbolisms (e.g., "rush" vs. "write").

Lambert and Jakobovits (1960) studied satiation effects using the Semantic Differential scale to measure meaning before and after satiation. They compared a group of experimental subjects with different groups of control subjects. The (Semantic Differential) meaning of the word "child" was determined for the experimental group before and after the repetition of the word. It was found that semantic satiation did occur for the experimental subjects as compared with 1) a silence control group, for whom the word was not repeated; 2) a different-word control group for whom the word "war" was repeated and the meaning of the word "child" measured, and 3) the retest control group, who rated the word "child" on the SD, then repeated the rating of the same word after a period of time. They also found that the forced repetition of a nonsense item having the same vocalic form as the word "child" failed to produce satiation. The same two authors (Jakobovits and Lambert, 1961) studied cross linguistic satiation effects, wherein the subjects repeated the word "home" and were tested with the word *maison*. They found satiation in compound bilinguals but not in coordinate bilinguals. Furthermore, they found that the forced repetition of a number prior to an addition task involving that number significantly increased the time required for the addition task. However, Messer, Jakobovits, Kanungo, and Lambert (1963), using the Semantic Differential scale, found satiation of words but not of numbers.

Using Noble's m as a measure of meaningfulness, and Noble's method of continuous association, Kanungo and Lambert (1963) explored the relation between semantic satiation and verbal association. Using four sets of words with similar m ratings as stimulus words in continuous association tests replicating Noble's technique, each subject was tested twice, with a 24-hour interval between test and retest, under three different conditions. The m value was determined for each test and retest under each condition.

The three conditions were as follows:

1) *Control Condition*
   The same set of words was used as stimuli in the continuous-association test and retest.

2) *Experimental Condition I*
   A second set of stimulus words was used in the test and, after satiation, in the retest.

3) *Experimental Condition II*
   The two other sets of stimulus words were combined. m values were obtained both before and after satiation, but from two different groups of subjects. This eliminated the effect of the subject's responses to words before satiation upon his responses to the same words after satiation.

Both relevant and irrelevant responses were considered in the analysis, although only relevant responses contribute to the m value. There was a significant increase in m in the control (nonsatiated) condition and in experimental condition I, and a decrease in experimental condition II, which suggests that some variable other than satiation was operating. Since, however, in condition II the decrease in relevant responses was coupled with a significant increase in irrelevant responses, the authors concluded that satiation leads to blocking of relevant associations and simultaneously modifies irrelevant associations. The "relevance" and "irrelevance" of the associates were estimated on a "common sense" basis according to the authors' own intuitive judgment.

In the above experiment it was the stimulus word that was satiated while the following study used satiation of the response word. The same authors (Kanungo and Lambert, 1964) had three groups of subjects learn a paired-associate list after a 5-, 15-, or 25-second period of repetition of the response members of the pairs, and another three groups after repetition periods of the same durations for nonresponse words. They found that the repetition reduced the intensity of the meaning of the words (according to Semantic Differential ratings), and that learning time increased after repetition of the response words. Repetition time (i.e., the length of the satiation period) was not significantly related to either meaning loss or learning time.

Schwartz and Novick (1964), using the method of Lambert and Jakobovits to assess satiation effects, but elaborating upon it by the use of pictures in addition to a typescript, found satiation effects with the typescript but not with pictures, from which they concluded that the effect is due to specific inhibition of associative activation, but may also involve unspecific factors such as boredom or other motivational changes.

Fillenbaum (1963) had his subjects repeat a given word for 30 seconds. They then repeated a second word until they reported loss of meaning. The time to subjective loss of meaning was recorded. The second word was the same as the first word for group 1; it was a synonym of the first word for group 2; and it was an unrelated word for group 3. He found that the immediately prior repetition of a synonym led to a more rapid loss of meaning than was the case in repetition of an unrelated word, which he concluded to be evidence for mediated or semantic generalization of verbal satiation. Gumenik and Spencer (1964), however, contended that loss of meaning following repetition of the word's synonym results from set rather than from generalization of satiation effects. Fillenbaum (1964) further argued that if continued exposure to a word results in loss of or changes in meaning, there should be, immediately following repetition of a word, an increase in the time required to perform some task or make some decision necessitating knowledge of the word's meaning. He found that decision latency was shorter when the repeated word was identical with one of the decision words than when it was a synonym or unrelated. He concluded from these results that repetition may alert the subject to specific word features and also result in changes in meaning, thus either facilitating or impairing subsequent performance involving the word or its synonym. Das and Cook (1964) also found facilitation in response speed with increased satiation although Semantic Differential ratings showed a strong satiation effect (loss of "meaning").

Yelen and Schulz (1963) showed generation as well as satiation of meaning as a result of repetition, but Ehrlich (1964) argued that such generation is also a satiation effect in that it indicates a change in established patterns of arousal. Schulz, however, indicated (see Underwood and Postman, 1963) that neither generation nor satiation occurred when a slight change was made in the experimental design.

Amster (1964) reviewed the semantic satiation literature and pointed out some of the uncontrolled variables in these experiments. Work in this area is interesting and suggestive, and if pursued and elaborated in a systematic way might shed some needed light upon the association process. So far it is not adequately related to association studies, which in turn are not sufficiently related to the more inclusive aspects of the problem of meaning, to illuminate the overall problem of meaning.

Associative clustering

Another method of studying meaning through associative processes is based on a phenomenon called "associative clustering." Randomized or structured lists of words are presented to a subject who is later asked to reproduce the list. Related words which appear together in recall, although they did not appear together in the presentation list, are called clusters. The clusters are then studied in a variety of ways, mostly in terms of some measure of association. Nearly all of the experimental work thus classified uses some variation of this basic method, and all such experiments have demonstrated through ingenious variations of the technique that clustering does occur in recall. Earlier experiments demonstrated that the clustering is related to associative strength however one chooses to define and measure it, but later work raised some questions about simple explanations. Several investigators have suggested a distinction between word relatedness, or associative strength, and meaning similarity. Other than these general findings, there is little agreement as to what attributes are involved in clustering, or whether the phenomenon requires the postulation of mediating mechanisms.

ASSOCIATIVE INDICES

One of the ways in which the phenomenon of clustering has been used has been to establish or to test out the effectiveness of various associative indices. For instance, Jenkins and Russell (1952) and Jenkins, Mink, and Russell (1958) showed that the mean clustering in recall varied directly with the magnitude of the Mean Associative Index of word relatedness (see p. 131 above). Bousfield, Whitmarsh, and Berkowitz (1958, 1960) obtained an $r = .578$ between clustering in specific word pairs in recall and the MR measure (see p. 132f. above). This correlation was lower than that obtained by Jenkins, Mink, and Russell when they used the MA index, but this could be expected in view of their use of specific word association pairs, whereas Jenkins, Mink, and Russell correlated clustering with the average associative frequency scores across four lists.

Bousfield, Cohen, and Whitmarsh (1958a and b) drew ten frequent and ten infrequent responses from the Connecticut Norms of associative frequency of categorized nouns (Cohen, Bousfield, and Whitmarsh, 1957) for each of eight categories. From these they composed two lists of high frequency responses, and administered each of the lists to a different group. Using their Taxonomic Index (see p. 137) as a criterion, they found values for total recall as well as category-clustering to be greater for the lists with a high index than a low. Cofer and Segal (1959), Holroyd and Holroyd (1961), and Bousfield, Steward, and Cowan (1961) replicated these results. The latter study also compared Deese's Index of Inter-Item Associative Strength (see p. 134ff.) with their own Measure of Stimulus Equivalence (see p. 137), using two lists of 40 words each. In both lists two categories were represented with low frequency associates to the category names, and two categories were represented with high frequency associates to the category names. Deese's index ordered categories in exact accordance with the obtained clustering, but there were two inversions on list two, along with more clustering for the low category-associate set than the index would predict. The Measure of Stimulus Equivalence ordered the category sets as to clustering in both sets. Across the two lists, $Rho = .91$ between the amount of clustering and the Index of Stimulus Equivalence, while $Rho = .72$ between clustering and the Index of Inter-Item Associative Strength. The authors demonstrated that clustering is unaffected by fairly wide variation in frequency of usage (from the Thorndike-Lorge tables), but Deese (1960) showed that more words were recalled from high-frequency-usage lists and also that the index of inter-word association was larger.

ORGANIZATION IN RECALL

The major experimental use of the clustering phenomenon has been in the study of what Cofer (1965) called organization in recall. In his review paper he summarized the experimental literature on associative clustering, organized the findings and conclusions, and discussed the progress in theoretical thinking within this area. Since his presentation of the experimental literature is fairly exhaustive, the reader is referred to this review for details of experimental development in this field. Cofer concluded that although he had previously contrasted associational and categorical bases for clustering, "It now seems to me . . . that such a contrast is neither useful nor heuristic" (p. 23). He went on to shift his attention to the experimental subjects, and stated that

> . . . evidence suggests (that) subjects will use either or both of these bases to accomplish their recalls and will find ways to organize recalls even though the experimenter has not provided means in the list he presents. Free recall can tell us something of the way verbal organization is set up, but we are largely in the dark as to how this organization acts to bring related items together whatever the basis of their relationship. How do associations and category relations lead the subject to put this with that?

This is perhaps another way of asking, "What is meaning?" It would seem, then, that experiments with associative clustering have finally led to a consideration of variables *within* the subject, and thus to posing the question about meaning rather than answering it.

CLUSTERING AND SEMANTIC GENERALIZATION

In an attempt to relate associative clustering and semantic generalization, Dicken (1958) designed an experiment using Mink's method. Mink (1957) had tested for generalization by means of a motor response. The subject, having learned to associate a key press with each word of a list of words was then presented, one word at a time, with a long list of words and told to respond by pressing the key whenever a word appeared that had been on the former list. There was generalization of the response to associates even when the associates were antonyms of the words on the original list. Mink had then concluded that semantic generalization was a simple associative phenomenon, since antonyms, although highly associated, do not have the same meaning. In order to test the validity of this assumption, Dicken selected clustering words which also had close interword meaning relations according to the Semantic Differential. The subject learned a list containing half of these words together with filler words. The list of words which the subject was to recognize included the learned half of the cluster, control words, and the other (unlearned) half of the words in the meaning cluster. On the average, there was generalization to the words of the same Semantic Differential cluster but this was not consistent, and associative overlap did not account for the difference. However, in his estimate of associative overlap he did not use an associative index which uses all the words which *two* response distributions have in common, thus it is unclear whether the use of another associative index might have reduced the ambiguity of the results. What *is* clear is the danger inherent in reading the results and conclusions of experimental work based upon relatively untested and unvalidated measuring instruments.

CLUSTERING AND AGE

Bousfield, Esterson, and Whitmarsh (1958) and Wicklund, Palermo, and Jenkins (1964b) studied developmental aspects of the clustering phenomenon. The latter study showed that the amount of clustering increases with age. It would be interesting to know how these results relate to Pollio's (1964) finding that although there is a significant and positive correlation between the experimental subjects' Semantic Differential ratings of a word and its primary associate, this correlation decreases with the age of the subjects. It is obvious that the number of possible associates to any word should grow with expanding experience (age), and the broader the associative "field," the greater the number of words which would tend to cluster. But the broader the associative field and the greater the clustering tendency, the greater would be the necessity to differentiate between items in an associative cluster in order for a word to have differentiated meaning as opposed to broadly generalized meaning. Pollio's study suggests that differential meaning involves some process beyond the associative process. Kalish and Haber (1962) pointed out that overgeneralization at first is advantageous, since it permits the inclusion of all possible relationships, but later a class must be delimited. This, they thought, was accomplished by a series of progressive discriminations which reduces generalization and excludes nonmembers of a class.

RECOGNITION AND RECALL

Several studies of recognition and recall phenomena have made use of threshold presentations of either stimulus words or test words in a variety of ways and with varying results. Spence and Holland (1962) presented a stimulus word, "cheese," tachistoscopically to their subjects prior to their reading and subsequent recall of a list of words. The list consisted of words half of which were associates to the stimulus word, half of which were unrelated. The stimulus word was presented to one group subliminally, to another supraliminally. To the third group, a blank card was flashed. There was no preferential recall of "cheese" associates in the second and third groups, but the first group with the subliminal presentation showed significantly better recall for the "cheese" associates. The authors postulated three levels of "awareness": 1) subliminal without partial cues; 2) near liminal with partial cues; and 3) supraliminal, to account for the fact that some of the group 1 subjects recalled more "meaning" associates, whereas others recalled more structurally related words. This looks like the old "conditioning (or learning) without awareness" bugaboo, which keeps raising its head in a variety of contexts.

Bousfield, Cowan, and Steward (1963) used a variation of this technique in which the projection of the stimulus word was designed to focus attention upon it and away from the associates which were being "learned." They had their subjects first identify the stimulus word as it was projected at successive levels of clarity, then indicate when the word appeared in a series of projected items which contained associates of the stimulus word along with other words having no apparent relationship with the stimulus word. In the test phase, the subjects were asked to recall the projected list. The results indicated incidental learning of the associates of the stimulus word, but the authors accounted for this in terms of a set to emit the stimulus word, which, supposedly, would then produce its associates through a direct associative process. In the case of Spence and Holland's subjects, since the stimulus word was not recognized, such a set could hardly be assumed to account for their recall of associates.

In a reversed version of this threshold technique and using recognition instead of recall, Cofer and Shepp (1957) asked subjects to recognize words presented for brief exposures, following presentation of standard words bearing either no relation or some degree of synonym relationship to the tachistoscopically presented stimulus word. Recognition of the stimulus words was facilitated when they were close synonyms of the standard words. But Howes and Solomon (1951) and Howes (1954) accounted for recognition thresholds for words simply in terms of their frequency of usage. Goldiamond and Hawkins' (1958) rather startling results surely tend to confirm Howes' hypothesis so far as perceptual recognition is concerned at least. Using the same method of limits, they found the same relationship between accuracy of recognition and word-frequency as obtained in the perceptual recognition studies *even when the stimuli were omitted entirely* and only blank cards were flashed. Jenkins reported [15] some beginning work using signal detection techniques adapted to a generalization task.

This leads into another vast area of investigation whose significance for the understanding of meaning is intriguing but too inexplicit for consideration here. It is plain that there is sufficient confusion in the areas already under consideration without adding to it the confusion in the area of perceptual awareness and perceptual defense.

Summary

Such experiments in associative clustering and related associative phenomena as we have examined may represent a beginning toward

---

[15] See Underwood and Postman (1963).

the clarification of the role played by association and meaningfulness in the recall of learned material, but they have contributed little to the broader understanding of meaning. They may, however, have pointed up the importance of understanding meaning. Since the associative process is surely at the very least an important component of meaning, it is imperative that this process be better understood than—judging from the experimental material reviewed—it is at present. Systematic development of some of the suggestive leads revealed in this work might contribute to progress toward an enhanced understanding.

Paired-associate learning

Various forms of paired-associate learning have nearly superceded other types of learning methods in the study of meaning. This method had its parenthood in the classical conditioning paradigm. Words were substituted in place of the unconditioned stimulus and the unconditioned response, the connection between S and R usually being assumed on the basis of established word association norms of some kind. It is at once apparent that in the paired-associate learning experiment, then, we are dealing with second order conditioning, since the response to the stimulus is merely a probabilistic learned response and far from a relatively invariant "innate" one, as in classical conditioning. Thus a so-called "three-stage" or "four-stage" learning paradigm is, in the classical conditioning sense, in actuality a four- or five- or *n*-stage model. The results are thus not directly comparable to those from a three-or four-stage classical conditioning experiment using, as a base for pairing, unconditioned stimuli with unconditioned responses. Nevertheless, as we shall see, comparisons are made as if the two situations were directly comparable.

There may be some value, however, to making these comparisons if the essential differences between the classical conditioning experiments and the learning experiments are kept clearly in mind. It is possible that through pursuing such comparisons the essential features of the mediating process, or meaning, may be discovered, refined, and elaborated. Some of these problems and possibilities will be discussed in a subsequent chapter. In order to establish a base for fruitful discussion, some characteristic examples of paired-associate learning experiments will be reviewed here. For a more complete coverage, the reader is referred to Cofer and Musgrave (1963).

Yavuz and Bousfield (1959) paired Turkish words with their supposed English equivalents selected because of their known position on the Semantic Differential evaluative scale. Subjects learned these pairs, and at a later time, were asked to rate the Turkish words on the Semantic Differential scale. The results indicated generalization of the connotative meaning of the English to the Turkish words, even when the subjects were unable to recall the "translation," or English "meaning" of the words.

Following a similar model, Pollio (1963) paired three nonsense syllables (CS) with three sets of nine meaningful words each (UCS). Word associations to the CS syllables were collected from two groups of 40 and 37 subjects, respectively, after the conditioning (learning) process. A third group of 25 subjects rated the obtained associates on the evaluative scale of the Semantic Differential. Pollio found that the Semantic Differential ratings of the associates were congruent with ratings of the UCS word group, whether the associates were from the original UCS words or cued from the connotative characteristics of the CS syllables. He concluded that in the absence of word-word associative habits, word association may be determined by the connotative characteristics of the stimulus word. That is, associative connections may be determined by meaning—a complete turning about of the notion that meaning is determined by associative bonds.

INDICES OF ASSOCIATION

The method of paired-associate learning has (like associative clustering) been used to test measures of relatedness or meaningfulness. Bastian (1957) supported the Index of Associative Frequency when he found that learning a second list of paired-associates was facilitated when the responses in the two lists were associatively related. Ryan (1960) found the same effect when the words on the stimulus side of the pairs were related. However, Carlin (1958) found no difference in the extent of mediation in pairs in which the associative strength varied. Radomisli (1962) observed differences in learning rates for variously related S-R pairs.

As a test of their Index of Generalization (see p. 133) Bousfield, Whitmarsh, and Danick (1958) had their subjects associate a number from one to ten to each of ten words, then learn the associated word-number pairs. They found generalization from the numbers to other stimulus words, r between the index for the test words and the actual generalization being .589. In addition, the latencies of the generalized responses were shorter to the test than to the control words.

As a test of the Index of Dominance Level (see p. 137), Underwood and Schulz (1960) constructed a 16-item list, pairing nouns as stimuli and adjectives as responses. The dominance level of the words was varied, and the results demonstrated a linear relationship, positive between dominance level and the number of errors in recall.

MEDIATION

In general, the experimental work in paired-associate learning is the most systematic and exhaustive of any of the American methods which seem to have the most relevance for understanding meaning. Most of this work is less directly concerned with the problem of meaning than with the role of mediation in the learning process, but it has important implications for the investigation of meaning. It is basic work, utilizing simple methods, but it is a necessary and solid beginning giving us a clearer notion as to where simple defining operations fail to be fruitful.

THREE-STAGE PARADIGM

Using the simplest mediation paradigm with three elements (A, B, and C) so that two elements were associated with the third, Kjeldergaard and Horton (1960) tested each of the eight possible patterns of arrangement,

two of them resulting in simple chaining (A → B → C),
two in reverse chaining (A ← B ← C),
two in stimulus equivalence (A → B ← C),
and two in response equivalence (A ← B → C).

Using the paired-associate method, low frequency words as elements (with half the pairs mediated and half not), and the subjects as their own controls, the results demonstrated highly significant overall facilitation of the mediated pairs, with no difference between the various paradigms, in all paradigms but one. This was the reverse chaining paradigm, where B→ A and C → B were learned, and A → C tested. The results of this extensive study were confirmed by Cramer and Cofer (1960).

Horton and Kjeldergaard (1961) elaborated upon their previous design in order to elucidate the role of mediate association in verbal generalization. They used a three-stage paradigm in which stimuli or responses were equated, or in which response chains were formed in the first two stages. They used a test stage in which the equated stimuli or responses, or the first and last members of response chains, were paired with each other, and the amount of generalization was noted. Again, they used all eight paradigms, finding generalization effects for all except one chaining model. None was significantly different from another, and the authors concluded that their results confirmed the importance of both forward and backward mediate associations in verbal generalization.

Until 1960 or thereabouts, most of the paired-associate learning experiments fell into one of the three basic types of three-stage paradigms shown in Table 2.

TABLE 2.
THREE-STAGE EXPERIMENTAL PARADIGMS
From: Kjeldergaard (1961).

		I	II	III
Stage 1	(Assumed or Learned)	A → B	A → B	B → A or A → B
Stage 2	"	B → C	C → B	B → C or A → C
Stage 3	(Test)	A → C	A → C	A → C or B → C

The first paradigm (I) is called response-chaining (Morgan and Underwood, 1950). Russell and Storms (1955) used this paradigm when they paired nonsense syllables with Kent-Rosanoff stimulus words (e.g., CEF with "stem"). A high-frequency associate of "stem" is "flower" and a high-frequency associate of "flower" is "smell." After learning a list like CEF (A) → "stem" (B), the subjects were tested with CEF (A) → "smell" (C). For pairs in which there was this implicit association, assumed from associative frequency norms, learning was significantly facilitated as compared with control pairs. This experiment is usually referred to as a three-stage model. Upon closer analysis, it can be seen that it can be viewed as a four-stage rather than a three-stage paradigm. As such, it will be considered below.

Cofer and Yarczower (1957) replicated the Russell and Storms experiment and confirmed their results, but found that the facilitation was a function of the direct associative connection, since synonymity, without associative connection, failed to facilitate learning. Kincaid, Bousfield, and Whitmarsh (1962), using a method of forced choice between low-frequency associates and non-associates, also showed that paired-associate learning of a meaningful response word to a nonsense syllable established connections between the nonsense syllable and members of a group of associative responses to the learned response word. However, their experiment did *not* support the contention that the strength of connections established between nonsense syllables and associates of the learned response word is a function of the strength of the cultural associative bonds between the learned word and its associative responses.

The second paradigm (II) is called acquired stimulus equivalence, since each of the two stimuli (A and C) produces the response B. Foss (1964) arranged the S-R pairing relation between first and second list learning so that he obtained facilitation, interference, and control word groups. In three experiments using the same stimulus equivalence design, but varying the number of stimuli which converged upon a common response, he found that both facilitation and interference effects increased with the number of convergent stimuli.

Kendler (1961) maintained the view that similar responses to different stimuli are primarily attributable to acquired rather than primary stimulus equivalence and that this can explain a common response to stimuli where there is no ostensible physical resemblance. For example, "food" is a concept that applies to watermelon and cornflakes which certainly have no physical similarity. What these two share is a common response which may be covert but which can nevertheless serve to mediate the final overt response.

A variation of this design was used to study facilitation in relearning rather than new learning. Ryan (1957) had his subjects learn a list of pairs (A → B), then another list of pairs (C → B) followed by relearning the first (A → B) list. (B) was a nonsense syllable and constant, and the (C) words were varied. For example, if (A) was "slow," (C) of the list would be "fast," which is a high-frequency associate to "slow" but has no meaning similarity, since it is an antonym of "slow." On another list, (C) might be "dim" which has high meaningful similarity but low frequency as a response to "slow." On the third list (C) would be "flaming" which bears no relationship to "slow." In the early relearning trials there was more facilitation when (C) was a high-frequency associate of (A), but with further trials the difference disappeared.

The third paradigm (III) is called acquired response equivalence, since two responses have the same stimulus. For example, Bastian (1957) had subjects learn successively pair list A → B and pair list A → C, where (A) was a nonsense word. To illustrate how the pairs were constructed, in one pair (B) was the word "sickness," and (C) was either "health" or "disease." Different subjects learned either an A → C pair in which (C) was "health" or one in which (C) was "disease." "Health" is a frequent associative response to "sickness." "Disease" is synonymous, but an infrequent associative response to "sickness." He found that there was more facilitation where there was a strong B-C association than where the relationship between B-C was weakly associative but strongly meaningful.

Experiments such as these emphasize the question as to the independence of meaning and associative processes raised in some of the studies using associative clustering. Staats, Staats, Finley, and Heard (1961) claimed to have demonstrated the independence of meaning and associative processes by means of the separate manipulation of the two processes. Five groups of words, having the same word association value *(m)* but differing in meaning as measured by the Semantic Differential, were presented with nonsense syllables to 40 subjects in a modified paired-association learning task. Three word groups, each consisting of two words, were learned as associates to different syllables. The groups consisted of two words of positive evaluative meaning, two that were neutral, and two of negative value. *m* was held constant while the evaluative (Semantic Differential) meaning was varied. In the second part of the experiment, four neutral words were learned as associates to a fourth syllable, and four positive words were paired with a fifth. Then the subjects rated each of the five syllables on the pleasant-unpleasant Semantic Differential scale. The problem posed with respect to interpreting the importance of such distinctions rests in the persistent confusion surrounding the very definition of meaning. When the term is used in the summary or discussion of any experiment, it is necessary to go to the method itself in order to determine which meaning of meaning is being referred to— whether it is the position of a word on the Semantic Differential scale, or whether it is its associative index and if so, which index, etc. Such distinctions raise questions as to the validity either of these interpretations or of other experimental results showing high correlations between the Semantic Differential ratings of words and their *m* value or some other associative index. Their contribution to any real understanding of meaning is still to be demonstrated.

FOUR-STAGE PARADIGM

In order to be clear about the nature of the current problems and controversies in the special area of inquiry devoted to paired-associate learning, it is necessary to go back in history.

In 1935 Shipley did a classical conditioning experiment using a four-stage paradigm. Using a tap on the cheek as UCS, a light (A) was paired with the UCS to produce a reflex eye-blink (B) (stage 1). Then a buzzer (C) was paired with the UCS to produce the eye-blink (B) (stage 2). In the third stage the light (A) was paired with shock, which produced finger withdrawal (D). Finally, the buzzer (C) was presented, and finger withdrawal (D) occurred in the absence of shock. The conditioning paradigm thus was as follows:

$$\text{Conditioned} \begin{cases} A \text{——} B \\ C \text{——} B \\ A \text{——} D \end{cases} \qquad \begin{array}{l} \text{Test} \\ C \text{——} D \text{ Generalization} \end{array}$$

It was on the basis of these experimental results that Hull (1939) had developed his theory of stimulus equivalence, and on which Foley and Cofer (1943, see p. 41 above) and Osgood (1956b) had built their elaborations and extensions to include language or verbal behavior (semantic generalization).

In 1951, Wickens and Briggs paired first a tone (A) and then a light (C) with the same verbal response (B). They then paired the tone (A) with shock to elicit a GSR (D). They found that the GSR (D) transferred, or generalized, to the light (C).

It is apparent that this experiment is designed according to the Shipley paradigm, although the response conditioned in the first two stages is a voluntary, verbal response rather than an unconditioned or reflex response.

In 1963 Jenkins reported a systematic investigation of 16 four-stage learning paradigms, eight of which were designed to test acquired stimulus equivalence, and eight, response equivalence. In the stimulus equivalence paradigms, it was assumed that (A) and (C) became functionally equivalent in the first two stages. Where a new response (D) is learned to (A), then (D) is more likely to occur as a response to (C), the transfer (generalization) being mediated by the implicit occurrence of (B) in the last two stages. In all these models, (stimulus) A—D (response) is learned in the third stage, and (stimulus) C—D (response) tested for in the fourth stage. In the first and second stages, each model contains one of all possible combinations of A and B, B and C. Of the resulting eight combinations, two test the capacity of a chain to mediate stimulus equivalence; two test the capacity of a reverse chain to mediate stimulus equivalence; two are paradigms of "pure" stimulus equivalence (the Shipley paradigm), and two test the transfer of equivalent responses to equivalent stimuli.

The elements of the Russell and Storms (1955) experiment referred to above (see pp. 131, 156) can be analyzed into a four-stage model of response, rather than stimulus, equivalence. In terms of the Jenkins four-stage paradigms, these subjects learned a list like CEF (D) → *stem* (A), tested with a list like CEF (D) → *smell* (C) in the last two stages of the model. The first two stages, *stem* (A) → *flower* (B), and *flower* (B) → *smell* (C) were assumed connections established by previous experience, the assumption of the connection being based on word association norms. Thus the paradigm:

Assume	A — B	
from		Test D — C
norms	B — C	
Learn	D — A	

The Russell and Storms results, showing facilitation in the final learning stage were confirmed by Cofer and Yarczower (1957), and Schulz and McGehee (1960).

Jenkins' (1963) eight arrangements to test response equivalence included the Russell and Storms paradigm. In these arrangements, the last two stages consisted of a D — A list to learn, and a D — C test list. Again, all possible combinations of A — B and B — C were made for the first two stages. The resulting eight combinations consisted of two models of chain-produced response equivalence; two of reverse-chain-produced response equivalence; two transfer of equivalent stimuli to equivalent responses; and two of "pure" response equivalence.

Each of the 16 models was tested with 16 subjects. No mediation effects whatever were demonstrated. Furthermore no single paradigm gave results significantly different from chance. However, Marshall (1964) found mediation effects in a four-stage paradigm when categorized pairs were used. When non-categorized pairs were employed, transfer effects were obtained in the three-stage, but not in the four-stage paradigm. Martin and Dean (1964) found that with a four-stage paradigm, superior learning was demonstrated only for those pairs which the subject reported as mediated, and the amount and kind of mediation reported varied as a function of the nature of the pair and of the conditions of the second-list learning. Other experiments, e.g., Palermo and Jenkins (1964), and Jakobovits and Lambert (1962), demonstrated facilitation in four-stage paradigms under certain conditions. Hakes and James (1964) found highly significant transfer in the four-stage stimulus equivalence paradigm when the first three stages were presented as a self-paced paired-associate task and the test stage as a matching task. They also found that subjects who mediated on any pairs did so on all, and concluded that if this all-or-none character of mediation is a general phenomenon, a reexamination of the theories of mediation is required.

Jenkins (1963), too, thought a reappraisal necessary. He presented an exhaustive discussion of the possible explanation of the failure of these methods to produce mediation effects, comparing the procedures and variables involved here with those involved in other, successful experiments. His conclusions were that the assumptions of mediation in the four-stage paradigm are valid, but that inadequate account has been taken of the mediational response as a response which is itself subject to reinforcement, interference, and inhibition. Thus the likelihood of eliciting the mediational process in any given experiment may be a function of the character of the tasks and/or situations presented to the subject in a given experimental setup, and also of the subject's previous history of reinforcement.

This brings us back to the subject of meaning. Jenkins (1963) stated that research in mediation has mainly been concerned with two points: 1) to demonstrate that mediation effects can be found, and 2) that mediation effects can properly be inferred only by such and such a technique because the nature of mediation *really* is thus and so. He felt that the first point had already been well established and no more research effort should therefore be expended on it. Finally he contended that the second point should be given less emphasis because the large amount of agreement among investigators was in danger of being obscured in the small details of difference.

Summary

Work on the development of measures of meaningfulness, word relatedness, association, and on paired-associate learning has contributed to the understanding of meaning mainly through the demonstration of the complexity of the problem. It seems fairly clear that simple defining operations will not suffice. The question still remains as to how or in what ways complexities need to be introduced into the experimental situations and into the theoretical framework in which they are embedded. Some experimenters choose to solve the problem by resorting to intervening variables or hypothetical constructs, such as the concept of mediating responses. Others take the position that such concepts are likely to be introduced as *post factum* explanations when explanatory dilemmas arise,[16] whereas they should be regarded as permissable only when the properties of the "intervening environment" can be described in an *a priori* manner and when its influence on behavior can be specified.[17] According to this position, to redefine the concept of stimulus would be more fruitful than to resort to concepts of mediation or other hypothetical constructs.[18] MacCorquodale and Meehl (1948) warned many years ago that explanations utilizing hypothetical constructs should be such that they need not remain metaphors. Rather, the metaphors themselves should suggest new ways of empirically attacking the unknown.

Some of the verbal learning theorists argue that the existence of some sort of mediating response has been adequately demonstrated and the next step is to study it directly. Others, notably Berlyne[19] and his associates have submitted telling arguments in support of a particular direction. He asserted that the neglect of motivational factors constitutes a "glaring inadequacy" in the work in this field. Berlyne (1964b, p. 7) summed up the situation as follows:

---

[16] e.g., see Goss (1964).
[17] See Kendler (1964, p. 217).
[18] See also Reese (1963).
[19] See, for example, Berlyne (1964a).

. . . The neo-behaviorists were fully aware that there is no one-to-one correspondence between stimulus conditions and response conditions. They recognized that the overt response depends jointly on the external stimulus situation and on conditions inside the organism. To take care of this difficulty, their theories tend to be replete with references to intervening variables, mediating processes, and implicit stimulus-producing responses, the function of all these devices being to make manageable the conceptual treatment of intricate input-output relations.

As Nash (1963, p. 343) pointed out, Morgan's cannon[20] which was designed to minimize the risk of overexplaining animal behavior, has often been evoked to justify underexplaining human behavior.

There may well be times when a theory that reduces some of our uncertainty about an important set of phenomena is preferable, both from the point of view of individual satisfaction and from that of the advancement of science, to a theory that tells us everything about matters of negligible intrinsic interest [Berlyne (1964c) pp. 15-16].

Whatever the research strategy adopted to tackle the complex problems involved in the study of verbal behavior, and in particular meaning, it is to be hoped that efforts will be directed toward collecting and establishing new and substantially supported factual data without prejudice from already existing theoretical systems.

References

AMSTER, H. Semantic satiation and generation: Learning? Adaptation? *Psychol. Bull.,* 1964, *62(4),* 273-286.

ASTRUP, C. *Schizophrenia: Conditional Reflex Studies.* Springfield, Ill.; Charles C. Thomas, 1962.

BASTIAN, J. R. Response chaining in verbal transfer. *Tech. Rep.,* #13, Contract Nonr. 66216, ONR & Univer. Minn., 1957.

BERLYNE, D. E. Curiosity and education. Lecture, Soc. Sci. Resrch. Council's Resrch. Conf. on Educ., Stanford, Cal., 1964a.

——. Behavior theory as personality theory. (b)
In: BORGATTA, E. F. & LAMBERT, W. W. 1964.

——. Emotional aspects of learning. (c)
In: FARNSWORTH, P. R., ET AL. XV. 1964.

---

[20] The Law of Parsimony.

BETTINGHAUS, E. P. Cognitive balance and the development of meaning. *J. Communications,* 1963, *8(2),* 94–105.

BORGATTA, E. F., & LAMBERT, W. W. (Eds.). *Handbook of Personality Theory and Research.* New York: Rand McNally, 1964.

BOUSFIELD, W. A., & PUFF, C. R. Clustering as a function of response dominance. *J. exp. Psychol.,* 1964, *67,* 76–79.

——, COHEN, B. H., & WHITMARSH, G. A. Associative clustering in the recall of words of different taxonomic frequencies of occurrence. *Psychol. Rep.,* 1958a, *4,* 39–44.

——, ——, ——. Verbal generalization: A theoretical rationale and an experimental technique. *Tech. Rep.,* #23, Contract Nonr. 631(00), ONR & Univer. Conn., 1958b.

——, COWAN, T. M., & STEWARD, J. R. The incidental learning of associative responses to given stimulus words. *J. gen. Psychol.,* 1963, *68,* 325–331.

——, ESTERSON, J., & WHITMARSH, G. A. A study of developmental changes in conceptual and perceptual associative clustering. *J. genet. Psychol.,* 1958, *92,* 95–102.

——, STEWARD, J. R., & COWAN, T. M. The use of free association norms for the prediction of clustering. *Tech. Rep.* #36, Contract Nonr. 631(00), ONR & Univer. Conn., 1961.

——, WHITMARSH, G. A., & BERKOWITZ, H. Partial response identities in associative clustering. *Tech. Rep.* #27, Contract Nonr. 631(00), ONR & Univer. Conn., 1958.

——, ——, ——. Partial response identities in associative clustering. *J. gen. Psychol.,* 1960, *63,* 233–238.

——, ——, & DANICK, J. J. Partial response identities in verbal generalization. *Psychol. Rep.,* 1958, *4,* 703–713.

CARLIN, J. E. Word-association strength as a variable in verbal paired-associate learning. Ph.D. thesis, Univer. Minn., 1958.

COFER, C. N. Associative commonality and rated similarity of certain words from Haagen's list. *Psychol. Rep.,* 1957, *3,* 603–606.

——. An experimental analysis of the role of context in verbal behavior. *Trans. N. Y. Acad. Sci.,* 1960, *22(5),* 341–347.

——. Inter-item associative strength and immediate free and forced recall. *Tech. Rep.* #1, Contract Nonr. 285(47), ONR & N. Y. Univer., 1961a.

——. Further studies of clustering in the recall of nouns embedded during presentation in sentences. *Tech. Rep.* #2, Contract Nonr. 285(47), ONR & N. Y. Univer., 1961b.

—— (Ed.). *Verbal Learning and Verbal Behavior.* New York: McGraw-Hill, 1961c.

——. Classification of effects of modifiers on discrete free associations made to verbal compounds. *Tech. Rep.* #8, Contract Nonr. 285(47), ONR & N. Y. Univer., 1962.

——. On some factors in the organizational characteristics of free recall. *Amer. Psychologist,* 1965, *20(4),* 261–272.

——, & MUSGRAVE, B. S. (Ed.). *Verbal Behavior and Learning: Problems and Processes.* New York: McGraw-Hill, 1963.

——, & SEGAL, E. M. Certain modifier effects with nouns varying in degree of clustering tendency. *Tech. Rep.* #29, Contract Nonr. 595(04), ONR & Univer. Maryland, 1959.

——, & SHEPP, B. E. Verbal context and perceptual recognition time. *Percept. mot. Skills,* 1957, *7, 215–218.*

——, & YARCZOWER, M. Further study of implicit verbal chaining in paired-associate learning. *Psychol. Rep.,* 1957, *3, 453–456.*

COHEN, B. H., BOUSFIELD, W. A., & WHITMARSH, G. A. Cultural norms for verbal items in 43 categories. *Tech. Rep.* #22, Contract Nonr. 631(00), ONR & Univer. Conn., 1957.

CRAMER, P., & COFER, C. N. The role of forward and reverse association in transfer of training. Abstr.: *Amer. Psychologist,* 1960, *16, 463.*

DAS, J. P., & COOK, C. H. On the development of an associative response time (RT) measure for semantic satiation. *Psychol. Rep.,* 1964, *15, 52.*

DEESE, J. Influence of inter-item associative strength upon immediate free recall. *Psychol. Rep.,* 1959a, *5, 305–312.*

——. On the prediction of occurrence of particular verbal intrusions in immediate recall. *J. exp. Psychol.,* 1959b, *58, 17–22.*

——. Frequency of usage and number of words in free recall: The role of association. *Psychol. Rep.,* 1960, *7, 337–344.*

——. Form class and the determinants of association. *J. verb. Learn. verb. Behav.,* 1962a, *1, 79–84.*

——. On the structure of associative meaning. *Psychol. Rev.,* 1962b, *69, 161–175.*

——. The associative structure of some common English adjectives. *J. verb. Learn. verb. Behav.,* 1964, *3, 347–357.*

DICKEN, C. F. Connotative meaning as a determinant of stimulus generalization. *Tech. Rep.* #23, Contract N8onr. 66216, ONR & Univer. Minn., 1958.

DREVER, J. On the non-existence of English associationism. *Proceedings, 1963 International Congress of Psychol.,* 1964, *17, 179–180 (Abstr.).*

EHRLICH, N. J. Arousal, meaning, and verbal satiation. Unpub. paper, *Ref.: Amer. Psychologist,* 1964, *19(9), 726.*

FARNSWORTH, P. R., ET AL. (Eds.). *Annual Review of Psychology.* XII. Palo Alto, Calif.: Annual Reviews, Inc., 1961.

——. *Annual Review of Psychology.* XV. Palo Alto, Calif.: Annual Reviews, Inc., 1964.

FILLENBAUM, S. Semantic generalization in verbal satiation. *Psychol. Rep.,* 1963, *13(1), 158.*

——. Semantic satiation and decision latency. *J. exp. Psychol.,* 1964, *68(3), 240–244.*

FLAVELL, J. H. Meaning and meaning similarity: I. A theoretical reassessment. *J. gen. Psychol.,* 1961a, *64, 307–319.*

FLAVELL, J. H. Meaning and meaning similarity: II. The semantic differential and co-occurrence as predictors of judged similarity in meaning. *J. gen. Psychol.,* 1961b, *64,* 321–335.

——, & FLAVELL, E. R. One determinant of judged semantic and associative connection between words. *J. exp. Psychol.,* 1959, *58,* 159–165.

FLUCKIGER, F. A. The interaction of verbal mediators following the acquisition of new meanings. An investigation of changes in the meaning of stimulus signs occurring with the acquisition of meaning for an initially meaningless assign, as reflected by a form of the Semantic Differential. Abstr.: Ph.D. thesis, N. Y. Univer. (Order No. 62-5329), 1962.

FOLEY, J. P., JR., & COFER, C. N. Mediated generalization and the interpretation of verbal behavior: II. Experimental study of certain homophone and synonym gradients. *J. exp. Psychol.,* 1943, *32,* 168–175.

FOSS, D. J. Acquired stimulus equivalence as a function of the number of converging stimulus items. Unpub. paper. Abstr.: *Amer. Psychologist,* 1964, *19(7),* 578.

GOLDIAMOND, I., & HAWKINS, W. F. Vexierversuch: The log relationship between word-frequency and recognition obtained in the absence of stimulus words. *J. exp. Psychol.,* 1958, *56(6),* 457–463.

GONZALES, R. C., & COFER, C. N. The effects of modifiers on the organization of verbal material as shown in clustering in free recall. *Tech. Rep.,* #6, Contract Nonr. 595(04), ONR & Univer. Maryland, 1956a.

——, ——. Evidence for mediational processes in free recall as exhibited by clustering of modifiers. *Tech Rep.,* #7, Contract Nonr. 595(04), ONR & Univer. Maryland, 1956b.

——, ——. The clustering of nouns through mediation by adjective categories. *Tech. Rep.,* #17, Contract Nonr. 595(04), ONR & Univer. Maryland, 1957.

——, ——. Exploratory studies of verbal context by means of clustering in free recall. *J. gen. Psychol.,* 1959, *95,* 293–320.

GOODALE, R. A. Meaningfulness: The correlation between *m* and some aspects of *D.* Unpub. Paper, *Ref.: Amer. Psychologist,* 1964, *19(9),* 732.

GOSS, A. E. Verbal mediation. *Psychol. Rec.,* 1964, *14,* 363–382.

GUMENIK, W. E., & SPENCER, T. Verbal satiation and changes in meaning of synonyms: Satiation or set? Unpub. Paper, *Ref.: Amer. Psychologist,* 1964, *19(9),* 725.

HAAGEN, C. H. Synonymity, vividness, familiarity, and associative value ratings of 400 pairs of common adjectives. *J. Psychol.,* 1949, *27,* 453–463.

HAKES, D. T., & JAMES, C. T. Mediated transfer in a four-stage, stimulus-equivalence paradigm. Unpub. paper. Abstr.: *Amer. Psychologist,* 1964, *19(7),* 561–562.

HOLROYD, R. G., & HOLROYD, J. C. Associative clustering in a retroactive paradigm. *J. gen. Psychol.,* 1961, *64,* 101–104.

HORTON, D. L., & KJELDERGAARD, P. M. An experimental analysis of associative factors in mediated generalization. *Psychol. Mon. gen. app.,* 1961, *75(11),* 1–26.

HOWE, E. S. Verb tense, negatives, and other determinants of the intensity of connotative meaning. Abstr.: *Amer. Psychologist,* 1964, *19(7),* 569.

HOWES, D. H. On the interpretation of word frequency as a variable affecting speed of recognition. *J. exp. Psychol.,* 1954, *48,* 106–112.

——. On the relation between the probability of a word as an associate and in general linguistic usage. *J. abnorm. soc. Psychol.,* 1957, *54,* 75–85.

——, & OSGOOD, C. E. On the combination of associative probabilities in linguistic contexts. *Amer. J. Psychol.,* 1954, *67,* 241–258.

——, & SOLOMON. R. L. Visual duration threshold as a function of word probability. *J. exp. Psychol.,* 1951, *41,* 401–410.

HULL, C. L. The problem of stimulus equivalence in behavior theory. *Psychol. Rev.,* 1939, *46,* 9–30.

JAKOBOVITS, L. A., & LAMBERT, W. E. Semantic satiation among bi-linguals. *J. exp. Psychol.,* 1961, *62,* 576–582.

——, ——. Mediated satiation in verbal transfer. *J. exp. Psychol.,* 1962, *64(4),* 346–351.

JENKINS, J. J. Mediated associations: Paradigms and situations.
In: COFER, C. N., & MUSGRAVE, B. S. 1963.

——, & COFER, C. N. An exploratory study of discrete free association to compound verbal stimuli. *Psychol. Rep.,* 1957, *3,* 599–602.

——, & RUSSELL, W. A. Associative clustering during recall. *J. abnorm. soc. Psychol.,* 1952, *47,* 818–821.

——, ——. Basic studies on individual and group behavior. *Annual Tech. Rep.,* Contract N8onr. 66216, ONR & Univer. Minn., 1956.

——, MINK, W. D., & RUSSELL, W. A. Associative clustering as a function of verbal association strength. *Psychol. Rep.,* 1958, *4,* 127–136.

JENSEN, A. R., & ROHWER, W. D. The effect of verbal mediation on the learning and retention of paired-associates by retarded adults. *Amer. J. ment. Defic.,* 1963, *68(1),* 80–84.

KALISH, H. J., & HABER, A. Generality of stimulus generalization. *Psychol. Rep.,* 1962, *11,* 741–746.

KANUNGO, R., & LAMBERT, W. E. Semantic satiation and meaningfulness. *Amer. J. Psychol.,* 1963. *76(3),* 421–428.

——, ——. Effects of variation in amount of verbal repetition on meaning and paired-associate learning. *J. verb. Learn. verb. Behav.,* 1964, *3,* 358–361.

KENDLER, H. H. The concept of the concept.
In: MELTON, A. W. 1964.

KENDLER, T. S. Concept formation.
In: FARNSWORTH, P. R., et al., XII, 1961.

KIMBROUGH, W. W., & COFER, C. N. A method for evaluating discrete, continuous association. *J. Psychol.,* 1957, *44,* 295–298.

KINCAID, W. D., JR., BOUSFIELD, W. A., & WHITMARSH, J. A. The parasitic reinforcement of verbal associative responses. *J. exp. Psychol.,* 1962, *64,* 572–579.

KJELDERGAARD, P. M. The psychology of language. *Rev. educ. Res.,* 1961, *31,* 119–128.

——, & HORTON, D. L. An experimental analysis of associative factors in stimulus equivalence, response equivalence and chaining paradigms. *Studies in verbal behavior.* Tech. Rep #3, NSF Grant, Univer. Minn., 1960.

LAFFAL, J., & FELDMAN, S. The structure of single word and continuous word associations. *J. verbal Learn. verbal Behav.,* 1962, *1,* 54–60.

LAMBERT, W. E.. & JAKOBOVITS, L. A. Verbal satiation and changes in intensity of meaning. *J. exp. Psychol.,* 1960, *60,* 376–383.

MAC CORQUODALE, K., & MEEHL, P. E. On a distinction between hypothetical constructs and intervening variables. *Psychol. Rev.,* 1948, *55,* 95–107.

MANDLER, G. Associative frequency and associative prepotency as measures of response to nonsense syllables. *Amer. J. Psychol.,* 1955, *68,* 662–665.

MARSHALL, G. R. The effects of associative specificity and patterns of association on mediation in the four-stage paradigm. Abstr.: *Amer. Psychologist,* 1964, *19(7),* 561.

——, & COFER, C. N. Associative indices as measures of word relatedness— A summary and comparison of ten methods. *Tech. Rep.* #10, Contract Nonr. 285(47), ONR & New York Univer., 1962.

——, ——. Associative indices as measures of word-relatedness—A summary and comparison of ten methods. *J. verb. Learn. verb. Behav.,* 1963, *1,* 408–421.

MARTIN, R. B., & DEAN, S. J. Implicit and explicit mediation in paired-associate learning. *J. exp. Psychol.,* 1964, *68(1),* 21–27.

MELTON, A. W. (Ed.). *Categories of Human Learning.* New York: Academic Press, 1964.

MESSER, S., JAKOBOVITS, L. A., KANUNGO, R., & LAMBERT, W. E. Semantic satiation of words and numbers. Unpub. paper, 1963.

MILLER, G. A. Some preliminaries to psycholinguistics. *Amer. Psychologist,* 1965, *20(1),* 15–20.

MILLER, N. E. The influence of past experience upon the transfer of subsequent training. Unpub. Ph.D. thesis, Yale Univer., 1935.

MINK, W. D. Semantic generalization as related to word association. *Tech. Rep.* #17, Contract N8onr. 66216, ONR & Univer. Minn., 1957. See also *Psychol. Rep.,* 1963, *12,* 59–67.

MORGAN, R. L., & UNDERWOOD, B. J. Proactive inhibition as a function of response similarity. *J. exp. Psychol.,* 1950, *40,* 592–603.

NASH, H. The role of metaphor in psychological theory. *Behav. Sci.,* 1963, *8(4),* 336–345.

NEWMAN, S. E., & TAYLOR, L. R. Context effects in paired-associate learning as a function of element-sharing among stimulus terms. *J. verb. Learn. verb. Behav.,* 1963, *1(4),* 243–249.

NOBLE, C. E. An analysis of meaning. *Psychol. Rev.,* 1952, *59,* 421–430.

O'NEIL, W. M. The effect of verbal association on tachistoscopic recognition. *Tech. Rep.* #4, Contract N8onr. 66216, ONR & Univer. Minn., 1953.

OSGOOD, C. E. Behavior theory and the social sciences. *Behav. Sci.*, 1956, *1*, 167–185. (a)

——. *Method and Theory in Experimental Psychology.* New York: Oxford, 1956. (b)

——. Comments on Professor Bousfield's paper. *In:* COFER, C. N. 1961(c).

PALERMO, D. S., & JENKINS, J. J. Paired-associate learning as a function of the strength of links in the associative chain. Unpub. Paper, *Ref.: Amer. Psychologist,* 1964, *19(9),* 723.

POLLIO, H. R. Word association as a function of semantic structure. Unpub. Ph.D. thesis, Univer. Mich., 1962.

——. Word association as a function of conditioned meaning. *J. exp. Psychol.,* 1963, *66,* 454–460.

——. Some semantic relations among word-associates. *Amer. J. Psychol.,* 1964, *77(2),* 249–256.

PORTNOY, S., PORTNOY, M., & SALZINGER, K. Perception as a function of association value with response bias controlled. *J. exp. Psychol.,* 1964, *68(3),* 316–320.

RADOMISLI, M. The structure of the word association networks of high and low commonality individuals. An investigation independent of word association performance. Unpub. Ph.D. thesis, N. Y. Univer., 1962.

RAZRAN, G. H. S. Semantic and phonetographic generalizations of salivary conditioning to verbal stimuli. *J. exp. Psychol.,* 1949, *39,* 642–652.

REESE, H. A reply to Youniss and Furth. *Psychol. Bull.,* 1963, *60(5),* 503–504.

ROSEN, E., & RUSSELL, W. A. Frequency characteristics of successive word association. *Amer. J. Psychol.,* 1957, *70,* 120–122.

ROTHKOPF, E. Z., & COKE, E. U. The prediction of free recall from word association measures. *J. exp. Psychol.,* 1961a, *62,* 433-438.

——, ——. Intralist association data for 99 words of the Kent-Rosanoff word list. *Psychol. Rep.,* 1961b, *8,* 463–474.

RUSSELL, W. A., & JENKINS, J. J. The complete Minnesota norms for responses to 100 words from the Kent-Rosanoff Word Association Test. *Tech. Rep.* #11, Contract N8onr. 66216, ONR & Univer. Minn., 1954.

——, & STORMS, L. H. Implicit verbal chaining in paired-associate learning. *J. exp. Psychol.,* 1955, *49,* 287–293.

RYAN, J. J., III. An experimental comparison of response transfer facilitated by meaningfully similar and associated verbal stimuli. *Tech. Rep.,* #21, Contract N8onr. 66216, ONR & Univer. Minn., 1957.

——. Comparison of verbal response transfer mediated by meaningfully similar and associated stimuli. *J. exp. Psychol.,* 1960, *60,* 408–415.

SCHULZ, R. W., & McGEHEE, N. E. Mediation in verbal paired associate learning. Unpub. paper, 1960.

SCHWARTZ, F., & NOVICK, T. N. An associative explanation of verbal satiation. *Psychol. Rep.,* 1964, *15(2),* 404.

SHIPLEY, W. C. Indirect conditioning. *J. gen. Psychol.,* 1935, *12,* 337–357.

SMITH, D. E. P., & RAYGOR, A. L. Verbal satiation and personality. *J. abnorm. soc. Psychol.,* 1956, *52,* 323–326.

SPENCE, D. P., & HOLLAND, B. The restricting effects of awareness: A paradox and an explanation. *J. abnorm. soc. Psychol.,* 1962, *64(3),* 163–174.

STAATS, A. W. Verbal habit families, concepts, and the operant conditioning of word classes. *Psychol. Rev.,* 1961, *68,* 190–204.

——, STAATS, C. K., FINLEY, J. R., & HEARD, W. G. Independent manipulation of meaning and (*m*). *Tech. Rev.,* #15, Contract Nonr. 2794(02), ONR & Ariz. State Univer., 1961.

SUNDBERG, N. D. A method for studying sensitivity to implied meanings. Abstr.: *Amer. Psychologist,* 1964, *19(7),* 475.

UNDERWOOD, B. J., & POSTMAN, L. Second California conference on verbal learning and verbal behavior. *J. verb. Learn. verb. Behav.,* 1963, *2(2),* 203–215.

——, & RICHARDSON, J. Some verbal materials for the study of concept formation. *Psychol. Bull.,* 1956a, *53,* 84–95.

——, ——. Verbal concept learning as a function of instructions and dominance level. *J. exp. Psychol.,* 1956b, *51,* 229–238.

——, & SCHULZ, R. W. *Meaningfulness and Verbal Learning.* Philadelphia: J. B. Lippincott, 1960.

——, HAM, M., & EKSTRAND, B. Cue selection in paired-associate learning. *J. exp. Psychol.,* 1962, *64(4),* 405–409.

WERTHEIMER, M. The relation between the sound of a word and its meaning. *Amer. J. Psychol.,* 1958, *71,* 412–415.

——, & GILLIS, W. M. Satiation and the rate of lapse of verbal meaning. *J. gen. Psychol.,* 1958, *59,* 79–85.

WHITMARSH, G. A., & BOUSFIELD, W. A. Use of free associational norms for the prediction of generalization of salivary conditioning to verbal stimuli. *Psychol. Rep.,* 1961, *8,* 91-95.

WICKENS, D. D., & BRIGGS, G. E. Mediated stimulus generalization as a factor in sensory pre-conditioning. *J. exp. Psychol.,* 1951, *42,* 197–200.

WICKLUND, D. A., PALERMO, D. S., & JENKINS, J. J. The effects of associative strength and response hierarchy on paired-associate learning. *J. verb. Learn. verb. Behav.,* 1964a, *3,* 413-420.

——, ——, ——. Associative clustering in children during the recall of randomly presented pairs of varying associative strengths. Unpub. Paper, *Ref.: Amer. Psychologist,* 1964b, *19(9),* 724.

WOLFENSBERGER, W. Conceptual satiation: An attempt to verify a construct. *Amer. J. ment. Deficiency,* 1963, *68(1),* 73–79.

YAVUZ, H. S., & BOUSFIELD, W. A. Recall of connotative meaning. *Psychol. Rep.,* 1959, *5,* 319–320.

YELEN, D. R., & SCHULZ, R. W. Verbal satiation? *J. verb. Learn. verb. Behav.,* 1963, *1,* 372–377.

PART
THREE
Discussion

Contemporary American Theory

I think it should be considered perfectly fair for one theorist to be ego-involved in two incompatible theories. In fact, to have only one is dangerous, for it leads him to overprotect something he should have constructed mainly to attack [Licklider (1959) p. 50].

Beware of the man of one method or one instrument, either experimental or theoretical. He tends to become method-oriented rather than problem-oriented. The method-oriented man is shackled; the problem-oriented man is at least reaching freely toward what is most important [Platt (1964) p. 351].

General considerations

The theoretical controversy in the area of meaning seems to epitomize a regrettable tendency in American psychological experimentation. It is the tendency, growing out of a non-inductive research orientation, for experimenters to become too enamored of their hypotheses and methodological strategies, with the result that the experimenters sometimes become more concerned with demonstrating the appropriateness of their models than with coping with the problems being investigated.[1] It also frequently leads to hassles over rarefied and overgeneralized theory which loses sight of its concrete roots in the specific experiment, or over interpretations of concrete instances at the expense of larger issues and at the risk of ignoring significant phenomena. An example of the latter is suggested by an argument put forward by Bousfield (1961) in a discussion of the difference between a mediating and a mediated response. Using as a hypothetical example a situation in which, through a series of conditioning processes involving a painful stimulus and the word "bad," the word "evil" comes to elicit the word

---
[1] See Kendler (1964).

"bad" as a response, Bousfield asserted that "bad" is a mediating response while the negative feeling of pain is a mediated response. He then asked which response is meaningful, and continued,

the verbal behavior theorist would be well advised to favor the assumption that "bad" is a meaningful response to "evil" because "bad" has acquired mediational properties. Though a case may be made for regarding the representational response to the pain stimulus as a meaningful response to "evil," *this incurs a penalty for the verbal behavior theorist who wishes to manipulate and measure meaningful responses.* While verbal responses are distinctive and their strengths measurable, we can't identify distinctive nonverbal response patterns for different verbal stimuli. Certainly the subject should show a PGR and changes in heart rate when the word "evil" is presented and such changes are measurable, but can it be shown that such patterns vary distinctively when different verbal stimuli are presented?[2]

It would appear that one way of resolving such a theoretical conflict would be to attempt to answer the last question empirically rather than to deny the significant implications of the fact that it can be asked.

Premature overgeneralization tends to lead to rigid theories, which in turn lead to a compounding of the assumptive sin and the tightening of the circular relationship between theory and method. What seems to become of prime importance then is not the discovery of new facts or the accumulation of evidence, but the proof that a given hypothesis is *right*. This tends toward a perversion of the scientific method which views hypothesis, or theory, simply as a vehicle which makes possible the exploration of a given territory. Obviously, the territory will yield different views depending upon whether the observer is crawling on his hands and knees; riding on a bicycle, in an automobile, a helicopter, a jet plane, or a satellite; whether he uses the unaided eye, a microscope, a telescope, a camera, or radar.

It would be an interesting and instructive exercise if the proponents of opposed theoretical camps would switch roles, design experiments in terms of the others' hypothesis, and then try to interpret the results in terms of both. Theory is of course essential to systematic experimentation; yet it should not be adopted to be proven right but simply to provide a flexible frame of reference. Mono-

---

2 Bousfield (1961, p. 83); *Italics* added.

gamous union between experimenter and theory should not be a culturally approved or even tolerated relationship; theory should never be more than the experimenter's light-o'-love.

The possibility that the myth of the hypothetico-deductive method is supported and honored often in the breach, if not *more* often in the breach than in the observance, has been suggested at no less an august gathering than the 1958 Estes Park Conference on graduate training for research.[3] There a group of eminent psychologists admitted in public that they themselves did not (always) operate the way they (often) pretended in print that they did; that is, from hypothesis (theory) to deductive consequence to experimental design, and so on. Yet somehow, in experimental and even in clinical psychological research, the myth persists that this is the only respectable model to follow.

BACKGROUND

American controversy about the definition and theory of meaning is intimately related to three facts. One is that the earliest studies were concerned with semantic generalization, followed the Pavlovian model, utilized the classical conditioning paradigm, and demonstrated generalization of the conditioned response to stimuli which were related to the conditioned stimulus by semantic rather than physical similarity. The second fact is that most of the subsequent experimental work has taken place in the context of learning theory, and interest in meaning has been primarily restricted to its importance as a variable affecting the acquisition, retention, and recall of verbal material. The third fact is that contemporary verbal learning experimentation and theory has one foot in simple association theory, the other foot in the classical conditioning paradigm used in the early studies of semantic generalization, and its head in the clouds of Skinnerian behaviorism.

As a consequence of this mixed parentage and ecology, attempts to reduce meaning to definable and measurable terms have taken varied forms with varied results. Important among the methods used were 1) conditioning methods employing several physiological measures, with the major emphasis in the United States on the GSR; 2) scaling methods, with the most important being Osgood's Semantic Differential; and 3) associative indices with many differ-

---

[3] See Festinger *et al.* (1959).

ent methods of arriving at many different (but certainly highly correlated) measures of associative strength.

Associationistic theory

Those experimentalists who had the strongest heritage of associationistic influences tended to feel that meaning presents no problem to verbal learning theory. Bousfield, for example, stated flatly (1961) that meaning is not only an unnecessary concept in the area of verbal learning, but one which inevitably leads to confusion, and that the term is not required to describe any of the research. However, he admits that one might be able to support the contention that verbal associations are meaningful.

The term "meaningful" represents one attempt to resolve theoretical difficulties by differentiating between "meaning" and "meaningfulness," and by disclaiming any generality for the concept of meaningfulness. But this device fails to satisfy other workers who are looking for a more inclusive theory.

In contrasting his own position with Osgood's, Noble (1963, p. 98) summed up the position of two of the camps as follows:

> It is fairly obvious that he [Osgood] . . . wants his notion of *meaning* (r_m) to be multidimensional. . . . More than this, Osgood is after a supertheory of meaning; by contrast, *m* is (or began as) merely an associational addendum to Hull's system.

But Osgood (1961) argued that Noble's *m* takes into account only sheer availability, whereas associative meaning takes into account the nature of the mediating associations. The fact that subjects' reactions are not predictable from knowing word-association hierarchies constitutes evidence that there are representational processes functioning in meaningful behavior that are not of the same form as the overt verbalizations used to express them.

Lachman and Sanders (1963) suggested that the frequent unidirectional relationships observed in word association tests may be a serious limitation of the direct association hypothesis. For example, they found that prepotent stimulus-response connections produce transfer effects in concept shifts. As Perls (1947) and other theorists in the psychotherapeutic area have pointed out, the significance of association lies not in the associative connections themselves, but rather in the existence of specific spheres of which they form a part. Underwood and Schulz (1960), too, questioned the adequacy of the direct association hypothesis as either a definition of or means of "measuring" meaning. Measures stemming from association theory, such as many of the associative indices, are often gross kinds of measures which are derived from other gross kinds of measures. By and large, they are "outcome" measures based upon frequency counts, or upon the significance of differences between groups (averaged measures). However, Jenkins (1963) insisted that associations proved to be effective indices of certain kinds of studied behaviors, that they served to draw attention to the fact that some mediational phenomena are asymmetrical, and what is needed now is more data on how the various indices function with respect to each other.

Learning theory models

Learning theory models as applied to language behavior embrace various levels of complexity, the more comprehensive the less parsimonious. Each incorporates the assumptions of simpler models, and adds further assumptions in order to encompass phenomena which defy explanation in a more parsimonious system. These models fall into two major classifications: 1) a simple, singlestage stimulus response model (S-R), and 2) a two- (or more) stage mediation model (S-O-R).

S-R THEORY OF MEANING

That the simple S-R model is no longer so simple has been made abundantly clear by Goss (1963). Staats and Staats (1963) made it sound simple, but their book was written as an elementary text and is addressed to students who are naive with respect to learning theory. Staats (1964) asserted that some unconditioned stimuli are also primary reinforcers (UCS^R). A response elicited will be conditioned to any neutral stimulus with which a UCS^R is paired. The neutral stimulus then becomes a conditioned stimulus, acquires the reinforcement value of the UCS^R, thus becoming a CS^R. Words may then become conditioned eliciting stimuli and will also be reinforcing stimuli (CS^R).

Essentially, those definitions of meaning in terms of direct association can be classified as strict single-stage S-R theories. The meaning of a stimulus is determined by the response or responses it evokes, and the meaning of a response is determined by the stimulus or stimuli which evoke it. Yet even at this solipsistic level there seems to be confusion as to what meaning is. Is it stimulus generalization, or response generalization? Is it stimulus discrimination, or response discrimination? Is it some kind of associationistic bond, and if so what kind? Or is it perhaps some process of which all these are varieties or manifestations?

Staats and Staats (1963), along with the more avowed Skinnerian operant conditioners, are among the few behavioristic experimentalists in the field of verbal behavior who are satisfied with the most parsimonious explanation. They presented a systematic theoretical S-R framework for the unification of the subareas in the investigation of verbal behavior, but it remains to be seen how it will hold up under experimental testing, and how heuristically fruitful it will be. Their theory of verbal learning and verbal behavior, seductively simple and admirably systematic and inclusive, deals with meaning as a response, learned according to the principles of classical conditioning and maintained by reinforcement. According to the principles of operant conditioning, conditional components of sensory, and perhaps even autonomic, responses elicited by an object may be conditioned to a word stimulus to form its meaning. Furthermore, speech responses can be conditioned to the sensory responses. In this way, a speech response is reinforced in the presence of sensory responses and the stimuli producing them, thus forming associative bonds between them. The meaning of a word would then tend to elicit a word response, with the word becoming the stimulus that would elicit the meaning of the word.

Generalization and differentiation occur according to the simple laws of stimulus and response generalization. Concept formation, or abstract processes, involve nothing more than extensions of these principles. To apply the Russian terminology, first signalling system signals (concrete meanings) are formed by first order conditioning, second signalling systems signals (abstract meanings) are formed by second order conditioning. This formulation represents the systematic elaboration of Staats' (1963) view that verbal behavior should be regarded as a single, unitary field. The principles studied in the various methodological subareas of investigation (e.g., operant conditioned, paired-associate, and serial learning; word association norms and mediation; semantic conditioning and mediation) are *all* operative when detailed studies are made of complex situations. He held that it should not be a matter of arguing for any one principle against any or all others, but rather that efforts should be made to see what the data reveal about how these various principles interact.

The Staats and Staats view, incorporating and underlining Skinner's notion that "the private event is at best no more than a link in a casual chain, and it is usually not even that . . ." (Skinner, 1953, p. 279), accepts the assumption that both conscious (and "unconscious") experience and its report are themselves determined by the same variables they purportedly explain. It dispenses with the notion of mediators, and meaning is regarded not as a hypothetical construct but (and only until such time as it may be possible to observe directly all its response elements) as an intervening variable.

The theory is so neat, clean, and reasonable that it is to be hoped that its proponents will be able to generate experiments which can account adequately for such frequently observed phenomena as the discrepancy between "experience" and/or verbal report and actual behavior. Bridgeman[4] remarked that "the true meaning of a term is to be found by observing what a man does with it, not by what he says about it."[5] Yet, "what he says about it" may, at least in some instances, imply meaning at another level; e.g., his conception of what he *ought* to think about it. This is clearly shown in an investigation (Kyriazis, 1963) of Semantic Differential ratings from prisoner patients.

Additional experimental evidence of these discrepancies can be adduced from some of the Russian work demonstrating failure of the first signalling system to be accurately reflected in the second signalling system, from such experiments as one by Cowden, Reynolds, and Ford (1961), and also from Hefferline's work.[6] The former experiment tested with a live snake a group of schizophrenic patients who had previously verbalized an intense fear of snakes. In the actual situation with a live snake, they displayed no fear at all, although continuing to verbalize it (the fear). The discrepancy between the verbal behavior and the actual behavior was reflected in the negative correlation ($r = -.54$) between measures of both. As to Hefferline's experiment, it would have been interesting to know what would have occurred with his subjects if they had been

---

[4] Quoted by Hayakawa (1958).
[5] Carnap's verification principle: see Malcolm (1964, p. 144).
[6] See p. 118f.

informed, after they had "hallucinated" the tone as a stimulus for their motor response, that there was indeed no tone delivered. Would they have continued to respond to the muscle twitch, and to "hear" the tone (first signalling system) in spite of "knowing" (second signalling system) that there was none? Or would the discrepancy between the two systems have disappeared?

This kind of discrepancy, frequently observed by the psychotherapist, is one which is epitomized in the cry of the patient, "I *know* such and such, but I *feel* thus and so, and somehow I always wind up acting the way I feel rather than in accordance with what I know." In other words, the patient's verbal behavior (knowledge) is at variance with his visceral behavior (feelings, emotions), and his behavior within the external environment may correspond with neither. What is the meaning of his behavior, then? And what is the meaning of the objects or events which elicit the inconsistent and incompatible behaviors?

Within the more strictly operant S-R framework, Salzinger and others spoke of word classes, but this notion seems inadequate as a definition of meaning. Word classes are formed, according to this view, when the same discriminative stimulus (S^D) controls the various words. Staats, Staats, and Finley (1961) showed that a group of word responses, each of which elicits a common meaning component, can be operantly conditioned as a class. Yet, Staats himself (1963) raised the question as to why it is that word responses controlled by one stimulus behave as a class in the absence of the S^D. He further pointed out that many word responses reinforced by the same social reinforcers are not members of the same response classes, and that some words in the same response class are reinforced by different stimuli. Even such a staunch Skinnerian as Lindsley (1959) admitted that verbal responses of hallucinating psychotic subjects appear to be under some strong control that resists direct differential positive reinforcement. Mann (1954) pointed out that although operant procedures may produce certain phenomena, in men and pigeons, that look alike, "between the stimulus and the response lie the differences, somatically and emotionally, between men and pigeons" (p. 405). "The way people manipulate their environment has incomplete meaning unless one also considers what it is in people that influences their method of manipulation" (p. 404).

The phenomenon of semantic generalization is one that created problems for a single-stage S-R model, although more recently

Staats and Staats (1963) accounted for it in terms of the simple reinforcement of implicit meaning responses. Razran's results (1939) were analyzed in terms of secondary generalization (Hull, 1939), a concept having something in common with both the fractional anticipatory goal response and the notion of the "pure stimulus act" (Hull, 1930). The pure stimulus act was defined as a cue-producing response with the sole function of providing stimuli for other acts—one which can generate stimuli that interact or compete with environmental stimuli to control behavior. Thus the mediation model was born.

MEDIATION THEORIES OF MEANING: S-O-R.

In their early work with word association, Cofer and Foley (1942)[7] adopted the Hullian notion of "implicit" responses for their model of mediation processes, as did Mowrer (1954), Osgood (1956), and Staats and Staats (1959). That is, when a word is contiguously presented with a stimulus object (unconditioned stimulus, or UCS), some of the unconditioned response (UCR) to the UCS will be conditioned to the word, and those responses, when stably conditioned, become the meaning of the word. Meaning can thus be treated as a conditioned response, and higher order conditioning can be accomplished by pairing a given word, which already elicited a conditioned meaning response (CR), with a stimulus to be conditioned to elicit that meaning.

Bousfield (1953) adopted a Hebbian model of supraordinates[8] and later developed his theory of partial response identities, asserting that a repeated particular stimulus results in the development of a representational sequence, comprising both a representational response (R^{rep}) and a representational stimulus (S^{rep}), the R^{rep} being a fractional part of the total response to a given stimulus, the S^{rep} being a stable pattern of feedback stimuli consequent on the occurrence of a given R^{rep}, and new responses being attached to it by conditioning.[9]

Osgood (1952, 1956) extended the notion of fractional or implicit responses into a general conception of meaning. When a word,

---

[7] See also Foley and MacMillan (1943), Foley and Matthews (1943), Foley and Cofer (1943), Cofer, Janis and Rowell (1943).

[8] See Bousfield and Cohen (1955).

[9] See Bousfield, Whitmarsh, and Danick (1958), Jenkins and Cofer (1957), Jenkins, Mink, and Russell (1958), and Deese (1959a and b) for further development with respect to response identities.

for example, is continuously presented with a stimulus object, some of the unconditioned response to the object will be conditioned to the word. These responses, when stably conditioned, became the meaning of the word. Representational mediators, then, are derived from detachable portions of responses made in the presence of stimuli in the past experience of the individual. This sounds identical with the Staats and Staats (1963) model, except that they chose to regard meaning responses as intervening variables, whereas Osgood (1963) thought that they could best be treated as hypothetical constructs having both stimulus and response properties. In addition, Osgood (1961) distinguished between two different kinds of meaning, denotative and connotative, which not only refer to different processes but vary independently of each other.

Early mediation theory split into two conceptions of the simple two-stage model. One stressed meaning similarity, the other associative bonds. According to the first conception, if A and B are close synonyms, and C is a high frequency associate to A, generalization will occur from A to B rather than to C. Transfer from A to other words would vary as a function of the magnitude with which the transfer stimuli elicit common, fractional *meaning* responses, and assumes previous formation of conditional responses or associations.[10] Experimental evidence[11] was inconclusive with regard to this assumption. According to the second conception, which focused on associative connections rather than meaning, generalization would be predictably greater from A to C than from A to B.[12] Support for this hypothesis was adduced from associative clustering experiments,[13] and from experiments showing facilitation in recognition and recall.[14] Yet there was sufficient uncertainty generated by experimental inconsistencies[15] so that it was necessary to reassess the previous interpretations of results from experimental work based on mediation models (Jenkins, 1959).

Note here that some of this controversy might be viewed as an artifact of the measuring instruments used (e.g., associative indices and/or the Semantic Differential), which in turn defined or at least

---

[10] See Osgood (1946).

[11] For example, see Cofer (1959), Russell and Storms (1955), Cofer and Shepp (1957), Cofer and Yarczower (1957), Cofer (1957), and Dicken (1958).

[12] See Jenkins and Russell (1952, 1956), Bousfield, Cohen, and Whitmarsh (1958), and Noble (1952).

[13] See pp. 147ff. above.

[14] See O'Neil (1953), Bastian (1956), and Mink (1957).

[15] e.g., See Ryan (1957, 1960), Carlin (1958), Mink (1957), and Moss (1960).

contributed to the definition of the terms "meaning" versus "associative strength." It would seem logically evident that any adequate definition of meaning must include the process of discrimination as well as of generalization. If one looks upon an antonym as an implicit response to the stimulus word, or a response tendency which is inhibited, then an antonym could be viewed, even in S-R terms, as a part of the total *meaning* of a word, not as only an associate to the word.[16] It seems rather difficult to understand, furthermore, why such a distinction should be made between an associative response and a meaning response. Surely no one would argue that the associative process is not involved in meaning, whatever meaning may be. Yet bitter controversies break out over whether it is "meaning" *or* "association" that facilitates learning, forgetting that "meaning" here refers to something that is represented by a word which has some score determined by the Semantic Differential, and "association" refers to something that is represented by a word which has some score determined by some index of association value, or frequency of occurrence as a response to a given stimulus.

Remember that Kjeldergaard and Horton (1960) had systematically tested the various combinations of elements in a three-stage learning paradigm[17] showing facilitation of mediated pairs in all combinations except the reverse chaining model; and that Jenkins (1963) extended the investigation to four-stage paradigms,[18] results showing no facilitation whatsoever.

Jenkins wrote (1963, p. 220):

> At this point an agonizing reappraisal took place . . . The paradigms contained the same model as that used by Russell and Storms and subsequently confirmed by Cofer and Yarczower (1957) and Schulz and McGehee (1960) as well as the famous Shipley paradigm (Shipley 1935) on which Hull (1939) had based his analysis of stimulus equivalence and on which Cofer and Foley (1942) and Osgood (1956) had built their theoretical extensions to language behavior.

Possible explanations of these inconsistencies included consideration of various differences in the experimental situation in terms of the strength of the association experimentally established; the degree of reinforcement of the mediating response; different degrees or kinds of associative arousal; and differences in the nature of the

---

[16] See p. 150 above.
[17] See p. 155ff. above.
[18] See p. 159ff. above.

response involved, whether instrumental or classical conditioning was involved. Jenkins' (1963) discussion of these points is exhaustive, and need not be reviewed here. He concluded that the difference in outcome of the various experiments points to two powerful considerations not dealt with in association studies in mediation: 1) the reinforcement of specific mediational processes, and 2) the likelihood of eliciting the mediational process as a function of the characteristics of the task confronting the subject, or his past history of reinforcement for mediating in the specific situation.

What seems even more cogent is the failure to distinguish between the paired-associate learning model and the classical conditioning model with respect to the nature of the unconditioned stimulus and the unconditioned response, or to the order of conditioning involved (e.g., first order or higher order). The classical definition of a UCS is a stimulus which consistently produces an innate, unlearned response (the UCR). The Shipley experiment referred to by Jenkins (above) was a classical conditioning experiment in the classical sense, using touch as UCS and eye-blink as UCR for the experimental first order conditioning, then elaborating the second order conditioning on this experimentally controlled base.

When stimulus and response are rendered by letters of the alphabet and relations by arrows, a verbal learning model looks exactly like the classical conditioning paradigm. Yet there is no evidence that any word consistently produces any other word as a response in free association or even following training (conditioning). The association between single words is merely a probabilistic matter, not a matter of either organismic or behavioral invariance. Connections between words must be the product of higher-order conditioning, and thus temporary, unstable, variable. Yet in paired-associate learning tests of mediation effects, the assumption is made that a word can be regarded as a UCS. It seems likely, therefore, that this confusion between the paired-associate learning model and the classical conditioning model—or at least the failure to control for the conditioning order of the conditioned verbal stimulus—is to a large extent responsible for the learning theorists' bewilderment over the failure of mediation paradigms to demonstrate mediation effects in learning.

Taylor (1953, 1955, and 1956) has shown in his work with the Cloze procedure that a given linguistic context may produce a *nearly* invariant verbal response. Other kinds of studies also have been done to assess linguistic contextual effects, but the notion that words may exist in nonverbal contexts has been neglected experimentally and theoretically. Consider, for example, the implications of Razran's finding[19] that words lost generalization strength when combined into sentences which were true or false. That the truth or falsity of the statements influenced both conditioning and generalization suggests that meaning may involve values or attitudes, however one may define these terms. It is too obvious to ignore that higher-order conditioning must be a much more complex matter than "simple" first-order conditioning, or even than a chaining process.

Mandler (1963) pointed out that we know from experimental evidence that meaningfulness on the response side of an S-R pair is more powerful in mediation than on the stimulus side, and (in agreement with Jenkins) that "actual responding" seems to have something to do with mobilizing meaningfulness or arousing mediates. However, he expressed his uncertainty as to just what "actual responding" means and asked (p. 247) : "Does it have something to do with attention, with activation and effort?" In his statements and questioning, it should be noted that he used such terms as "mobilizing," "arousing," "activation," "attention," and "effort," but failed to define these terms operationally, or to ask what they mean, or where they should be located in the S-R chain.

Jenkins (1963) likewise referred to "associative arousal" and "emotional involvement" without being explicit about how such concepts might be handled in an S-R model. He used the terms within the context of a discussion of two instances of successful four-stage mediation (Shipley, 1935; and Wickens and Briggs, 1951), which were both extensions of classical conditioning models. It should be noted that the Wickens and Briggs (1951) experiment was designed to show that sensory preconditioning could be viewed as a special case of mediated generalization.

In reviewing the Russian literature on interoceptive conditioning, Razran (1961) constructed a case for viewing the American concept of sensory preconditioning as equivalent to the Russian concept of first signalling system formation, and second-order conditioning as equivalent to the development of the second signalling system from the first. If we remember that sensory preconditioning involves organismic response variables, it should be fairly clear that Jenkins and Mandler are invoking concepts which refer to the interior of the "black box." Razran (1961) recanted his previous position (Razran, 1955) with respect to the infrequency of occurrence of

---

[19] See p. 40 above.

second-order conditioning, and adopted the position that the supposed infrequency was due to experimenter failure to observe certain stimulus sequences. It seems pertinent to raise the question as to whether or not the failure to demonstrate mediation effects in the four-stage learning paradigm as applied in paired-associate learning experiments may be due, not only to the failure to observe certain stimulus sequences which are present, but also to the careful exclusion from the experimental setup of variables which might produce such stimulus sequences, on the grounds that they are unknown or unknowable because they are unobservable.

In analyzing the Mink (1957) and Razran (1949) experiments which yielded exactly opposite results with the same experimental paradigm, Jenkins (1963) spoke of "effort" and "attention," and explained the difference in results in terms of conditions favoring "associative arousal" in the first stage in one experiment, and in the second stage in the other. He dismissed the difference in the nature of the response involved in the two types of experiments as of no importance. Here again one might raise the question as to what the "actual" response was. What is "associative arousal?" Could not the *arousal,* or whatever that is, be considered the "actual" response to the "functional" stimulus?

Mandler's question[20] as to what constitutes a "functional stimulus" in an experiment has sometimes been raised outside the S-R fold but it is a strange question to occur in an S-R context. If "functional" refers to what the stimulus *does,* then the question should be answerable in terms of the response to it. But if the response is a "mediating" response, thus covert and hidden in the "black box," then essentially we are again asking, "What is the mediating response?", or in effect, "What does the stimulus *mean* to the subject?", or, "What is the nature of *meaning*?" We are also admitting that the application of S-R theory to the problem of meaning has been fruitful mainly in that it has reemphasized the importance and significance of the question it was supposed to answer.

It seems that a simple theory based on the preexperimental or experimental formation of associative bonds between and among words is not sufficient to account for either the positive or negative experimental findings in studies of verbal behavior, let alone to constitute an adequate definition of meaning. Procedural proposals for tackling the problem all seem to head in the direction of concept formation experiments, based on the proposition that words are

---

20 See Cofer and Musgrave (1963).

conceptual tools, associated only through logic, grammatical structure, context, and shared referents. It is implicit in these proposals that mediators are assumed to be verbal, or that the mediating process is a verbal process. Yet experimental studies, such as Furth's work (1964) with deaf subjects, have clearly demonstrated that it is important to differentiate verbal from conceptual performance as such. Werner and Kaplan (1963, p. 15) complained that

. . . the widespread view which treats symbolic vehicles and referents as two fully formed entities that are externally linked to each other through continuous pairing and reinforcement. . . denies to symbolization (including language) any creative role in cognitive organization of experience and thought. Symbolic vehicles thus become reduced to a complex system of markers, useful merely for routine indicators of referents and for communication about preformed judgments and concepts.

Brown (1958) denied that meaning, for the psychologist, is any particular response, even a mediating response. He saw meaning rather as a disposition to behave in certain varying ways with respect to the form (e.g., word, object, event, person) as the contingent circumstances change. Meaning "is not a learning, a beginning, a miniature reaction. It is a response potential," (p. 103) and has no substantive character aside from the structure of the nervous system. Since, he proposed, a disposition is discovered by creating various contingencies and observing the various responses, meaning could then be discovered by these means. He continued:

The task is not to find the constant reaction (e.g., the mediating reaction) that lies behind the varying overt behavior, but rather to find functionally central responses within the overt behavior.

Brown admitted that there might be some kind of subtle response of muscle or gland originally released by the referent object which through conditioning might also be released by the sign or symbol of the object, but he also seemed to feel that the psychologist can safely leave such central reactions to others and focus on overt behavior. This is essentially the same attitude as that espoused by the mediation theorists. But what if the "subtle reaction of muscle or gland" is not "released by" the referent (and thus will extinguish, as in classical conditioning) but is instead the fortuitous background or internal context within which the direct associative connections take place? If Gendlin's (1962) hypothesis is correct that meaning is formed in the interaction between "experiencing" and symbols, and if "experiencing" is understood to mean not just the perception of, let us say, an object, but this perception's-taking-place-in-the-context-of-an-internal-state of an object-in-an-external-context, then even first-order conditioning is a far more complex process than the formation of a simple connection between an object and its name.

Hebb (1960) asserted that it is essential to distinguish between the kind of sense-dominated behavior[21] which is embraced under the S-R formulation and behavior which is not sense-dominated. He maintained that references to mental processes are not inconsistent with a behavioristic analysis, since consciousness, sensation, perception, feeling, emotion can all be regarded as intervening variables or constructs. He said (p. 740):

> ... the camel already has his nose inside the tent—the learning theorist's tent, I mean. Seward ... Lawrence ... Meehl and MacCorquodale ... Osgood ... Berlyne ... and Kendler suffice to show that the mediating process is quite compatible with Hullian theory.

Razran (1961a and b) has proposed that we alert ourselves to the implications of recent Soviet experimental findings concerning the nature of proprioceptive, interoceptive, and orienting reflex conditioning. Russian experiments have demonstrated generalization produced by secondary conditioning of these processes that appear to be "almost constant concomitants of primary exteroceptive and primary sensory-interoceptive conditioning" (1961a, p. 1070).

Although the trend in theory seems to be away from emphasis on over-simplified, two-dimensional, chaining-type associational process, even Mandler's (1963) proposal that verbal response units might be considered as n-dimensional spaces implies, although it is not explicitly stated, that the unit space is a verbal-associate space. Yet in his comments here he employed other terms which suggest the possibility that other than strictly cognitive, verbal processes may be involved in mediation or meaning. For a closely reasoned discussion of the inadequacies of both S-R and mediation theories of meaning, see Fodor (1965).

Jenkins (1963) summarized the situation with regard to mediation as one of essential agreement among investigators about the existence of a mediating process which is an implicit and unobservable response with stimulus properties, but one of uncertainty with

---

[21] In Russian terms, first signalling system activity.

respect to how these implicit processes are acquired, activated, inhibited, or employed. He warned (p. 212) that:

> So long as we work within a natural language framework, all
> our inference bases are confounded with hosts of overlapping
> processes, any or all of which may be intimately associated with
> the effects we observe.

It should be kept clearly in mind that in speaking about mediation
theory, we are referring fairly exclusively to theory within the realm
of verbal learning and verbal behavior. The reason for this is contained in the basis for selection of the experimental work covered
in this review.

Summary

To recapitulate, the area of verbal learning and verbal behavior is
the only contemporary experimental area in which there is anything
remotely approaching a systematic consideration of the questions
posed by the unsolved problem of meaning, or an attempt to give
the problem definition. Comments made here are not necessarily
globally applicable to any theory of behavior, or of learning, but
only to an assumptive extrapolation from such theory or theories
to "meaning theory."

With regard to meaning, the views of American theorists range
from the contention that any concept of meaning is unnecessary and
irrelevant, to rather reluctant admissions of the possibility that
meaning may be a critical variable which must be understood in
order to account for anything but the simplest forms of behavior.
It would appear that the concept of meaning is even moving beyond
the realm of intervening variable or of mediating response to another realm in which it may color, to some unspecified extent, the
heretofore clear concept of stimulus. At any rate, such a term as
"functional stimulus" has appeared in discussions within an S-R
context. The heritage of the study of meaning in the Pavlovian,
physiologically based classical conditioning model maintains in its
descendants an uneasy awareness of the neglected interior of the
"black box," but the pull of S-R simplicity mitigates in favor of its
denial.

It is always difficult to abandon simple models for more complex
ones. Simplification has obvious virtues, but the virtue dims when
the model fails to fit the growing body of evidence. It sometimes

seems as though simplicity is clung to for its own sake, rather than because it helps to separate the essential from the nonessential. With respect to meaning, it might be salutary for both the S-R and mediation theorists to pay heed to the admonition of one of their most distinguished spiritual progenitors who said:

It is the requirement that rules be communicable and teachable that makes simplicity desirable.. . . . It is men that are simple, not nature. The simplification of nature that is achieved by scientific laws is achieved at the expense of prediction. [Guthrie (1959) p. 162] and (p. 172) that

. . . models serve to help us conceive the relations between stimuli and responses, but they follow theory and do not lead.

The numerous theories of meaning should not be the source of quarrels and controversies, but should rather alert their adherents to the variety of psychological levels and aspects to which this one overworked and little understood term is applied. One research strategy, based on one theoretical position, may uncover significant factors which—although they may have to do with only a small portion of the total meaning of meaning, or only one level of meaning—may illuminate one corner in the darkness. Rather than to argue about which approach or theory is right, it might be more fruitful to see where each small piece fits into the total picture. The important thing is that experimenters in this area not be misled by preconceptions growing out of experience in other fields so that "trivial features may be unduly emphasized, while crucially important aspects may be postponed, neglected, or even overlooked entirely."[22]

References

BASTIAN, J. R. Response chaining in verbal transfer. Unpub. Ph.D. thesis, Univer. Minn., 1956.

BOUSFIELD, W. A. The occurrence of clustering in the recall of randomly arranged associates. *J. gen. Psychol.,* 1953, *49,* 229–240.

——. The problem of meaning in verbal learning.
In: COFER, C. N. 1961.

——, & COHEN, B. H. General review of a program of research on associative clustering.
In: JENKINS, J. J. 1955.

---

[22] Miller (1965, p. 15); see also Laffal (1964).

BOUSFIELD, W. A., COHEN, B. H., & WHITMARSH, G. A. Verbal generalization: A theoretical rationale and an experimental technique. *Tech. Rep.,* #23, Contract Nonr. 631(00), ONR & Univer. Conn., 1958.

——, WHITMARSH, G. A., & DANICK, J. J. Partial reponse identities in verbal generalization. *Psychol. Rep.,* 1958, *4,* 703–713.

BROWN, R. *Words and Things.* Glencoe, Ill.: The Free Press, 1958.

CARLIN, J. E. Word-association strength as a variable in verbal paired-associate learning. Unpub. Ph.D. thesis, Univer. Minn., 1958.

COFER, C. N. Associative commonality and rated similarity of certain words from Haagen's list. *Psychol. Rep.,* 1957, *3,* 603–606.

——. A study of clustering in free recall based on synonyms. *J. gen. Psychol.,* 1959, *60,* 3–10.

——. *Verbal Learning and Verbal Behavior.* New York: McGraw-Hill, 1961.

——, & FOLEY, J. P. Mediated generalization and the interpretation of verbal behavior: I. Prologomena. *Psychol. Rev.,* 1942, *49,* 513–540.

——, & MUSGRAVE, B. S. (Eds.). *Verbal Behavior and Learning: Problems and Processes.* New York: McGraw-Hill, 1963.

——, & SHEPP, B. E. Verbal context and perceptual recognition time. *Percept. mot. Skills,* 1957, *7,* 215–218.

——, & YARCZOWER, M. Further study of implicit verbal chaining in paired-associate learning. *Psychol. Rep.,* 1957, *3,* 453–456.

——, JANIS, M. G., & ROWELL, M. M. Mediated generalization and the interpretation of verbal behavior: III. Experimental study of antonym gradients. *J. exp. Psychol.,* 1943, *32,* 266–269.

COWDEN, R. C., REYNOLDS, D. J., & FORD, L. I. The verbal-behavior discrepancy in schizophrenia. *J. clin. Psychol.,* 1961, *17(4),* 406–408.

DEESE, J. Influence of inter-item associative strength upon immediate free recall. *Psychol. Rep.,* 1959a, *5,* 305–312.

——. On the prediction of occurrence of particular verbal intrusions in immediate recall. *J. exp. Psychol.,* 1959b, *58,* 17–22.

DICKEN, C. F. Connotative meaning as a determinant of stimulus generalization. *Tech. Rep.* #23, Contract N8onr. 66216, ONR & Univer. Minn., 1958.

FESTINGER, L., ET AL. Education for research in psychology. Seminar, 1958, ETB of APA. *Amer. Psychologist,* 1959, *14,* 167–179.

FODOR, J. A., Could meaning be an r_m? *J. verb. Learn. verb. Behav.,* 1965, *4(2),* 73-81.

FOLEY, J. P., JR., & COFER, C. N. Mediated generalization and the interpretation of verbal behavior: II. Experimental study of certain homophone and synonym gradients. *J. exp. Psychol.,* 1943, *32,* 168–175.

——, & MACMILLAN, Z. Mediated generalization and the interpretation of verbal behavior: V. "Free association" as related to differences in professional training. *J. exp. Psychol.,* 1943, *33,* 299–310.

——, & MATTHEWS, M. A. Mediated generalization and the interpretation of verbal behavior: IV. Experimental study of the development of inter-linguistic synonym gradients. *J. exp. Psychol.,* 1943, *33,* 188–200.

FURTH, H. G. Conceptual performance in deaf adults. *J. abnorm. soc. Psychol., 69(6),* 676-681, 1964.

GENDLIN, E. T. *Experiencing and the Creation of Meaning.* Glencoe, Ill.: The Free Press of Glencoe, 1962.

GOSS, A. E. Comments.
    In: COFER, C. N., & MUSGRAVE, B. S. 1963.

GUTHRIE, E. R. Association by contiguity.
    In: KOCH, S. 1959.

HAYAKAWA, S. I. How words change our lives. *Adventures of the Mind* #17. *Saturday Evening Post,* Philadelphia: Curtis, 1958.

HEBB, D. O. The American Revolution. *Amer. Psychologist,* 1960, *15,* 735–744.

HULL, C. L. Knowledge and purpose as habit mechanism. *Psychol. Rev.,* 1930, *37,* 511–525.

——. The problem of stimulus equivalence in behavior theory. *Psychol. Rev.,* 1939, *46,* 9–30.

JENKINS, J. J. (Ed.). Associative processes in verbal behavior: A report of the Minnesota Conference. Univer. Minn.: Dep't. Psychol., 1955.

——. A study of mediated association. *Studies in Verbal Behavior. Tech. Rep.* #2, NSF Grant, Univer. Minn., 1959.

——. Mediated associations: Paradigms and situations.
    In: COFER, C. N., & MUSGRAVE, B. S. 1963.

——, & RUSSELL, W. A. Associative clustering during recall. *J. abnorm. soc. Psychol.,* 1952, *47,* 818–821.

——, ——. Basic studies on individual and group behavior. *Annual Tech. Rep.,* Contract N8onr. 66216, ONR & Univer. Minn., 1956.

——, MINK, W. D., & RUSSELL, W. A. Associative clustering as a function of verbal association strength. *Psychol. Rep.,* 1958, *4,* 127–136.

—— & COFER, C. N. An exploratory study of discrete free association to compound verbal stimuli. *Psychol. Rep.,* 1957, *3,* 599–602.

KENDLER, H. H. The concept of the concept.
    In: MELTON, A. W. 1964.

KJELDERGAARD, P. M., & HORTON, D. L. An experimental analysis of asso-ciative factors in stimulus equivalence, response equivalence, and chaining paradigms. *Studies in Verbal Behavior. Tech. Rep.* #3, NSF Grant, Univer. Minn., 1960.

KLINE, N. S. (Ed.). Pavlovian Conference on Higher Nervous Activity. *Annals of N.Y. Acad. Sci.,* 1961, *92(3),* 813–1198.

KOCH, S. (Ed.). *Psychology: A Study of a Science.* I. Sensory, perceptual, and physiological formulations. New York: McGraw-Hill, 1959.

—— (Ed.). *Psychology: A Study of a Science.* II. General systematic formu-lations, learning, and special processes. New York: McGraw-Hill, 1959.

—— (Ed.). *Psychology: A Study of a Science.* VI. Investigations of man as socius: Their place in psychology and the social sciences. New York: McGraw-Hill, 1963.

KYRIAZIS, C. A comparison of semantic structures of ideal and actual concepts of the self and certain important socializing agents in male prisoner mental patients who have expressed aggressive behavior in the form of criminal assault, homicide, or rape. Unpub. Ph.D. thesis, George Washington Univer., Washington, D. C., 1963.

LACHMAN, R., & SANDERS, J. A. Concept shifts and verbal behavior. *J. exp. Psychol.*, 1963, *65(1)*, 22–29.

LAFFAL, J. Psycholinguistics and the psychology of language. *Amer. Psychologist*, 1964, *19(10)*, 813–815.

LICKLIDER, J. C. R. Three auditory theories.
In: KOCH, S. I. 1959.

LINDSLEY, O. R. Reduction in rate of vocal psychotic symptoms by differential positive reinforcement. *J. exp. Anal. Behav.*, 1959, *2*, 269.

MALCOLM, M. Behaviorism as a philosophy of psychology.
In: WANN, T. W. 1964.

MANDLER, G. Comments on Professor Jenkins' paper.
In: COFER, C. N., & MUSGRAVE, B. S. 1963.

MANN, J. Comments.
In: SKINNER, B. F. 1954.

MELTON, A. W. (Ed.). *Categories of Human Learning.* New York: Academic Press, 1964.

MILLER, G. A. Some preliminaries to psycholinguistics. *Amer. Psychologist,* 1965, *20(1)*, 15–20.

MINK, W. D. Semantic generalization as related to word association. *Tech. Rep.* #17, Contract. N8onr. 66216, ONR & Univer. Minn., 1957. See also *Psychol. Rep.*, 1963, *12*, 59–67.

MOSS, S. A. A study of the semantic generalization effect. Unpub. Ph.D. thesis, Univer. Calif., 1960.

MOWRER, O. H. The psychologist looks at language. *Amer. Psychologist,* 1954, *9*, 660–694.

NOBLE, C. E. An analysis of meaning. *Psychol. Rev.*, 1952, *59*, 421–430.

——. Meaningfulness and familiarity.
In: COFER, C. N., & MUSGRAVE, B. S. 1963.

O'NEIL, W. M. The effect of verbal association on tachistoscopic recognition. *Tech. Rep.* #4, Contract N8onr. 66216, ONR & Univ. Minn., 1953.

OSGOOD, C. E. Meaningful similarity and interference in learning. *J. exp. Psychol.*, 1946, *36*, 277–301.

——. The nature and measurement of meaning. *Psychol. Bull.*, 1952, *49*, 197–237.

——. *Method and Theory in Experimental Psychology.* New York: Oxford, 1956.

OSGOOD, C. E. Psycholinguistics.
  In: COFER, C. N. 1961.
——. Comments on Professor Bousfield's paper.
  In: KOCH, S. VI. 1963.
PERLS, F. S. *Ego, Hunger and Aggression.* London: George Allen & Unwin Ltd., 1947.
PLATT, J. R. Strong inference. *Science,* 1964, *146,* 347–353.
RAZRAN, G. H. S. A quantitative study of meaning by a conditioned salivary technique (semantic conditioning). *Science,* 1939, *90,* 89–90.
——. Semantic and phonetographic generalizations of salivary conditioning to verbal stimuli. *J. exp. Psychol.,* 1949, *39,* 642–652.
——. A note on second-order conditioning—and secondary reinforcement. *Psychol. Rev.,* 1955, *62,* 327–332.
——. Discussion. (a)
  In: KLINE, N. S. 1961.
——. The observable unconscious and the inferable conscious in current Soviet psychophysiology: Interoceptive conditioning, semantic conditioning, and the orienting reflex. *Psychol. Rev.,* 1961, *68,* 81–147. (b)
RUSSELL, W. A., & STORMS, L. H. Implicit verbal chaining in paired-associate learning. *J. exp. Psychol.,* 1955, *49,* 287–293.
RYAN, J. J., III. An experimental comparison of response transfer facilitated by meaningfully similar and associated verbal stimuli. *Tech. Rep.* #21, Contract N8onr. 66216, ONR & Univer. Minn., 1957.
——. Comparison of verbal response transfer mediated by meaningfully similar and associated stimuli. *J. exp. Psychol.,* 1960, *60,* 408–415.
SCHULZ, R. W., & MCGEHEE, N. E. Mediation in verbal paired-associate learning. Unpub. paper, 1960.
SHIPLEY, W. C. Indirect conditioning. *J. gen. Psychol.,* 1935, *12,* 337–357.
SKINNER, B. F. *Science and Human Behavior.* New York: Macmillan, 1953.
——. A new method for the experimental analysis of the behavior of psychotic patients. *J. nerv. ment. Disease,* 1954, *120,* 403–406.
STAATS, A. W. Comments.
  In: COFER, C. N., & MUSGRAVE, B. S. 1963.
——. Conditioned stimuli, conditioned reinforcers, and word meaning. *Tech. Rep.* #27, Contract Nonr. 2794(02), ONR & Ariz. Sta. Univer., 1964.
——, & STAATS, C. K. Meaning and *m:* Separate but correlated. *Psychol. Rev.,* 1959, *66,* 136–144.
——, ——. *Complex Human Behavior.* New York: Holt, Rinehart & Winston, 1963.
——, ——, & FINLEY, J. R. Operant conditioning of a semantically identified word class. *Tech. Rep.* #14, Contract Nonr. 2794(02), ONR & Ariz. Sta. Univer., 1961.
TAYLOR, W. L. "Cloze Procedure": A new tool for measuring readability. *Journalism Quarterly,* 1953, *30,* 415–433.

——. Application of "Cloze" and entropy measures to the study of contextual constraint in samples of continuous prose. *Dissertation Abstr.*, 1955, *15*, 464-465.

——. Recent developments in the use of "Cloze Procedure." *Journalism Quarterly*, 1956, *33*, 42-48.

UNDERWOOD, B. J., & SCHULZ, R. W. *Meaningfulness and Verbal Learning.* Philadelphia: J. B. Lippincott, 1960.

WANN, T. W. (Ed.). *Behaviorism and Phenomenology.* Chicago: Univer. Chicago Press, 1964.

WERNER, H., & KAPLAN, B. *Symbol Formation.* New York: John Wiley and Sons, 1963.

WICKENS, D. D., & BRIGGS, G. E. Mediated stimulus generalization as a factor in sensory pre-conditioning. *J. exp. Psychol.*, 1951, *42*, 197-200.

Russian Theory

As long as we lack a generally accepted system incorporating all the available psychological knowledge, any factual discovery inevitably leads to the creation of a new theory to fit the newly observed facts. . . . In modern psychology great discoveries are made daily only to be shrouded in ad hoc *theories. . . .* [Vigotsky (1962) p. 10].

General conclusions

Keeping in mind that the Russian material covered in this context was selected on the basis of its availability in translation, and that much of the work referred to was available only in secondary sources, the conclusions offered can only be tentative. First, there is no apparent Russian controversy with respect to theories of meaning. Furthermore, it is really inaccurate to speak of Russian theories of meaning, for there is no research which is directly addressed to this problem. Russian experimentalists have traditionally been concerned primarily with theories of central nervous system functioning. Psychology as the science and practice is defined in the United States hardly exists in the Soviet Union. Psychology *qua* psychology is largely pedagogical, or developmental. Scientific or experimental psychology is solidly grounded in dialectical materialism[1] and uses as its experimental model the Pavlovian classical conditioning paradigm.[2]

---

[1] See Pick (1964), and Tucker (1956).

[2] It should be noted that most of the Russian work covered in this book was published before 1957, consequently these remarks and generalizations apply only to pre-1957 Russian work. In a symposium (Cole, Maltzman and Brozek, 1965) on current trends in Soviet psychology, Cole pointed out that recent trends in the USSR are away from Pavlovianism. Brozek added that American psychologists are much more Pavlovian than the Russians. Although Soviet psychologists are oriented toward working on Pavlovian-type problems, they are very familiar with the Western literature, and more general psychological theories are becoming more important (e.g., information theory, mathematical models, cybernetics). They are interested in teaching machines, but find Skinner's ideas strange, and

Lenin stated that the scientific psychologist should study the nervous processes—"the material substrate of psychic phenomena."[3] This "material substrate" which is the proper object of psychological investigation is the physiological *function,* or neurodynamics, not the anatomical structure of the brain and central nervous system. Thus the major tasks are to explore the laws of movement and interaction of nervous processes.

Soviet psychological experimentation seeks to elaborate and explicate the known laws of radiation of excitatory and inhibitory processes and their mutual induction, as well as to discover new ways to investigate and analyze those forms of neural activity which cannot be understood in terms of known laws. Russian psychological experimentation is therefore not concerned with working toward theories of meaning, or perception, or learning as such, but instead utilizes these processes to study neurodynamics. Consequently, anything that is said about Russian theory of meaning is inferred from theories of functional systems.

Meaning and the signalling systems

However, with respect to *a* theory of meaning, Russian theories of the development and functioning of the signalling systems[4] seem most relevant. It should be remembered that according to Russian theory, there are three major functional levels or systems:

1. The reflex system, consisting of the inborn, phylogenetically determined connections between unconditioned stimuli and unconditioned responses.

2. The first signalling system, consisting of ontogenetically determined conditional reflexes. Connections are formed through the experience of the individual with the objects and events in his environment. Such linkages are formed according to the laws of physical similarity, spatial and/or temporal contiguity, or through the mediation of biological activity. That is, dissimilar stimuli

---

favor Piaget's more cognitive theories of learning. Maltzman reported that studies in problem solving and concept formation are popular, that these studies emphasize cognitive functions, and follow the conceptions of Miller, Galanter and Pribram (1960). Maltzman added that Russian psychologists seem to regard Tolman as the greatest American psychologist.

3 See Boiko (1961, p. 1).

4 Most of the material on signalling systems and orienting reflex is from Luria's, Sokolov's, and Bridger's chapters in Brazier (1960), see also Ban (1964).

having no obvious physical or logical connection with each other may become linked during the satisfaction of some biological need. The content of the first signalling system in man is determined by the society in which the individual lives, but the mechanism is biological. Conditioning learning theories are relevant to this level, and aspects of human cognition which are perceptual, sensory, primitive, or prelogical are governed by first signalling system laws. Although this sensory mode of cognition shows its influence in many areas of human development, in man it does not normally exist isolated from the second signalling system.

3. The second signalling system is formed from the first signalling system through the process of substituting verbal symbols for verbal designations of the direct sensory or perceptual impressions. Thus man is able to manipulate and group reality not only with respect to its form and appearance, but also in terms of relationships and interactions. The second signalling system makes it possible for man to acquire, store, and communicate knowledge without direct immediate experience of things.

Words as such may belong to either the first or second signalling systems or to both simultaneously. Having attributes of both signals and symbols, they are used not only to indicate objects but also to represent them, taking the place of objects or events not present, yet *not* replacing the emotional situation in which the objects or events may have occurred.

Meaning, central processes, and language

From this we might infer, with additional evidence from the nature of the Soviet semantic-proprioceptive experiments, that the Russian concept of the *meaning* of the symbol would include not only the representation of the object (e.g., its image, or its verbal description) but also the emotional situation, and that the processes involved would be differentiated in some way from, even though interacting intimately with, the cognitive, second signalling system processes.

Language, as the basis for the second signalling system, has as its principal feature the symbol, and specifies alternatives and ways of measuring these alternatives. Having an alphabet and a grammar, language is both measurable and programmed. It is acquired by the individual child first through imitation, then through linkage of the word and object by means of direct experience of the word and object together (first signalling system). Two requisites, one biological and the other social, are essential to the development of the signalling systems. The biological prerequisite is a self-signalling system having two aspects to its development: 1) the ability to produce the signals through imitation, and 2) the repetition of the signals in conjunction with activity with and manipulation of the objects signalized. Through repeated activity with an object in a variety of contexts, the child develops generalized sensory representations of the object, and this generalization or process of abstraction serves to separate the meaning of the word from the action or the object itself.

The reverse process, in which different words are used along with similar objects and actions, serves to differentiate the essential and the nonessential qualities and features of an object or an action. By acquiring the ability to delay the response to an object or an event (which may be due to a biosocial maturation process, or possibly to the acquisition of language itself) a self-signalling system is interposed between stimulus and response, and operations can be carried out internally rather than externally.

In the structure of the connections of the second signalling system, certain complexes of stimuli, through "intersystem" connections, determine the variable relationships between direct stimuli and responses. The entire nervous activity represents a continuous conditioning of current reactions by past experience and, simultaneously, modification of existing structural traces (temporary connections) under the influence of new combinations of external conditions. The latter partly strengthen, partly differentiate, and partly extinguish previously existing conditioned reflexes (Boiko, 1961). The role of temporary connections which are of an associative type and unreinforced, is decisive in the transfer to a new stimulus of a response developed to another stimulus (Degtyar', Znanenskaya, and Kol'tsova, 1959, p. 54).[5]

Sokolov (in Luria, 1960, pp. 409-410) asserted that although such a specific stimulus as a word can be precisely differentiated from other words, it can at the same time evoke strong generalized involuntary responses. He theorized that the cortex, which influences the activating system, is itself activated by generalized responses through the reticular formation. During the course of the elaboration of conditioned reflexes, some facilitory mechanisms are operative which are specifically connected with the meaning

---

[5] See also Bridger (1960).

of the stimulus. Although meaning is not defined here, but is rather employed as an explanatory concept, it might be possible to view the "facilitory mechanism" *as* the stimulus meaning itself.

Razran (1961, p. 126) summarized the Russian position as follows:

> Language . . . is not just an array of second-order conditioned responses or signals, of which animals also are capable, but it is a special higher level human system characterized by being not a signal of one signal . . . but a signal of many signals, a second-order conditioned response to a compound conditioned stimulus . . . a system that by its very nature does not merely link and analyze but synthesizes . . . its acquired information.

Signalling system transfer and interaction

Much of the Russian experimental work is addressed to the problem of transfer from the first to the second signalling system (concept formation), and to the interaction between the two systems. Since responses in the second signalling system are closely dependent upon the first, the study of the second in isolation is impossible. However, reaction time, or response latency, has often been used as a measure of inhibition in the second system, and it is thought that word association tests give the most valuable information with respect to other kinds of disturbances in the second system. Responses conditioned with verbal commands have been used extensively to study functions in the first system and the interactions between the two systems (Astrup, 1962). Faddeeva (1956, p. 171) stated that

> with the aid of electively generalized verbal impressions and the reactions connected with these, the second signalling system regulates within the complex dynamic pattern the interrelations of the multitude of impressions of related specific objects and their verbal designations, as well as the dynamic interrelations between the patterns of direct connections and verbal associations.

Meaning and the central nervous system

According to Bridger (1960), it is the neocortex which is electrophysiologically able to differentiate signals from what is signallized, something the limbic system cannot do. Thus the more the limbic system is activated, and the stronger the emotion aroused by a stimulus, the more likely it is that motor activity will be involved, and the more difficult differentiation will be. Likewise, inhibition of the neocortex—as in sleep, hallucinogenic drugs, sensory deprivation, and hypnosis—tends to shift cognitive processes toward first signalling system activity and to lessen the gap between the signal and the signified (e.g., the phenomenon of chronogenetic disinhibition).

Objects or events are similar when and because they share common elements. According to Boiko (1961) identical stimulus elements activate the same complexes of cerebral cells. Chuprikova (1961) speculated that the cortical representation of verbal stimuli is such that "cell structures related to logical structures similar in meaning have also correspondingly tighter functional and spatio-structural relations in the cerebral cortex, as compared with cell-systems related to words dissimilar in meaning" (p. 80). However, lest we slip into an entirely solipsistic frame of reference, let us reiterate the fact that it is not possible to detect, from the Russian literature available in the form of translation or review articles, any definition of meaning or any theory as to how meaning is acquired, although there are references to meaning and the effects of meaning on neurodynamic processes. It might be assumed that meaning is formed by the elaboration of conditioned reflex connections and their systematization, and

> . . . radiating over the cerebral cortex, colliding with each other, summating and entering into complex inductive relations, these processes (of excitation and inhibition) give origin to a multitude of new functional connections and determine the whole complex picture of the system of dynamics which is expressed in the external effects of reactions [Boiko, (1961) p. 10].

General theoretical orientation

Some references to a biologically based and determined system of self-stimulation which is involved in transfer from the first to the second signalling system are highly reminiscent of Osgood's notion of the mediating process. It can be inferred that this system of self-stimulation includes, in Osgood's system as well as the Russian formulation, affective as well as cognitive elements. Osgood (1961) explicitly stated that mediating responses are largely based on visceral responses because the latter are readily available and widely generalized. Furthermore, he asserted that, because affect *is* massive and widely generalized, its relevant aspects can be picked up on a verbal instrument such as the Semantic Differential and need not be directly investigated. Russian experimenters, conversely, use physiological measures of affective processes to investigate the function of the signalling system. That is, instead of inferring some kind of mediating response, and utilizing it as a hypothetical construct in theory, or as an intervening variable in experimentation, Russian experimenters are more likely to attempt a direct investigation on the self-signalling system, or at least of elements thereof, as a means of studying neurodynamics.

The rationale for particular kinds of studies possibly suggests a kind of theoretical orientation toward the matter under investigation. Semantic conditioning studies, for example, are thought to lend themselves to the uncovering of an area of experimentally separable meaning-units which continually enter into complex functional relationships with each other and with non-meaning-units. These units, existing both in and out of awareness, form controlling rather than controlled systems, whether they are conscious or not. Razran (1961, pp. 108–109) emphasized the fact that

> Russian psychophysiology accords a *sui generis* status to verbal conditioning, regarding it as not merely a case of simple second-order conditioning but as a special higher-level 'signal-of-signals', conditioned response basis of abstraction or high-level generalization. That a word is by its very nature an abstraction is taken very seriously in both its genetic and ontological aspects as a problem fit for both experimental analysis and clinical research.

Some of the experimental findings from such investigations, which are discussed in less global theoretical terms than neurodynamic theory and which have to do with the formation and development of the second signalling system and with transfer between the two signalling systems, might have some implications for the pursuit of a theory of meaning, and will be discussed in the following chapter.

Differences between American and Russian theory and experimentation

What seems to be strikingly different about American and Russian theory is first the noncontroversial nature of Soviet theory, and second something that is difficult to label, but is related in some way to the first point. To a large extent the first difference may be due to the dogma of Marxist dialectic materialism which provides the frame of reference for all efforts, artistic as well as scientific, and which rejects and suppresses whatever tends to break or even stretch its boundaries. The effect is what appears to be a unified effort toward common goals.

The second difference has to do with the way in which experimental results are handled. Interpretations of the data from any given experiment are at once more specific and more general than is the case with American analyses. That is, conclusions are generally limited to the concrete area under particular investigation and, in some cases, to possible generalizations in terms of the data's significance to neurodynamic theory. As Berlyne (1964) pointed out, the theoretical arguments of Russian researchers often bear little relationship to hypotheses implying distinct empirical consequences.

Berlyne (1964) quoted Zinchenko (1962) as taking to task the psychologists' operating in the empiricist-associationist behaviorist tradition. The Russian researcher views this notion of associative bonds as too mechanical and too passive, citing Pavlov's dictum that association involves both analysis and synthesis. Russian experimenters criticize the "sterile S — R formula" that responses are determined solely by external stimuli as indicating a failure to recognize the importance of internal processes, including consciousness, and of physiological experimental findings and explanations.

Russian theory seems to contain no body of subtheory, such as learning theory, theory of perception, or personality theory, as does American psychology. This may have the advantage of keeping the experimenters' eyes more firmly fixed on the ultimate goal: namely, to understand the total functioning of the whole individual, even though part-functions may be studied in individual experiments.

References

ASTRUP, C. *Schizophrenia: Conditional Reflex Studies.* Springfield, Ill.: Charles C. Thomas, 1962.

BAN, T. *Conditioning and Psychiatry.* Chicago: Aldine, 1964.

BERLYNE, D. E. Haply I may remember and haply may forget. *Review of:* ZINCHENKO, P. I. 1962. *Contemporary Psychol.,* 1964, *9(8),* 323–324.

BOIKO, E. I. (Ed.). *Studies in Higher Neurodynamics as Related to Problems of Psychology.* Washington, D.C.: Office Tech. Serv., 1961.

BRAZIER, M. A. B. (Ed.). The Central Nervous System and Behavior. (Transactions of the third conference sponsored by the Josiah Macy, Jr., Foundation and the National Science Foundation). New York: Josiah Macy, Jr., Foundation, 1960.

BRIDGER, W. H. Signalling systems in the development of cognitive functions. *In:* BRAZIER, M. A. B. 1960.

CHUPRIKOVA, N. I. Dynamics of nervous processes at the differentiation of direct and verbal stimuli in adults. *In:* BOIKO, E. I. 1961.

COFER, C. N. (Ed.). *Verbal Learning and Verbal Behavior.* New York: McGraw-Hill, 1961.

DEGTYAR', YE. N., ZNANENSKAYA, A. M., & KOL'TSOVA, M. M. Physiological mechanisms of certain forms of generalization in young children. *In: Works of the Institute of Physiology.* VIII. (Trans. from Russian). Foreign Tech. Div., Air Force Systems Command, Wright-Patterson AFB, Ohio: 1959.

FADDEEVA, V. K. On the role of elective irradiation and induction in certain complex forms of joint activity by the two signalling systems. *In:* IVANOV-SMOLENSKY, A. G., ET AL. II. 1956.

IVANOV-SMOLENSKY, A. G., ET AL. (Eds.). *Works of the Institute of Higher Nervous Activity: Pathophysiological Series.* II. Moscow: Academy of Sciences of the USSR, 1956. Jerusalem: Israel Program for Scientific Translations, 1960. (Office Tech. Serv., U. S. Dep't. Commerce, Washington, D. C., 20025, PST Catalogue #72).

LURIA, A. R. Verbal regulation of behavior. *In:* BRAZIER, M. A. B. 1960.

MILLER, G. A., GALANTER, E., & PRIBRAM, K. H. *Plans and the Structure of Behavior.* New York: Holt, 1960.

OSGOOD, C. E. Comments on Professor Bousfield's paper. *In:* COFER, C. N. 1961.

PICK, H. L., JR. Perception in Soviet psychology. *Psychol. Bull.,* 1964, *62,* 21–35.

RAZRAN, G. H. S. The observable unconscious and the inferable conscious in current Soviet psychophysiology: Interoceptive conditioning, semantic conditioning, and the orienting reflex. *Psychol. Rev.*, 1961, *68*, 81–147.

SOKOLOV, E. N. Neuronal models and the orienting reflex. *In:* BRAZIER, M. A. B. 1960.

TUCKER, R. C. *Stalin and the Uses of Psychology.* Santa Monica, Calif.: Rand, 1956.

VIGOTSKY, L. S. *Thought and Language.* Cambridge, Mass.: The M.I.T. Press, 1962.

ZINCHENKO, P. I. (Involuntary Remembering). Moscow: Academy of Pedagogical Sciences RSFSR, 1962.

Implications

Meaning is a harlot among words, it is a temptress who seduces . . . from the path of intellectual chastity [Cherry (1961)].

General: The definition of meaning

One conclusion seems eminently clear from the material here presented: meaning, the elusive Cinderella, is still at large, evading identification and capture. Perhaps one of the difficulties lies in the various images that her various suitors have of her—images that have led them to seek her in different places, using different ways. Some see her as a simple-minded creature, some as complex, subtle, and sophisticated. Some have focused on her intellectual qualities, and some imagine her to be sensitive and emotional. Some, overwhelmed by her mystery, have from the first contented themselves with living with her only in fantasy, concluding that she is essentially unknown and unknowable.

Since it is not yet possible to describe the lady in any detail, the appropriate question to ask seems to be whether we have any clues as to where she might be hiding. If so, which clues might be worth pursuing, and which ones seem to lead to dead ends?

In the course of presenting experimental work, selected because it presumably is in some way related to the problem of "meaning," we have encountered four major, explicit or implicit hypotheses: 1) the meaning of anything (stimulus) can be defined in terms of the response to it; 2) meaning can be understood in terms of simple associative (direct) connections between stimulus and response; 3) meaning can best be conceptualized as a hypothetical construct or as an intervening variable—a mediating process which is essentially unobserved and unobservable and consists of scaled-down versions of previously overt responses which, when elicited, serve as stimuli for other overt responses; 4) meaning might be regarded as a complex interconnected response system, including visceral, sensory, and cognitive elements.

It is important to keep in mind the fact that hypotheses arise out of experimental results, and in turn determine the structure of subsequent experimental investigations. Thus, when we classify hypotheses here, we are referring perhaps more to the methodological approach than to the general theoretical orientation of the investigators. It is an exaggeration to speak of clear-cut divisions in theoretical orientation regarding the meaning of meaning. What should be conveyed is that some investigators have chosen to approach the immensely complex problem in a direction that moved from the specific and simple to the more general, whereas others have moved in the opposite direction. Both ways can be fruitful so long as the experimental method is not mistaken for the psychological process itself, and so long as the limitations of the experimental findings are recognized as possibly a function of limitations in the method.

Contemporary American experimental efforts to cope with the problem of meaning seem to divide themselves into two major categories: 1) the "severed-head" approach of the verbal-learning theorists and 2) the "automatic machine" approach of the instrumental or operant conditioners. The first group, heirs to the associationistic theory of the past, has moved farther away from any concern with the emotional or autonomic-based processes toward more exclusive concern with cognitive or conceptual processes. The second group, heirs of Watsonian-Skinnerian behaviorism and still stoutly denying the relevance of anything within the "black box," is beginning to deal with the knotty problems posed by human experimental subjects by admitting verbal behavior to consideration. In operant experiments, verbal instructions on the stimulus side and verbal report on the response side are beginning to be studied. In verbal conditioning experiments, verbal behavior is boldly viewed as operant behavior, and verbal stimuli as reinforcement. Furthermore, verbal-learning theorists are beginning to sound more like operant conditioners when they speak of eliciting and reinforcing mediation responses, which suggests a rather strange and clandestine wedding of the scotomized interior and the more acceptable exterior of the "black box."

Meanwhile, Russian experimenters, heirs of a union of neurophysiological and psychological families and perhaps unaware of the inviolacy of the "black box," have proceeded to probe its interior by cutting new windows in the walls in the hope of letting in some light. Aware of the potency of the word, they have found new ways to observe the exercise of its power in the internal economy of the functioning human organism as well as to measure its efficacy in regulating the more grossly observable behavior of the individual human being. Thus, the movement in Soviet experimentation seems to be toward emphasis upon the essential interrelatedness and unity of emotional and cognitive function and process, of responsiveness *within* the individual organism and responses *of* the organism. A few American experimenters have begun to move in this direction too.

It would appear that we are still a long way from any kind of inclusive theory of meaning. What has emerged with considerable clarity is that the word "meaning" refers to so many different concepts, constructs, functional systems, processes, and areas of "experience" that it requires the flexibility of a mountain goat to leap from level to level. The word has been used as an explanatory concept (e.g., generalization takes place along a meaning dimension) and as the concept being explained (e.g., meaning *is* stimulus or response generalization). The literature is rife with such implied tautologies. To be fair it must be noted that much of this may be an artifact of the fact that we have included in our consideration both studies that have been directly concerned with the nature of meaning, and studies that have been concerned with some other problem into which meaning enters as a variable.

Nevertheless, this points up the necessity for arriving at a consensus with regard to what the referent is when we use the word "meaning" in psychological experiments, and highlights the lack of concensus at present. This is not to say that we must know what meaning *is,* or be agreed upon a global theory of meaning before we can use meaning as a variable. This would be as absurd as saying that we have to know what meaning is before we can proceed to try to find out what it is. It is to urge, rather, that we recognize that the word "meaning," as it is used at the present time, has not just a single, well-understood referent, but many and varied referents. It is to insist, furthermore, that we specify the particular referent of the term "meaning" if and when it is used as a variable, or as an explanatory principle, or as an interpretive base in experimentation.

There is little concensus even when we narrow the problem down to what we refer to when we speak not of meaning in general, but of the meaning of a word. The term is used in experimental work as variously referring to the assumed logical connections between a given word and other words, to a word's dictionary definition, to its denotative function in pointing to an object or event, to its connotative function (as in the Semantic Differential), to its associative value in a given context, to the frequency of its appearance as a response to something, and so on. Perhaps the very fact that a single verbal symbol is used to connote so many varied functions and processes with a minimum of communicational confusion suggests that a basic process is involved in all of them and that we have been studying the manifestations of a single process rather than the process itself.

Again, this does not suggest that it is not legitimate to approach the study of a larger process through observation, examination, and analysis of its manifestations. As a matter of fact, it may be not only a fruitful, but perhaps the only possible method of approach. But it is imperative that as experimenters we keep in mind what we are doing, and communicate the limitations when we report our findings.

It is more than probable that the only way open to us at present is to explore many avenues in many directions, some of which may bring us to way stations, some of which will be dead ends.

It is likely that the journey will be long and arduous, and that it will be accomplished by taking one small step at a time. Lest we lose our footing and stumble because we look up and ahead too much, we must concentrate on the terrain and on how and where we take each step. From time to time, though, it is salutary to look up and survey the broader countryside, and glimpse the heights toward which we struggle an inch at a time. The existence of the heights does not denigrate our plodding; it justifies the effort.

Methodology

One question raised by the Russian experimental work which has important methodological implications for the Amercian work in psychophysiology in particular, but less so for other kinds of experimentation, is: what is the difference between the orienting response and other kinds of responses?

Let us take a specific example: The GSR may appear as a response to a particular stimulus. It is also a segment of the response pattern (orienting reflex) to novelty. Is it possible to distinguish this response *qua* response from the "same" response as a part of the orienting reflex? If, for example, we condition, extinguish and recondition the GSR, do our results show conditioning and reconditioning, or are we merely showing a switch from the orienting response to a "real" response, and back to the orienting response as conditions change and, perhaps, introduce novelty? What constitutes "novelty"?

Are we justified in making logical assumptions with respect to the definition of novelty, or must we define as novel that which elicits the orienting reflex? Sokolov (1960), for example, showed that after the orienting response to a word stimulus disappeared, other words of similar semantic meaning did not evoke the orienting response, whereas words of different meanings did. Is a novel stimulus, then, one whose meaning in a given context departs from the meaning of the context within which it occurs? And if so, what determines the meaning of the contextual situation and of the deviant stimulus?

Answers to questions such as these, it would seem, are rather critical for the interpretation of even the most basic research on physiological measures. When it comes to the interpretation of results from experiments using physiological responses as measures of *other* processes, they are even more crucial. Again, we need more data from more refined experimental methods based upon the control of hitherto unrecognized variables, and more exhaustive analysis of the data thus obtained.

Related to the question of when a given reaction is a response to a specific stimulus and when it is an orienting response (to novelty of the stimulus) is another question of even broader scope and significance: what is a stimulus and what is a response? The adequacy of our current concepts of stimulus and response has persistently been questioned. Several American experimenters have raised questions about what the "actual" or "functional" stimulus in an experiment is,—whether it is an eliciting or a reinforcing stimulus—but there has been little if any systematic investigation of the importance or extent of the problem.

In Russia, Mkrtycheva (1956) showed that even the simplest stimulus, such as a spot of light, must be viewed as a complex stimulus, the individual qualities of which may be analyzed without the participation of the second signalling system (without verbalization.) When a subject was instructed to respond (press a balloon) at the appearance of a light spot, his responses were different from when he pressed at the cessation of the spot. In the latter case, the response latency was inversely related to the duration of the light stimulus, while the response duration was directly proportional to the stimulus duration. In the first case there was no such relationship. What is the stimulus in this experiment: the light spot, certain qualities of the light spot, the verbal instructions, something else, or all of these? Luria's experiments with children[1] also show how responses are affected by certain physical properties of the stimulus, and how they may be altered by the subject's own verbalizations. Are these verbalizations, then, responses, or do they constitute a portion of a complex stimulus?

Some of the questions raised about the definition of stimulus and response are conceptual problems with methodological practices which have conceptual consequence. But even the clear-cut operational definition of stimulus and response proposed by the operant conditioners is subject to question when verbal instructions are used with human subjects, when symbolic rewards and punishments serve as reinforcement, and when the subjects' verbal reports are considered along with their instrumental responses.

Along with the question as to what is stimulus and what is response comes the uncertainty as to what constitutes the connection between them. By and large, American behaviorists have been more interested in, and focused on, the stimulus and response and have been content to make assumptions about the connection in terms of some hypothesized mediating process—if they felt the need to explain the connection at all. Russian experimenters, however, have been more interested in the connection, and have utilized observable stimuli and responses to elucidate the central processes, pushing the limits of what was observable farther and farther into the internal functioning systems of the organism.

Perhaps the hypothesized mediating processes of some American theorists are not so implicit and unobservable as it has been thought. Perhaps the mediation hypothesis itself is a concept which interferes with rather than facilitates experimental development in American S-R theory.

In other words, the relegation to the never-never land of intervening variable—a land which need not be explored or mapped—of all phenomena defying explanation in terms of a simple model

---

[1] See p. 99–100 above.

or presenting methodological problems with respect to observation, may allow us to cling to an overly simplified theory long after it has served its usefulness, at the expense of moving on to more fruitful models and methods.

In general, S-R theory is unidirectional and unidimensional. The feedback concept of information theory and of instrumental operant conditioning theory has, to some extent, altered the directional aspects. Such developments as Osgood's Semantic Differential have added dimensionality, although the fact that it is grounded in verbal associationism tends to limit its generality if not its usefulness. Perhaps it is time to recognize the heuristic limits of oversimplification and face the hard reality of the complexity of the functioning human organism.

> A vital psychology must be rooted in . . . man . . . (a model) whose concepts will not be essentially derived from methods of study but rather from the functioning of human life. ... Explicit or not, the concept of human nature we hold guides our research directives [Feifel (1964, pp. 418-9)].

This is not to suggest that we substitute the "soft" methods of inference for the "hard" methodology of experimental observation and control; nor is it to suggest that we abandon the rich harvest of years of S-R experimentation and theorizing. It is to suggest, instead, that we acknowledge that even the most stripped-down experimental situation which includes a human animal as its subject is not necessarily simple just because the experimenter wills it so; that some single environmental event is the only thing being reacted to just because the experimenter calls it the stimulus; that a single observable motor or verbal bit of behavior is the whole of the reaction just because the experimenter designates it as the response. It is to suggest, as a first step, that we take an enlarged, multidimensional view of what is stimulus and what is response.

If stimulus is viewed as a patterning of internal and external events, and response as a patterning of behavior which includes events within the skin as well as the gross acts of the organism within the external environment, then the problem of mediation may be left to the physiologists and neurologists. It may make it possible for the phenomenologists and the behaviorist to communicate with each other in a common language to the enrichment of both. Would it not be possible to view "experience," or "experiencing" as the phenomenologist refers to it, as the totality of the organism's responsiveness—the patterning of changes brought about by and specific to the stimulus but taking place in a context of ongoing processes and in turn altering the context?

Is it not possible that meaning and the phenomenology of the experiencing organism are one and the same thing? In this case, the meaning of a stimulus could justifiably be defined in terms of the response to it, the term "response" being understood to refer to the pattern of changes-within-a-context.

Another possible way of looking at it would be to include the context—defined here as the particular state or pattern of the on-going processes *within* the individual respondent—as an integral part of the stimulus along with the *external* context of the stimulating event. In this case, the meaning of a particular event would be a patterned function of both stimulus and response elements, rather than single links in a chain.

It is certainly not inconceivable that the phenomenology of an individual, which consists of all possible meanings, is a product of the conditioning process—conditioning in both the classical and operant sense (if indeed they are different processes and not just different partial segments of the same process). That is to say that it is possible that what is referred to as "experiential" could be internal connections (CRs) which are felt rather than observed from the outside, and which, instead of being just a substrate for behavior, may be an integral part of the complex S-R network. Reflex "unconditioned" responses undoubtedly are occurring continuously, and are not just triggered off by external stimuli discretely applied. Connections between conditional stimuli and unconditioned responses must be continuously formed by chance as well as by design, many of them essentially inextinguishable either because of diffuse generalization or because they are sufficiently reinforced by their consequences (internal changes that are taking place).[2] Such a view, of course, assumes not just first- or second-order conditioning, but "*n*th-order," or "*n*th-dimensional," which we might possibly demonstrate in the laboratory, once we have taken the broader view of stimulus and response and/or of "consequences" (reinforcement).

To be sure, such a view implies staggering complexities which

---

[2] Many American experimenters have held that visceral responses are not subject to instrumental conditioning because they have no consequences and thus are not reinforced. It seems quite possible, however, that visceral responses *are* continuously reinforced by their consequences, the only difference being that the consequences do not occur in the external environment and thus are not observed. For a broader discussion of these questions, see Miller (1961).

cannot be dealt with all at once. It involves the exercise of tremendous ingenuity to devise new methods of observation, of simultaneously recording many variables, and new computer programs for processing masses of data. But it would seem that if man is ingenious enough to solve the complexities involved in launching a machine into the vastness of space; to guide it unerringly to its "small" target millions of miles away; to fill it with equipment that can observe and transmit the observations back to earth-bound recording devices; and to predict the exact moment in time when the half-year journey from earth to Mars will end, he should not be intimidated by the complexities of the workings within himself.

The real point is not how difficult the road, or how distant the heights may be. The important question is: can we, by taking a fresh and broader look at our objectives, devise better ways of reaching them, even though the new and better ways will still have to be traveled only with small plodding steps?

If the implications of the experimental work under consideration relating to the possibility of finding a simple definition of meaning or a simple method to continue the search are discouraging, the implications relating to a variety of areas of psychological interest are exciting.

Some areas of psychological concern

Sticks and stones
May break my bones
But words can never hurt me (Old Folk Saying).

When a child chants the above jingle to shield himself from hostile names hurled at him in lieu of brickbats, he may convince himself that he is well defended, but at some level even *he* knows that he is whistling in the dark. Words *can* hurt, and they can heal and help. Exchange of hurtful words has to a large extent replaced communication with fists, clubs, knives, swords, and guns in civilized societies. Parents and teachers use words to correct and punish, and sometimes the wounds thus inflicted never heal. Words of praise, encouragement, sympathy, and love from parents, friends, teachers, and ministers have long provided essential nourishment for growth and sustenance—something everybody knows. But how this comes about is quite another matter. The word as an instrument of influence, regulation, control is probably less understood than any other regulatory instrument, and at the same time it is the one most universally employed.

An increased understanding of how words function might lift the veil of mystery in which meaning still remains shrouded. To increase our understanding of how words function is essential not only for the optimal development of individual man, but perhaps even for the survival of mankind. The urgency is perhaps a function of the fact that in a complex society, second signalling system activity to a large extent replaces first signalling system activity. Our words and deeds are farther and farther removed from their simple referents on the one hand, and from the objects and events which are affected by them on the other hand. We live in an expanded and expanding world where we are influenced by, and in turn influence, things and events and persons which we will never know through sight, sound, or touch. Yet at the same time we, as human organisms, function in the world in terms of little understood interaction between three systems: the reflex system, and the first and second signalling systems. Can we discover how to control or integrate the interaction of these systems?

Although such areas of inquiry and operation as training, education, child rearing, psychotherapy, diplomacy are usually separate disciplines and approached in different ways, they are intimately related in that they depend upon words as their principal tools. We need to know the significance to such fields, for instance, of Luria's statement (1960) that the word replaces the object but not the emotional situation. We need to know more about the function of emotion: its role in meaning, in learning; whether emotion serves to organize or disorganize, facilitate or inhibit, or all of these; what determines which function it serves; how the exercise of the various functional properties of emotion can be regulated.

Razran (1961) showed how Russian experimentation has demonstrated not only the ready two-way conditionability of visceral action, but also the relative inextinguishability and resistance to reconditioning of autonomic responses. He also discussed the implications of the experimental evidence of conflicts resulting from juxtaposition of intero- and exteroceptive stimulation and the apparent dominance of reactions to interoceptive over exteroceptive stimulation. In view of the fact that interoceptive stimulation and response is continuous, periodic, and organism-bound, interoceptive conditioning is a built-in and relatively uncontrolled function. The experimental findings have such enormous implications that replication and the collection of additional data is imperative.

Questions that remain to be answered are many. How is the evidence from interoceptive conditioning, especially from the semantic conditioning of interoceptive responses, related to some of the inconsistencies in the findings with regard to the interaction between the first and second signalling systems and the dominance of one over the other? *Are* these actually inconsistencies or are they evidence of the varying effects of varying conditions? If the latter, what are the determining conditions and how do they operate?

Many experimenters, American and Russian, have demonstrated generalization on both the stimulus and the response side. Some have indicated the diffuse nature of generalization at early ages. What if, as they surely must, faulty generalizations occur? How can we limit generalization from inextinguishable responses (a perennial problem in psychotherapy, for example)? We need to know more about the relationships between vegetative, motor, and verbal generalization, and how they can be regulated and integrated. How significant to these problems, for instance, are findings such as Mednick's (1958) and others' that anxiety tends to increase both conditionability and generalization? What is the significance of Korbatov's[3] discoveries about an optimal level of conditioning? What is the significance of the persistent findings that old meanings persist and reassert themselves in certain states of impaired physiological functioning and under certain conditions of distraction (chronogenetic disinhibition)? What implications does this have for conditioning, deconditioning, and extinction? What implications does it have for the relation between physical and mental health, for the notion of regression?

We need to know also where the question of awareness fits in and whether this is simply an experimental methodological problem, or one having implications for the way in which we tend to conceptualize the nature of the conditioning process. We need to know how the question of awareness is related to hypotheses regarding self-stimulation, self-signalling and the implications these notions, and the experimental evidence which supports them, have for the development and functioning of self control.[4]

---

[3] See p. 104 above.

[4] The term "self-control" is used here not in the usual sense of suppression of feeling or action which is some kind of predetermined "natural" response to a stimulus, or inhibition of a conditioned S-R connection; it is used rather in the sense of selectivity or choice of a stimulus and/or response and implies the notion of indeterminacy rather than determinism.

CONCLUSIONS

Such questions as these and many others cry for answers. But in order to answer them, much more data are needed; and to accumulate the necessary data requires methodological development and refinement, and perhaps an expansion of our theoretical frames of reference.

What is required is 1) the systematic collection of data in many individually narrow band widths; 2) development of new techniques for the systematic observation of not only the motor and verbal levels of human behavior, but also the physiological level; 3) to refrain, until we have amassed more reliable interrelatable data, from over-generalizing and overtheorizing in a way that inhibits progress rather than facilitates it; and 4) to study carefully the errors committed and the partial insights gained from past efforts, as well as their significance to the prospective fruitfulness of future efforts.

References

BRAZIER, M. A. B. (Ed.). *The Central Nervous System and Behavior.* (Transactions of the third conference sponsored by the Josiah Macy, Jr., Foundation and the National Science Foundation). New York: Josiah Macy, Jr., Foundation, 1960.

CHERRY, C. *On Human Communication.* New York: Science Editions, 1961.

COLE, M., MALTZMAN, J., & BROZEK, J. Symposium: Some current trends in Soviet psychology. *Ref. Amer. Psychologist,* 1965, *20(7),* 591.

FEIFEL, H. Philosophy reconsidered. *Psychol. Rep.,* 1964, *15(2),* 415–420.

KLINE, N. S. (Ed.) *Pavlovian Conference on Higher Nervous Activity. Annals of N.Y. Acad. Sci.,* 1961, *92(3),* 813–1198.

LURIA, A. R. Verbal regulation of behavior.
In: BRAZIER, M. A. B. 1960.

MEDNICK, S. A. A learning theory approach to schizophrenia. *Psychol. Bull.,* 1958, *55,* 316–327.

MILLER, N. E. Integration of neurophysiological and behavioral research.
In: KLINE, N. S. 1961.

MKRTYCHEVA, L. I. Some mechanisms of cortical activity of man in the analysis of simple stimuli.
In: RUSINOV, V. S., ET AL. II. 1956.

RAZRAN, G. H. S. The observable unconscious and the inferable conscious in current Soviet psychophysiology: Interoceptive conditioning, semantic conditioning, and the orienting reflex. *Psychol. Rev.,* 1961, *68,* 81–147.

RUSINOV, V. S., ET AL. (Eds.). *Works of the Institute of Higher Nervous Activity: Physiological Series.* II. Moscow: Academy of Sciences of the USSR, 1956.
Jerusalem: Israel Program for Scientific Translations, 1960.
(Office Tech. Serv., U. S. Dep't. Commerce, Washington, D. C., 20025, PST Catalogue #71).
SOKOLOV, E. N. Neuronal models and the orienting reflex.
In: BRAZIER, M. A. B. 1960.

Author Index

Subject Index